On the Art of Doing Field Studies

An Experience-based Research Methodology

Ib Andersen
Finn Borum
Peer Hull Kristensen
Peter Karnøe

Handelshøjskolens Forlag
Distribution: Munksgaard

© Handelshøjskolens Forlag 1995
Printed in Denmark 1995
Set in Plantin by Grafisk Værk A/S, Denmark
Printed by AKA-Print, Århus
Cover designed by Kontrapunkt
Book designed by Jørn Ekstrøm

ISBN 87-16-13269-6

Series O, No. 18
Copenhagen Business School
Studies from the Institute of Organization and Industrial Sociology

Series edited by Finn Borum

Translation:
Marianne Risberg
Stephanie Hadler

Preface

This book is written for Ph.D. students and others who are about to explore a complex social field. Our target group is graduates in the social sciences – whether they work as researchers or not.

During recent years there has been a growing interest in the exploration of social fields: the life form of certain groups of people, organizations, networks, projects, or the social processes around a public issue. Thus far, the majority of studies of this type have been conducted according to the various principles of »take a deep breath and plunge« and/ or »necessity is the mother of invention«. This led to a difficult selection process and included no guarantees that the most talented researchers would be safe from the worst possible fates: death by drowning or death by exposure.

Having worked with field studies for a number of years where the above conditions were the predominant ones, we developed a desire to systematize our experiences in order to establish a tradition within this field. Field studies are both an art and a craft: nothing can replace learning by doing. On the other hand, junior researchers should not have to start from scratch when they embark on a project. We are convinced that it is possible to pass experiences on to future researchers and give them advice that will enable them to avoid the most mundane and traditional mistakes.

Therefore, this book has a practical orientation. First, like a map of the sea, it presents an overview – albeit incomplete – of the obstacles, challenges, high seas, and ultimate harbours and docks lying ahead in the waters for the researcher embarking on a field study project. Therefore, we recommend reading this book before starting such a project.

Second, the book gives instructions on how to attempt to avert the navigational obstacles that loom on the horizon – or how one, particularly in critical situations, can avoid the ultimate disaster: capsizing. Therefore, our advice is to use the book as a reference tool during the process as well.

We hope that current and future researchers, who are either in the midst of or already have embarked on the existential experience of field studies, will find assistance and consolation in this book.

Copenhagen, August 1995   *Ib Andersen – Finn Borum*
Peer Hull Kristensen – Peter Karnøe

Contents

Part 3: Elements For A Research Practice

Part 4: Conclusion

Part 1:
Introduction

1. The Need for a Research Methodology for Field Studies

Two Weaknesses in Contemporary Literature on Methodology

Books on methodology are by nature normative: they tell how research ought to be conducted and how concrete methodological problems ought to be solved. This is commendable, but it often embodies two important weaknesses in relation to the intensive field study.

First, methodological literature often refers to the researcher in the impersonal, third person singular. This is consistent with perceiving scientific activity as an activity independent of the person conducting it. Based on this perspective, therefore, it should be possible for other researchers to test or duplicate the study. This ideal, which is rooted in the research paradigm of the natural sciences, has had a great impact on methodological reasoning within the social sciences.

In relation to a research practice that emphasizes intensive field studies and qualitative methods, denying the importance of the individual researcher becomes problematic. Observations made during studies of complex social processes and structures are inevitably affected by the interests, selective perception, and specific talents of the concrete researcher. Ethnography is an example of a discipline in which the individual researcher shapes the practice and methodology. Naturally, this gives rise to a continuous debate about the scientific status of ethnography and the findings it produces (Van Maanen 1988).

Why conduct intensive field studies if they entail such problems? Primarily because, in some cases, it is the only way to produce the type of knowledge desired. This is the case, for example, if you are interested in studying how actors create a shared meaning system or world-view (cf. Blumer's formulation of »symbolic interactionism«, 1969: 2-26).

Another reason for applying the intensive field study may stem from a wish to explore a unique, complex case. Allison's (1971) analysis of the Kennedy administration's decision-making process during the Cuban missile crisis is perhaps one of the best known studies. It also illustrates that a field study not only produces insights into a concrete case, but that it may also result in knowledge that can be generalized. In this way,

Allison demonstrates that there is a connection between the models applied in interpreting a decision-making process and the findings that result.

A third and quite legitimate reason for applying the field study may be that it is a research methodology that a particular researcher masters and therefore wishes to use. The social sciences contain a rich repertoire of research methodologies; of these, most researchers use only a few throughout their career. Depending on the type of research environment in which a researcher has been trained, she becomes socialized into the limited, methodological repertoire in which that environment has established competence and that it views as legitimate. Unless she changes research environments or the environment itself undergoes a crisis (Kuhn 1970), she is very likely to identify herself with a trajectory that implies a pronounced rejection of certain methods and a corresponding specialization in others.

A fourth and crucial reason for applying field studies is that the phenomena to be researched can only be studied in their natural surroundings. Other available research designs, such as experimental design, are not applicable to the project in question.

Last, but not least, field studies are experiencing a renaissance due to the fact that social scientists within an increasing range of disciplines have lost faith in the »Grand Theories«. Micro actors do not seem to behave in the way macro theoretical structures lead us to expect. A radical example of this recognition is that we must study micro behaviour in order to discover what macro structures are significant to the acting subjects (compare Knorr-Cetina 1988). Such discoveries can only be made in social fields.

Second, the methodological literature's use of *ought to* often implies that the research process is interpreted in terms of the norms of rationality that dominate western societies. According to this line of thought, the research process should be guided by an overall objective that can be specified in a set of research questions – possibly specified in hypotheses that can be subject to testing. Based on this, a research design can then be chosen. The field study is seen as just one of many options. The research process is then subject to more detailed planning, and the study is subsequently conducted. Collected data are processed and interpreted, and the analysis is turned into a research report that answers the initially posed questions.

Yin's (1984) book on case study design is an example of a good book within this type of methodology. It is an important contribution to the development of field study methodology, but it rigidly adheres to the framework of the analytical rationality outlined above.

Based on this perception of research as a goal-directed, *approximated* rational process that follows a logical sequence of phases, at least the first three of this book's four examples of research projects represent deviations from acceptable research practice.

The projects' transgression of time schedules, the heterogeneity of data, and the participants' existential crises are, in this perspective, symptoms of deviations from traditional research practice. The conclusion is therefore simple: be prepared. Don't start a project until properly attired. Read all the relevant theory and define precise questions that will be able to survive the entire project. Don't start collecting data before the research design has been determined in detail. Be technically rational and stringent during the entire research project and stick to the course plotted!

Thus, the main conclusion is that deviations from the approximated rational model lead to unfavourable consequences, and these can be eliminated by returning to the approximated rational model!

Another conclusion is that such projects – even though their planning and execution are less appropriate – can lead to the discovery of smart techniques. These can be incorporated into the approximated rational research methodology and thus contribute to its further refinement.

Naturally, the research process is not quite that simple. Therefore, methodological literature usually apologizes for the capriciousness of life and the individual's limited rationality. This is done partly by allowing for feedback loops between the research phases, partly by admitting that translations from one phase to another are far from unambiguous.

In spite of these concessions to the limited rationality, the lingering and prevailing perception of the research process is still that it should be characterized by technical rationality: actions occurring at a later stage in the process must be justifiable as appropriate in relation to the initial objective. Consequently, errors are concealed along with irrational behaviour and accidental events, all of which, in our opinion, are significant aspects of normal research practice.

Within the social sciences there are examples of methodological literature that does not rigorously adhere to the result of the research process and its technical rationality (Argyris 1970; Enderud 1984, 1986; Bryman 1989; Flyvbjerg 1991). However, the gap between the research practice that evolves around field studies and the existing methodological literature is still too great. In our opinion, neither the experience nor the knowledge gained by individual researchers is processed and utilized sufficiently. There is a need for a methodological discussion and development that takes as its base both the distinctive characteristics of intensive field studies and the situation of the Ph.D. student.

Our research tales show that the research process is conducted in a complex, social context. During the project, the researcher weaves many contradictory considerations into a sensible whole. An awareness of the many contradictory forces that push and pull the researcher in different directions may aid in reducing the confusion that can eventually push a project, and thus the researcher, into a crisis situation.

The Need for Another Type of Methodological Literature

In 1967, an exciting book entitled *Sociologists at Work*, edited by the United States sociologist Phillip E. Hammond, was published. The book was a reaction to the traditional methodological books on social science that had been published by United States publishers. In his introduction to the book, Hammond quotes the famous sociologist Robert K. Merton's characterization of this literature:

> »This literature is concerned with ... ways in which scientists ought to think, feel, and act. It does not necessarily describe, in needed detail, the ways in which scientists actually do think, feel, and act.« (Hammond 1964: 3; Merton 1962: 19)

Conventional methodological literature was primarily concerned with the guidelines with which the »scientific craftsman« could work his way step by step through the research process. The guidelines greatly resemble cookbooks that provide step-by-step recipe preparation: »Finely chop three shallots. Sauté over low heat until transparent. Maintain at a simmer on low heat while ...« etc. This type of book is indeed necessary and it comes in many versions – good as well as bad. However, what bothered Hammond and Merton – and others as well – was that the repertoire of techniques was not the important, critical resource when producing good, exciting, and ground-breaking research. A cookbook can only be used to reproduce various dishes; it rarely (though exceptions do exist) describes how to produce new, exciting, gastronomic delights with the use of experimentation. But such books are very good as basic literature. If we first master the skills and the basic principles, we are usually better equipped for producing something new at a later time by experimenting with fantasy.

This applies not only to the social sciences but also to the natural sciences. In his book *On Understanding Science* (1947: 116) James B. Conant, professor of chemistry, says:

> »To my mind there has been too little said in the popular accounts of science about both the dynamic quality of the enterprise and the fact that it is concerned with evolving conceptual schemes rather than the classification of facts.«

The craft alone does not create new results; rather, it is our ability to develop concepts and conceptual couplings that produces knowledge. This is far more difficult to describe and prescribe than the various procedures for data classification. Possibly this is the reason why so few writers have dealt with the subject. Conant cites this quality as the ability to find sustainable and fruitful concepts and conceptual couplings for »the feel for tactics and strategy of science«. About this, Hammond says:

> »This component of research ... is admittedly illusive and hard to transmit. Some scientists would insist that it is not possible to give formal instruction in how to do research, and the history of science is full of the physicist's or mathematician's reference to his discoveries as »aesthetic« experiences, presumably because he indeed finds his creative researches difficult to describe. But though at some reaches the origins of ideas, the theoretical breakthroughs during the course of research, are to be described only as poetic, as mysterious or awesome, at some other level they can be understood, or at least described, as very human activities.« (Hammond 1964: 3).

As mentioned, Hammond's book was a reaction to the »cookbooks«. The resultant anthology presents the personal descriptions of 11 well-known United States sociologists on how they conducted their research projects. It is exciting and rewarding, for example, to read how *The Dy-*

namics of Bureaucracy (Peter M. Blau), *Union Democracy* (Seymour Martin Lipset), and *The Adolescent Society* (James S. Coleman) came into being. The tales reveal much valuable information about the research process: information not found in the »cookbooks«.

Hammond's initiative was commendable and inspiring. On the other hand, he wrapped up the task a little too easily. The book consists of 12 chapters: an introductory chapter and 11 ensuing chapters each telling a research tale. Following Hammond's instructions, each tale provides details of the specific research process and does not attempt to make any generalizations. Unfortunately, Hammond included no thirteenth chapter: he furnished us with no synthesis of the comprehensive field data he thus had collected. It is left to the reader to draw her own conclusions on how to proceed in case she wants to conduct a research project similar to those in the book (or of a different design, for that matter).

Our book contains four research tales. In that way, it resembles *Sociologists at Work*, although the field material is not as comprehensive as Hammond's. What distinguishes our book from Hammond's is that we attempt to take that next step (which Hammond did not) and draw some lessons from these tales. In existing methodological literature, such lessons are only mentioned fragmentarily or not at all. We leave it to the reader to assess the extent to which we succeed in breaking this pattern.

Research as a Learning Process

Like Hammond, we take our point of departure in the research process as it develops in practice. Basically, we conceive of the research process as a learning process. By nature, this is the case if it is your first (Ph.D.) project. However, the intensive exploration of social systems and processes represents a complex situation for senior researchers as well. Since the potential theoretical universe is infinite, the preparation will always be insufficient. And since the very reason for exploring the social field is that it is unknown or little known, the first problem definition will always be tentative.

Compared with Thompson & Tuden's typology for decision-making situations (Scott 1992: 296), the research process cannot be reduced to computations. This would require predetermined objectives and the technical mastering of methods for achieving them. When the objectives are not quite clear, but are developed during the process, and methods and techniques are not fully mastered or must be developed ad hoc, judgement and inspiration become inevitable and major components of the research process (Figure 1.1).

Decisions based on judgement and inspiration can be appropriate, but they may also prove erroneous. Research becomes a risky activity – contrary to what Argyris (1970) has labelled »mechanistic research«. The field researcher runs the risk of being wrong. But also of becoming wiser, as the recognition of mistakes has been known to produce wisdom.

Figure 1.1. Typology for Decision-Making Situations

	Agreement and clarity about goals	
Beliefs about causation	Yes	No
Unambiguous	Computation	Compromise
Ambiguous	Judgement	Inspiration

Surprises result when exploring the field. These unexpected occurrences may cause you to question the original problem definition: perhaps time has shown that it is too broad or aspects of it have become irrelevant. Furthermore, assumptions about cause and effect relationships and the nature of social processes may fall apart and have to be radically revised.

One possible reaction to this is to adhere to the original problem definition and conceptualization of the field. But this is synonymous to writing off the possibility of learning something beyond the initially developed frame of reference, cf. Argyris & Schoen's (1978) distinction between »single and double loop learning«. The first type of learning concerns that which takes place within a given perspective or set of rules, whereas the latter transcends these. We find that the first type of learning is an important element of a Ph.D. project: learning the methods for the application of theory and models as well as methodological rules and techniques is a necessary but insufficient precondition for a successful educational process. Ideally, the second type of learning should occur as well during the Ph.D. project – or, for that matter, during any field study.

There is another possible reaction to surprise: continuous redefinition and reconceptualization facilitate more fundamental learning and the production of significant knowledge. However, this is only possible if the researcher is willing to write off previous intellectual investments and accept the subsequent uncertainty and potential crises that arise. It is precisely here – from critical events and unpredictable consequences arising from decision-making – that experiential learning materializes.

To avoid being misunderstood, we wish to stress that we are not arguing in favour of a purely inductive research process. In our opinion, we have witnessed far too many examples of inductive research processes that did not sufficiently utilize the available resources of established theoretical knowledge. We have also seen induction used too often as nothing more than a poor excuse for the posing of very loose research questions.

Apart from field studies containing elements of surprise, another important characteristic is that they are social activities. The learning situation is not simply limited to an individual (the researcher) trying to learn from a problem-solving situation. Learning takes place in an organized context of which the main elements are the research environment and the field environment.

The researcher is subject to influence from both close and distant research communities and acts within an institutional framework that can be a facilitation as well as a hindrance. The institutional framework can be facilitating in that the professional and methodological orientation of an environment develops a certain competence that makes training and learning easier. However, this can become a hindrance, as well, as learning outside the specific competence is impeded and perhaps impossible. Furthermore, the degree of paradigm rigidity in the research environment is of decisive importance for the individual researcher's ability to acquire more fundamental (double loop) learning.

The field being explored also affects the researcher. The actors in the field provide interpretations of themselves and the researcher and add to the demands on, hopes about, and expectations of the researcher's behaviour and product. Moreover, the field – in the same way as the research environment – rarely speaks with one voice. Conflicting explanations and expectations often weave the researcher into a web of contradictory pressures. During an intensive field study, the researcher will feel that she is becoming part of the field and its social dynamics. This can be so intense an experience that the research becomes obscured or forgotten.

This interaction between researcher, research environment, and field infuses the field study with the features of an organic system. But in this disorder, we find inherent norms, routines, hierarchies, communities, demands, and expectations that, in relation to the learning process, represent both opportunities and limitations (March & Olsen 1979). The researcher will have to develop an ability to function and produce knowledge in this context. To the young researcher, this often represents the litmus test.

A Methodology for Intensive Field Studies

This book endeavours to contribute to the development of a methodology for the intensive field study. By *methodology* we mean the basic principles guiding the exploration of empirical fields. Our discussion is confined to the general principles, and we do not discuss the comprehensive repertoire of techniques available for data processing, data analysis, and reporting. As far as these issues are concerned, we refer the reader to the methodological literature on specific qualitative or quantitative methods (Burgess 1990; Fielding 1988).

We have chosen to work inductively and to refrain from general meta-theoretical discussions. Flyvbjerg (1991) has developed a field study methodology based on more general, epistemological considerations. It is interesting that his methodology and ours share several elements and both subscribe to a conception of the research process as a learning process (see Chapter 11).

Our point of departure is Blumer's (1969: 24-26) perception of what constitutes the basic elements of empirical, scientific exploration:

- the possession and use of a prior picture or scheme of the empirical world under study;
- the asking of questions of the empirical world and the conversion of the questions into problems;
- determination of the data to be sought and the means to be employed in getting the data;
- determination of relations between the data;
- interpretation of the findings; and
- the use of concepts.

This is not an argument in favour of a deductive research process, and the elements must not be interpreted as a linear, approximated rational process. Like Blumer, we argue that the researcher at any time during the process should try to explicate and continuously revise her perception of the field.

The Intensive Field Study

The term intensive field study covers the exploration of complex, social, empirical phenomena – either contemporary or historical – by applying multiple sources of data.

This definition is close to Yin's (1984: 23; 1991) definition of case study research, and we have chosen to view case studies and field studies as synonymous. However, we prefer the term field to case: partly because the word case is often used to describe a teaching method and partly because a field study often leads to the identification of several cases within the empirical field studied.

Contrary to Yin, we do not attempt to distinguish between contemporary and historical studies. Present time is elusive – a passage from the past to the future. Even studies of great topicality are inevitably forced to work with data reflecting what has been. Neither do we, as Yin does, intend to maintain a distinction between the case study and the ethnographic study. In view of the recent years' trend to focus on cultural phenomena and the development of cultural theories, ethnography has become a natural element of empirical, social research.

The complexity of field studies refers, first, to the fact that defining the empirical field in relation to its context is not an obvious task. Second, no definition of the empirical field will be able to neutralize the multifaceted nature of social phenomena. No matter how narrow the definition or how rich the repertoire of collected data, the exploration will never result in anything other than one of many possible interpretations.

Therefore, we fundamentally view the field study as a expedition into the unknown. We have no intention of eliminating this uncertainty. Rather, we wish to uncover some of the basic elements of uncertainty characterizing the intensive field study. In this way, we hope to be able to contribute to demystifying the method. Doing this should then reduce the tendency to view problems as manifestations of personal inability and make elements of uncertainty more tangible and to a certain extent preventable.

We have no intention of recommending the intensive field study as *the* method or of reducing it to a category that can be mastered by applying a specific approach. On the contrary, in our opinion the field study is merely one of an array of methods, and whether it is an appropriate method to apply must be determined based on a number of situational factors connected to the concrete research project. The most important of these factors are: the objectives and questions of the study, the theoretical perspective, the nature of the field studied, the researcher's skills, and the project's resources (Borum 1990). We do not discuss in detail the field study in relation to alternative methods but refer to Yin's (1984) and Carroll & Johnson's (1990) discussion of this issue.

The Basis and Genesis of the Book

In keeping with the objective of this book, our empirical point of departure is the (young) researcher's situation. The empirical basis is – as mentioned earlier – four intensive field studies conducted by the authors, each telling their own story. The rules guiding our tales are simple: a chronological account that, as honestly as possible, presents critical (positive as well as negative) events and experiences during the research process. When viewed in light of Van Maanen's (1988) three categories of tales from the field – realist, confessional, and impressionist – we subscribe to the category confessional tales. Through our four very personal tales on how field studies can be practised, we attempt to demystify the method. The confidences and confessions are, however, strongly selective and are restricted to the purpose and the content of the research process: we interpret the course of the research process and the results as conditioned by the interaction between the research field, researcher, and research environment. We maintain the right to privacy in our personal life, which excludes other possible and interesting interpretations.

Before writing our tales, we had several discussions in which we discovered that we shared certain assumptions about the specific characteristics of intensive field studies:

- They demand empathy, in other words, the ability to understand and share the feelings, experiences, etc., of another social system. This is something that can only occur if adequate humility and curiosity exist.
- They involve shocks and crises and necessitate continuous clashes with prior assumptions.
- They can neither be described nor understood from the perspective of the funnel of an approximated rational model for a research process. A logic tree of multiple branches is a much better illustration of the very different situations that may result from a given point of departure.
- They demand application or development of a theory for uncovering the elements that go beyond the field and that can make the study

something more than a merely interesting, unique tale.
- They demand adaptation of methods and techniques to the concrete field and the context of the study.
- A qualitative method is a question of a basic methodology and not a question of applying either qualitative or quantitative techniques (cf. Morgan & Smircich 1980).
- The traditional phase models for the research process have serious shortcomings. In the first place, they inappropriately place sharp distinctions between data collection, data analysis, and the writing of the report; secondly, as a principal rule, they ignore some specific demands that are placed on a researcher during the intensive study of a social system.

We then began to write with determination (as much as time allowed) and produced the first draft of the empirical basis of the book: four tales from the field. In the next phase we read, discussed, and reflected on one another's tales – most effectively during a week's seminar in the autumn of 1991. Apart from wanting to make the tales more comprehensible and informative, our comments endeavoured to provoke the storyteller's memory. Ignored areas, weak explanations, smooth accounts, and the absence of individuals or conflicts made the readers sceptical and brought about many probing comments. The comments had an effect on us similar to that of the *madeleine* that set Proust in search of lost times and caused rich and varied experiences to rise the surface. The storyteller »suddenly remembered« elements, experiences, and explanations – and in several cases he retrospectively gained a new understanding of the process and the events. In several situations we realized for the first time what we had learned from the original research process.

We are aware of the problems of retrospection and retrospective interpretation. However, we have basically attempted to help one another remember crises and ruptures – in other words, reduce repression. On the other hand, we have attempted to counteract tendencies towards ex post-rationalization: logical or smooth descriptions of the process were met with scepticism that, in several cases, led to the identification of forgotten ruptures or the discovery of ruptures that had occurred prior to the first defined period.

After we revised the first drafts of our tales, we discussed potential themes that were emerging from the research projects. The result of this inductive process was a long list of themes (the final version covered three and a half pages) that we tried to systematize according to major categories that could make up a cross-analysis of the research tales and the development of a unified methodology on field studies. Several times we had to face the fact that the categorizations did not hold – neither logically nor inspirationally – when they had to be specified.

We therefore chose to view the list of themes as a source of inspiration for the deductive phase. During this, we reread the four tales, keeping in mind our list of themes. At the same time we went through a great deal of the current literature on methodology. Through this process we developed the few dimensions that we have applied to this final interpretation of our experiences. Finally, based on our interests, we selected the dimensions with which we wanted to continue to work.

At this point, Peter Karnøe had to withdraw temporarily from the process for two happy occasions: the birth of his daughter and a prolonged stay in the United States as a visiting scholar. During the spring and summer of 1992, the remaining three authors wrote, discussed, and thoroughly revised the thematic analyses to such an extent that all three of us can be held to answer for the content of the book, even through it was produced with one of us as mainly responsible for each section.

All in all, this book develops a research methodology based on experience – inductively but not without presumptions. We have utilized the help of a wide range of theories and literature on methodology that reflects our different educational backgrounds and research experience.

The Empirical Field of the Book

Each of the four field studies has been completed and published. In other words, the selected tales are biased: a large number of research projects are not completed and some of the completed projects are not published. We find the absence of uncompleted projects to be a weakness of the book; however, for several reasons we dropped the idea of including tales about uncompleted projects. As a consolation, it is evident from the tales that, during the process, at least three of the four projects might have ended up as failures. We hope that, in spite of the biased selection of tales, we have uncovered some factors of significant importance as to whether a project results in research or non-research.

If judged according to the criterion of publish or perish, the four projects are tales of success: all results were published. Whether the quality and the content of the studies are to be regarded as successful and whether the proportion between the resources used and the knowledge gained is reasonable are other issues; however, we are hardly the proper people to answer the questions. But we are all deeply involved in our field studies: we learned a great deal from them; and we were deeply affected personally and professionally by them both during and after the process. None of us would give up that experience. The three older members of this team (the three first authors) conducted several field studies after these reported projects. The experiences from these have, of course, influenced our interpretations of former research projects. In the future we intend to apply the field study method and will continue to develop this research methodology – an outline of which is presented here.

Part 2:
Four Research Tales

2. From an Initial Evaluation of Treatment Centres to an Ultimate Evaluation of the Life Paths of Drug Addicts – A Research Odyssey

Ib Andersen

My Background and the First Steps

From 1967 to 1978 I worked part time at the University of Copenhagen teaching theoretical statistics to political science and sociology students. With the sociology students, the classes gradually began to focus on prevalent social science methodology. Thus, the course developed into a combination of qualitative and quantitative research methods with quantitative methods being primarily based on theoretical and mathematical statistics. In my final years at the University of Copenhagen, I taught primarily sociology students. During those years, I was involved in many exciting projects and, inevitably, some deadly boring.

In the autumn of 1971 I started – as usual – with a new class of sociology students. The students themselves chose the projects on which they wanted to work. Four students in this class were particularly interested in a subject that primarily involved the developments that had taken place in research on drug abuse in Denmark. The students were interested in the theoretical, sociological, and methodological aspects of this development, but in addition to these, they were interested in concrete research techniques that had been applied in the various studies on drug abuse.

The students defined their subject broadly, which basically entailed a general mapping out of how a new research field develops. That is, they were interested in the factors that influenced the development process. As a result of this problem definition, they then began to examine the existing Danish literature on the subject. Having defined its historical context, they then set out to examine which interest groups (public authorities, social groups, etc.) governed this development.

The first true studies on drug abuse were primarily descriptions of the scope of drug abuse and how it spread to larger sections of the population, especially to young people. They also offered explanations for why young people ended up in a drug addiction career (career is used here in the sense of how abuse is established and later developed): this is what psychiatrists call anamnesis (case history). However, these studies proposed many different explanations and covered wide spectra on several levels.

In the beginning, the interest behind these studies was mainly directed by curiosity. Drug abuse was a new phenomenon and had, therefore, certain sensational characteristics. Also, at that time increasing numbers of youths began to experiment with drugs – a development seen to have future, catastrophic consequences. Later, research within this field developed primarily into studies of institutional treatment centres or of the various methods of treatment, and they focused especially on the individual treatment centres. The quality of some of these studies was rather dubious. Some seemed to have been used only for the purpose of legitimizing individual centres and the treatments they offered.

The main results of the sociology students' project were published in Danish in 1972. I served as a co-author (Andersen, Bauter, Gregersen, Hultzrantz & Kirstein 1972).

Interest and Occasion – A Bargain is a Bargain

In May 1972, I graduated from the University of Copenhagen and subsequently received a research grant from the Institute of Organization and Industrial Sociology, Copenhagen Business School. During the preceding 30 months, I had collaborated closely with some of the Institute's researchers because I was employed from 1969 to 1971 by the Department of Mechanical Technology of the Technical University of Denmark as a research assistant for a project studying the introduction of participatory democracy at the Copenhagen Business School. This project was a collaboration between the Department of Mechanical Technology of the Technical University of Denmark and the Institute of Organization and Industrial Sociology of Copenhagen Business School. I was actually recruited for the project through the Institute of Organization and Industrial Sociology, but for practical reasons I was employed by the Technical University of Denmark, since it administered the grant. A fellow student, who at that time worked as a research assistant at the Institute of Organization, effected the contact. I was very interested in being attached to the Institute, where I had worked as a research assistant on a project for 5 months in 1965.

After finishing the editing of the previously mentioned book (Andersen, Bauter, Gregersen, Hultzrantz & Kirstein 1972), I became interested in the subject itself. Going over the research and project reports available at that time, it again surprised me to find that the methodological content of the studies seemed so dubious.

The idea of a specific study of this phenomenon became increasingly attractive. However, I was a bit doubtful about how to approach the matter. Naturally, the first question to occurr was how to get in contact with and gain access to the institutional treatment centres. What I was especially interested in was finding out to what extent the individual treatment centres offered anything that could be perceived as positive viewed from the perspective of an addict's drug career. In other words, I wanted to assess and evaluate the different types of drug abuse and addiction treatments used by these institutional treatment centres. How appropriate were the various treatments? Did they have any effect at all? Or even worse – did the treatment centres' activities trap the addicts in a continuing life of drug abuse?

My point of departure was critical: I was critical towards what these institutional treatment centres offered the addicts. The centres were very different in terms of organizational structure, ownership, financial base, and treatment of the individual addict. What characterized the field most was the fact that each institutional treatment centre had its own standard treatment programme: family care at one, withdrawal via methadone combined with some socioeducational activities at another, psychotherapy at a third, and at a fourth centre only medically supervised withdrawal and then back out onto the street again, etc.

As far as I could see, the drug addicts undergoing treatment in the various institutional treatment centres were a very mixed group in terms of age, social background, drug career, etc. It did not seem plausible that the standard programmes applied by these institutional treatment centres could be equally effective on all types of addicts. Nevertheless, all institutional treatment centres accepted all types of addicts. Poor or very few considerations were taken when deciding who should be admitted to a specific treatment centre. In other words, no analysis of the addict was carried out, and drug addicts were thus distributed randomly among the various institutional treatment centres. In my opinion, the reason for this was that the institutional treatment centres lacked any knowledge about which type of treatment might have a positive effect on the various types of addicts. And this was the issue I really wanted to explore.

In 1973, a former student of mine, Preben West Hansen, dropped in to see me. After having graduated from the Copenhagen Business School with a M.Sc. in Economics and Business Administration, he had chosen not to do his military service, and instead take a stand as a conscientious objector. In Denmark, this entails being assigned to do community service for 6 months. He was at that time stationed at Højbjerggård – an institutional treatment centre for drug addicts. The centre was located in Gladsaxe, a suburb of Copenhagen, and treated a considerable number of severe drug addicts. It was owned by an association of Christians and was thus private as most of this type of institutional treatment centre in the Copenhagen area. Preben West Hansen, who later became a research assistant, was very anxious to study the treatment being offered to drug addicts at Højbjerggård. He asked whether I would be interested. I certainly was – having had this type of project in mind for quite some time. Now the occasion presented itself, and luckily I was not committed to other projects at the time. We agreed to a provisional arrangement: he should try to find out whether the management at Højbjerggård would agree to participate in such a project.

At that time the management of Højbjerggård consisted of a psychiatrist and an academic with a background in educational theory and practice. They showed an immediate interest in the study and after a couple of preliminary discussions, we agreed that I, in collaboration with Preben West Hansen, should apply for a grant from the Danish Social Science Research Council. We agreed to take it easy until the Council had made its decision and not to do anything until we knew we had obtained the funding. The grant came through at the end of 1974.

Thus, it was relatively easy to get access to the institutional treatment centre we were to study, and there was no question about who the project participants were and who the project leader was. Preben West Hansen, whom the institutional treatment centre trusted, established contacts for me with the treatment centre's management. The terms of trade were reasonably clear: we had an exciting project and they counted on receiving a series of results that they could use to legitimize the continued existence of Højbjerggård. We did not sign any agreement of cooperation defining the implementation of the project, nor did we – as far as I can remember – make any verbal agreements. Luckily, this never became an issue.

What Did We Actually Want to Study and How?

We had numerous, lengthy discussions on the project's design and implementation. What did we actually want to study? Was it the institutional treatment centre as such or the various types of treatment offered to the drug addicts? Many of the previously published studies operated with an input-output design: they described the drug addict's situation when s/he was admitted to the institutional treatment centre (input). At the treatment centre, the addicts were subjected to treatment – this was perceived as a kind of black box. When addicts left the institutional treatment centre (output), the effect of the treatment was measured according to a number of variables considered relevant in view of the treatment. The difference between the input description of the drug addict and the subsequent output description of the drug addict was, therefore, the effect of the treatment they had undergone in the centre.

After a series of discussions, we rejected such a design as useless, since this process could not include a great number of considerations. What about the influences to which the drug addicts were subjected during their stay at the institutional treatment centre – influences that had nothing to do with the actual institutionalization? How could one filter out the effects of these influences? Also, we found it difficult to see the value of this type of result. There was very little explanatory value contained in such studies.

We were interested in finding explanations as to why certain types of treatment had a positive effect on some drug addicts and a negative or no effect on others.

The Project Team

Preben West Hansen and I soon reached the conclusion that we would have to enlarge the project team to get a more varied perspective on the study. Jørn Daugaard Pedersen, a sociology student who was in the process of finishing his studies and had shown an interest in the work at the Institute, was asked to join the project team, and he accepted. We also contacted Tore Jacob Hegland, an associate professor at the Institute of Organization and Industrial Sociology. He also accepted. Tore Jacob Hegland had previously been involved in studies of numerous social conditions, including institutional treatment centres. Furthermore, he was very competent methodologically. The main idea behind this project team composition was to create conditions for competent dis-

cussions about the progress of the project. The study was primarily conducted by Preben West Hansen, Jørn Daugaard Pedersen, and myself.
Tore Jacob Hegland functioned for the most part as our sparring partner. During the project, Tore Jacob Hegland was appointed professor at
Aalborg University Centre and thus had to leave the project team after
9 months. This occurred in the beginning of 1976.

What Do We Use to Replace the Input-Output Design?

Our original design operated with several different types of data collection: participant observation, discussions, intensive interviews, documentary material, etc. We spent most of 1975 on literary studies and
preliminary data collection. We participated in a number of meetings at
Højbjerggård, met with the management and staff in order to gather information – primarily at Højbjerggård, but also at other institutional
treatment centres. We conducted preliminary interviews with a number
of drug addicts at Højbjerggård, studied case records, and much more.
In 1975 and 1976 we visited research institutions in the Netherlands
and Great Britain that were conducting studies on the treatment of drug
addicts.

We had no intention of playing the role of neutral, objective, detached
researchers. Our approach was recognized as action-oriented, as were
most of the projects at the Institute of Organization and Industrial Sociology at that time. Therefore, we participated actively in discussions
that occurred in internal meetings and seminars and in open courses at
Højbjerggård as well as with representatives from other institutional
treatment centres. In other words we played – or in any case tried to play
– an active role in affecting the form of the treatment milieu for drug addicts in Copenhagen.

After Tore Jacob Hegland left the project in the beginning of 1976,
the team continued to discuss the few advantages and numerous disadvantages of the input-output model. The design of the study is illustrated in Figure 2.1.

As mentioned, this model requires that the drug addicts be measured
according to a number of variables before being enrolled in a treatment
centre and then again after being discharged from the centre. The difference between these two measurements is what occurs in the black box.

Such a design contains very crucial methodological problems. The
first is when to measure the clients. In this context, the greatest problem
is the timing of the measurement after completion of the treatment and

discharge: should this occur immediately on discharge or after a period of time? In the first case, there is a tendency for the results of the treatment to be shown as positive or good, for instance when measuring abstinence as an end result. In the second case, with the measurement being taken a longer period of time after discharge, the results tend to be negative or poor, since holding power is poor or nonexistent in the long run.

Figure 2.1. The Input-Output Model

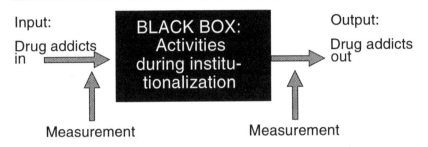

The results of such measurements thus depend on when the measurements are taken. Measuring the effects a longer period of time after the client has left the institutional treatment centre implies yet another methodological problem: what is the effect of the treatment and what is the effect of other influences after the client has been discharged? The longer the period of time the client has been out of the centre, the more difficult becomes the task of tracking the effect of the treatment.

A second fundamental problem that arises from applying the input-output model is whether or not the difference determined by comparing the two measurements can solely be attributed to what happens in the black box, in other words the actual treatment at the centre. It cannot. Institutional treatment centres are not hermetically sealed: exogenous factors are bound to influence the treatment. Furthermore, the backgrounds and experiences – the baggage each drug addict brings – is bound to decisively affect how they react to treatment.

Our problem was thus: if we are to find explanations for why treatments have one effect on some addicts and another effect on other addicts, it is not enough to examine the differences in input-output measurements. We have to include other explanatory factors in order to understand these relations; and this is the third fundamental problem of applying input-output models.

However, the difficulty in the development process of the design was finding a model that could replace the input-output model. For a long time we focused on the institutional treatment centre as the central unit of analysis (including the types of treatment offered). It was this dogged focus that hindered the needed shift in our perspective. We discussed the problem with the staff at Højbjerggård and other Copenhagen treatment centres without coming any closer to a solution.

The shift in perspective came – as I remember it – on a day when we had a longer discussion on »just exactly what kind of an animal is drug addiction treatment?« At that time we had interviewed staff members at the treatment centres as well as drug addicts themselves. When the institutional staff were asked what the treatment comprised, they answered, roughly speaking: »the activities occurring at the institutional treatment centre«! Therefore, eating with the drug addicts was treatment; playing billiards with the addicts was also considered treatment. When the drug addicts were asked what the treatment consisted of, they gave a description of their daily routine. The main difference from their everyday life outside the treatment centre was that at the treatment centre they had to comply with certain rules and they received legal drugs (although the dose was reduced daily).

These statements reflected, in our opinion, a very diffuse perception of the nature of treatment and possibly a conscious attempt to legitimize all activities in the institutional treatment centre as being treatment. Both the staff and the drug addicts were interested in sustaining this legitimation, since it represented a human system for both sides. In other words, their conception of treatment included much of what we considered to be everyday activities.

If one accepted this broad definition of treatment, one could justifiably claim that many everyday activities outside the institutional treatment centres could be defined as treatment. If this is true, focusing on the role of institutional treatment centres in a drug addict's career would be far too limiting if one was to understand the results occurring from a period of stay at an institutional treatment centre. The stay at the centre merely represented one element of a comprehensive set of factors that influenced the total course of development. The important question was which events in the life of a drug addict had a therapeutic effect (an effect that helped them out of a career of addiction and back into a more or less independent social life)? One could imagine that many things and events both inside and outside the centres had a therapeutic effect on their life.

One of the consequences of this discussion was that we drew, on the chalk board, a long horizontal line symbolizing the time line of the career of a drug addict. On this time line we indicated different events that might affect this career. An example is shown in Figure 2.2.

Figure 2.2. Events Affecting the Path of Life

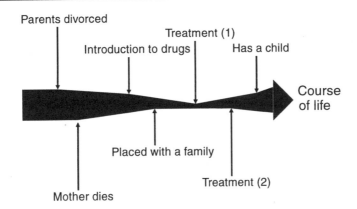

We had created the basis for a shift in perspective. It was clear that the fundamental unit that would be the point of departure for our analysis had shifted from a focus on the individual treatment centres and now focused on the individual drug addict's path of life. By operating with descriptions covering the drug addicts' complete life history, it now became possible to examine how the temporal occurrence of various events affected and shaped the individual drug addict's life. Also, it became possible to examine how the combination of various events had affected the drug addict's development. We were aware of the difficulties connected with such analyses, but we were convinced that this design had greater and more valid explanatory power in terms of producing explanations for why these individuals had developed into drug addicts and what could be done to intervene in this development. And that was our main interest.

Let me further the point. The study was explorative, but in the long run, we intended to design an intervention theory that, to a certain extent, could help identify when and how to intervene in the life of a drug addict in order to possibly get him or her off drugs and into an independent social life. As far as we knew, no literature in Denmark had dealt with this problem. The literature on drug addiction in Denmark only briefly discussed what one could call the social dynamics of drug addiction, that is, the psychological and sociological factors and mechanisms that push and pull young people in particular back and forth into drug addiction. We took the idea of push and pull from that part of demography that studies emigration and immigration (the movement of people). In an attempt to explain why people move from one place to another, researchers focus on circumstances that push people away (such as unemployment, lack of reasonable housing, etc.) and circumstances that pull people towards the new settlement (beautiful natural surroundings, better services, lower taxes, etc.). We transferred this idea to life paths in order to explain why drug addicts moved from one life situation to another. What pushed them away from their current situation and what pulled them toward the new life situation? If we could identify these pushes and pulls, we would have achieved much in terms of developing a theory on how to intervene in the life of a drug addict.

We felt that there was a great need for some applicable results from the study that could be used as input for designing the treatment of drug addicts as well as for designing preventive activities. We were interested in highlighting the following questions:

- Who becomes a drug addict?
- Why do some people become drug addicts?
- How do they become drug addicts?
- What does the drug addict's life look like later?
- Who succeeds in getting off drugs and how?
- What are the consequences of this recognition in terms of treatment?

As a result of the above-mentioned decisions, we needed to conduct lengthy, intensive interviews with a large number of drug addicts. In this way we could establish a considerable number of field studies rich in detail. In other words, the field study method became an important element of our research design. We engaged in extensive discussions with the management at Højbjerggård about how to get access to data on the individual drug addict, such as case records. We also discussed whom to include in the population of drug addicts, which questions it would be interesting to ask and what kind of literature we should study. We then embarked on a comprehensive study of the literature: it was a motley affair in which epidemiologists, physicians, biologists, psychiatrists, psychologists, social workers, sociologists, and many others all had their say.

Setting the Limits of the Empirical Field

Thus, the nature of the study on which we were to embark was retrospective. Our point of departure was a certain group of people: drug addicts registered at Højbjerggård, that is, severe cases of drug addiction. We would begin with their current situation and attempt to unravel their life history. This was important to the objectives and issues defined for the study. In other words, we selected a group of drug addicts at a fairly late point in their course of life (they were between 22 and 31 years old) and went back in time in an attempt to elucidate their path of development. Such a design makes it impossible to generalize about the connection between conditions existing in childhood and the subsequent path a life will take. We are, therefore, unable to say anything about how and under which conditions a troubled childhood and adolescence produces either a deviant or a conforming member of society – nor anything about the opposite – what an »untroubled« childhood and adolescence may lead to. Nor can we, based on the study, say anything about why some individuals become alcoholics and criminals and others become drug addicts. What we can attempt to explain is why the individuals in the study became drug addicts. That this is only part of the explanation appears from the fact that not all drug addicts have experienced a troubled childhood and adolescence – something our data clearly revealed. Therefore, several types of explanations are required to explain deviant behaviour. The conditions that exist during childhood and adolescence explain only in part an individual's subsequent development.

The Population of the Study

Our next step was to define and set boundaries for the population of drug addicts who were relevant viewed in relation to the study's objective and issues. This was not easy, as our perspective and hence, to a certain extent, our objectives and issues had shifted in relation to the original point of departure. At the same time, we were confined in practice to the population of drug addicts who had been enrolled at Højbjerggård. The study was dependent on Højbjerggård, since we had been granted access to its information on drug addicts. Viewed in the light of our shift in perspective, this could well seem problematic. Why base the study on this group of drug addicts and not on any other number of addicts registered at other institutional treatment centres, not to mention drug addicts who had never been in contact with the institutional treatment centres? This was clearly a weak point in our selection. Likewise, it could have been exciting to undertake a prospective study, in other words a future-oriented, running survey of a population of drug addicts. A retrospective study, such as ours, always implies problems of reliability and validity. The memory often fails the respondents, they turn to post-rationalization, and it is often difficult to produce historical documentary material to verify and supplement the respondents' information.

Our second criterion was to include only the drug addicts who had been abusing pure morphine, heroin, and the like for at least 3 years. Our final population thus comprised 65 individuals between the ages of 20 and 30 years who, on average, had been on drugs for approximately 6 years. At the start of the project, several of them had been abusing drugs for more than 10 years.

»The Turning Points of Life«: A Turning Point

Our main source was thus intensive interviews with drug addicts, but the question was, what should we ask them? We agreed on the need to construct an open-ended interview guide but otherwise left it to the drug addicts to decide which events they felt had decisively affected their lives. The point of departure was thus very open. On the other hand, we knew we needed to look into a number of additional factors. We were, among other things, interested in situations that we chose to label »turning points of life«. It seemed that in the life path of some drug addicts, a qualitative change suddenly took place that started a development that aggravated or improved their life situation. What was the nature of these turning points and how did they come about?

Furthermore, we were interested in the factors that impeded or promoted different developmental phases. We went through much literature on developmental psychology and clinical psychology before designing the final interview guide. We knew very little about these issues but were convinced that childhood and adolescent conditions and general psychological factors significantly affected the personality of drug addicts and hence their subsequent path of life.

Prior to the interviews we had our doubts. Would it be possible to track down the drug addicts and would they consent to being interviewed? Much of what we would interview them about was very sensitive issues that both involved their troubled past and pertained to their intimate relationships.

Travelling into the Universe of Drug Addicts

The data collection on which we were about to embark proved to be one of the most rewarding experiences of the study. I was taken by surprise again and again. I experienced and learned things that I had absolutely not expected.

All our worries about whether the drug addicts would agree to participate in the interviews proved to be groundless. Almost all of those with whom we succeeded in establishing contact agreed to participate. What proved to be more difficult was tracking them down. Højbjerggård provided us with their names and most recent addresses as well as their civil registration numbers. We wrote the Civil Registration System and asked for current addresses, which we obtained without too much trouble. So arose the next problem. They were invariably not living at the addresses we had received from the Civil Registration System. We then had to ask neighbours whether they knew where to find them. In some cases we obtained their parents' addresses through Højbjerggård and in this way succeeded in getting hold of many of those whom we failed to contact via the Civil Registration System. Ultimately, we had a population of 65 whom we interviewed.

There were absolutely no problems involved in getting the drug addicts to open up in an interview. They were willing to answer any question. The problem was rather to put an end to the interview. Many of them told us that this was the first time in their life that anyone had asked them to give a coherent account of their life history – and that included all types of professional counsellors with whom they had been in contact: social workers, psychiatrists, physicians, teachers, school counsellors, and others. For the first time in their life, they were encouraged to tell their own history. Some of them told us that the mere fact that they were encouraged to tell their story started them thinking about what they actually had been through. It also made them think about the future they were facing. The fact that the interviews started a cognitive process among the interviewees was food for thought. Many of them came from the lower strata of the working class in which there is no tradition for thinking in terms of the future. When asked what plans they had, they were unable to answer. They did not plan for tomorrow. They lived only in the present.

All the interviews were taped, and there were no objections – not even from those serving their sentence at the time of the interview. During the interviews, some of them even confessed criminal activities to which they had not confessed in court. Some told us that they had been sentenced for a crime they had not committed; but then, on the other hand, they had committed a series of crimes for which they had not been indicted; so all things considered, the criminal books balanced.

I do not think I have ever met such great openness in any interviews I have since conducted professionally as that I encountered with the drug addicts participating in this study. I think part of the reason may have been that, in general, very few people had ever shown any interest in them as human beings – very few had taken the time to listen to a full account of their life history. They felt that what they told us was of some value and could hopefully be used positively for others. In general, most of the people in a drug addict's environment were very sceptical: »Don't trust a drug addict; they bluff and they cheat.« These addicts immediately sensed during the interview that this was not our attitude.

As we worked our way through the interviews, we developed our interviewing technique further and added new questions to our interview guide. Therefore, the first interviews we conducted were very different from the final ones. Generally, this presents a problem when the material is subjected to analysis at a later date, and in principle the first interviewees should be re-interviewed and the material supplemented with the additional questions and points of view. We did not do this, and this might be a weakness of the study. The interviews were edited later. We did not transcribe the tapes in full but in an edited version, and these versions filled 400 standard-sized pages.

We checked the empirical information gathered during our interviews and supplemented with other empirical evidence from the participants' case records at Højbjerggård and information from other institutional treatment centres. We applied for access to the Criminal Record Office's files in order to subject their criminal career to analysis. It was extremely difficult to get access to the files, but after a long, complicated process in which we finally, in a last-ditch attempt, contacted the director, we ultimately received permission. However, by that point, the study was too far along, and we were unable to follow through on the offer. Due to the long investigative process, we had by then run short of both human and financial resources.

We also tried to get access to the files on individuals suffering from mental disorders via the Institute of Psychiatric Demographics. At that time, the files were located at the mental hospital in Risskov, Jutland, which by and large was solely staffed with psychiatrists. Our application was turned down on the grounds that we did not possess the necessary psychiatric insight to be able to understand the information. If the project team had included a psychiatrist, they would have granted us permission to look into the files. We perceived the refusal as outright professional tyranny.

Conducting 65 long, intensive interviews was hard work. Originally the group consisted of three interviewers (the remainder of the project team: Preben West Hansen, Jørn Daugaard Pedersen, and myself). As a result, we had to hire one more interviewer during the last part of this phase. We were almost driven to our knees with the amount of work and information. During weeks filled with numerous interviews, it was difficult to keep the information separate. However, it was also difficult to integrate a new interviewer into the team. We three had been on the project right from the start and had therefore generated considerable, shared knowledge about the field. The new interviewer unquestionably increased the interview effect in the data collection period – not because she was a poor interviewer, quite the contrary she was a trained and skilful interviewer, but because her premises and experience were significantly different from ours.

When semistructured, qualitative interviews are being conducted, it is extremely important to use, throughout the study, the same team of interviewers who are familiar with the issues and objectives of the study. Furthermore, it is important that interviewers exchange, on an ongoing basis, experiences during the data collection phase, discuss matters of dispute and resolve these mutually, and read each other's interviews immediately after editing. This work structure reduces the interview effect and constitutes the basis for a mutual, preliminary analysis of the material and makes the final analysis easier since one already has established a series of potential solutions to the puzzle.

Analysing the Paths of Life

The analysis actually started shortly after the first interview was conducted. The first interview attracted a great deal of attention: how much information had the interviewer been able to extract from the interviewee? Did the interview reveal anything exciting, surprising, or unexpected? Was it possible to find a pattern in the paths of life? I feel it is very important to start the analysis at this early stage, that is, to begin forming an idea about the crux of the information, to test various hypotheses, to seek explanations as to why it went as it did, etc. In relation to the next interview, it is then important to direct one's expectations towards certain relationships and, via that, to then test these conjectures. It is also decisively important to record these ongoing results so they are not forgotten during the process. They are crucial in connection with the final analysis and report.

The more in-depth analysis of the collected data, that is, the 65 interviews and life histories, was extremely complicated and time-consuming. Each of us read all of the interviews and noted the patterns and typical explanations emerging from the stories we could glean from the material. Aside from this, we were to highlight exceptionally interesting statements in the texts that could be used to illustrate some of our conclusions.

During the interviews, we were struck by the wide scope represented in the stories that we had collected. Some drug addicts had been able to conceal their abuse for years. They had been able to hold down normal jobs and abuse drugs at the same time. But they had been forced to frequent the drug milieu in order to purchase their drugs. There were the classic street junkies who survived though swindling and criminal activity and, among women, by prostitution. There was the rich drug dealer who hid his activities behind the acceptable façade of his own firm. There was the proper, middle-class individual who had become addicted to drugs, typically due to medically prescribed opiates for pain, etc. The wide scope we chronicled helped puncture the myth that drug addicts are merely drug addicts. They are many things, and their need for treatment and support differs greatly. Viewed in the perspective of the study, it became an objective in itself to demonstrate this profound variety.

However, it was not adequate to show just that they were different. We were interested in identifying types, each of which requires a specific kind of treatment or intervention. Establishing a typology of drug addicts that was relevant in relation to treatment or intervention was our most important task at that time. What characteristic drug addict types were contained in our material?

The first typology with which we operated was based on the theory of psychodynamics. According to this theory, the later progress in life is strongly determined by conditions existing in the early developmental years. Therefore, the conditions in childhood and adolescence became crucial to this typology, and we operated with three categories of drug addicts: those coming from a severely troubled childhood and adolescence, those coming from a median amount of trouble, and those who appeared to have had no noteworthy trouble in childhood or adolescence. We defined the three types in greater detail (which are not worth going into here), and then each of us classified the 65 interviewees accordingly. When we compared the results of this classification, there proved to be very poor agreement as to the way in which we should classify. We reviewed the classification criteria, tightened them up, and went through the process once more. After the second round, we were in almost total agreement.

However, we wanted to work with typologies other than those that only concerned conditions during childhood and adolescence. Therefore, we undertook an in-depth examination of the literature concerning drug addict typology in relation to their path of life, their connection to conventional society and groups of drug addicts, etc. In search of the literature on these aspects, we undertook an electronic, interactive, online search of the field that stretched to libraries within Scandinavia, Europe, and further to the United States.

The Long, Lonesome Trail

I was left with the comprehensive, time-consuming task of completing the qualitative analysis, which lasted from the middle of 1978 until the spring of 1983, when the manuscript was finished. Preben West Hansen had no permanent position at the Institute, so we applied jointly to the Danish Social Science Research Council for a grant to conduct a study on unemployment. For practical reasons in the application, I was named as project leader. It was easier to obtain a grant if the applicant had a permanent position at an institution of higher education. Our application for funding was granted, and Preben West Hansen therefore spent most of his time on that study. Even though he led the daily activities, I participated part time.

Jørn Daugaard Pedersen was interested in starting work on his dissertation in sociology. He was primarily interested in the organization of the treatment system for drug addicts. Even though the subject of his dissertation took its point of departure in our drug addict study, it involved neither the central problem nor the comprehensive qualitative data. Further data collection and processing were therefore needed. We applied for funding from the National Board of Social Welfare (Ministry of Social Affairs) and received it. I acted as Jørn Daugaard Pedersen's supervisor for his dissertation.

The last interviewer to be included on our team found another job – sensibly enough – since our resources had dried up.

In principle I was left alone to do the rest of the work – that is, complete the comprehensive qualitative analysis and write the report. At the same time, I had become involved in two new projects as project leader and supervisor, respectively.

Even though Preben West Hansen was very supportive and willing to participate in practical and theoretical discussions related to the original study, this period was extremely lonesome for me. I found it very difficult to accomplish anything. This situation led to much personal questioning about whether or not to continue my research career. The lack of daily, committed sparring partners who were jointly responsible for the study became increasingly pronounced.

A series of practical problems hindered a sensible organization of the further analysis. Any academic knows the problems: working at a university creates numerous commitments related to teaching, supervising, administration, other research projects and counselling students. The business community and other people often interfere in your planning and actually control much of your time. The time allocated for research tends to be whatever is left over after other activities are completed, so that you end up with 10 minutes here, half an hour there, etc. This means that in reality you do not have any time for research activities, because the costs of getting started are so great that you gain nothing from those short stolen moments available between other activities. During the period in which I was to complete the analysis, the Institute had lent me out for 2 years (1978-1980) to a centre at the Copenhagen Business School working on reforming the undergraduate studies. Work with this reform was very comprehensive and, combined with my other commitments at that time, I was left with very little time for the analysis. In addition to this, my wife began law school in 1978, which meant that she lived away from home for long periods, and I became a single parent responsible for two children, aged 7 and 12.

Planning and administering time includes noting planned activities in your diary. If you do not set aside the time necessary for carrying out these activities, others will use your time to their advantage. Consequently, what you spend your time on does not necessarily reflect your own preferences and interests. The remainder of the project team (Preben West Hansen, Jørn Daugaard Pedersen and myself) thus succeeded in setting aside 4 days in the middle of 1978, and we left the city to spend these days in a borrowed summer cottage. The purpose was to get started on the comprehensive analysis, but naturally there were limits to what we could accomplish in 4 days.

Days, weeks, and months passed during which I did not get around to work on the analysis and report. It hung heavily and constantly on my conscience. It became such a weight that I almost could not bring myself to take out the material, even though I had set aside an afternoon or a morning for the purpose of working on it. I made no progress at all; I went around and around in circles, thinking the same thoughts over and over – it was an awful period. But I was determined to finish the job – for my own sake and in order to redeem my self-respect. And I knew that I could. That I did not doubt. I also knew that it would be difficult.

During the summer of 1980, I finished my work with the undergraduate reform. I had generated a considerable amount of overtime and applied to my Institute for two sabbaticals – during the autumn semester of 1980 and part of the spring semester of 1981. I had previously agreed to run for the position as Institute head beginning in July 1981. My sabbaticals were granted, and I was elected head of the Institute starting in July.

The prospect of a long, coherent research period gave me a great deal of needed optimism. I gathered all the data on the study: notes, sub-reports, interviews, drafts for the sub-analyses, books, lists of literature. I acquainted myself thoroughly with the material: sorted it out in appropriate categories, drafted a preliminary framework for the research report and took stock of the situation to find out what was missing and needed to be done so a reasonable report could be written that presented the most significant results from the study. This process was very encouraging. I realized that much of the work had already been accomplished and, therefore, much of the report could be written right away. There were many exciting results I had forgotten. Many of these results were contained in my project journal. My desire to do something with this study returned in full force.

Preben West Hansen agreed to spend time with me discussing my ideas for the framework of the report, and we agreed to what extent he would act as co-author of the report that I intended to submit to one of the well-known Danish publishers. It did not take us long to compose the framework, and we each committed ourselves to specific sections.

The first draft of a great deal of the publication was written during September 1980. I applied to the Copenhagen Business School for a grant that would allow me to spend the month of October 1980 at San Cataldo near Amalfi in southern Italy. My application was granted.

San Cataldo is a former monastery owned by a groups of Danes. Its function is to act as a type of refuge where individuals can spend a period of time devoted exclusively to their art or science – in divine peace and quiet. My stay at San Cataldo was one of the events that gave great impetus to my research. Prior to the stay, I had spent much time studying literature on the typification of drug addicts and the paths of their lives. I was interested in the identification of typical phases that these lives went through, as well in identifying a typical path. I brought along a comprehensive selection of literature and a considerable amount of preliminary drafts. My intention was to finish this part of the study – the categorization of the phases and a typification of the life paths. I succeeded.

The very atmosphere in the monastery contributed to my personal success. Let me quote extracts from a letter that I sent to my family after the first week:

>»October 7, 1980
>
> I am writing to you from the balcony of the monastery. It is a bit past 10:00 in the morning – 25 degrees Celsius in the shade. Directly across from me – on the other side of the Dragon Valley – is the mountain village, Ravello. The area is beautiful. This monastery is surrounded on three sides by high mountains and its front faces the valley. To the south the Mediterranean has cut deep inlets into the cliffs. Here lie fishing villages, squeezed in between mountains and sea. The monastery and its surrounding garden are beautiful and well maintained. The interior has been kept strictly monastic – whitewashed walls and niches filled with terra cotta pottery. Its hallways are arched and pillared and contain large vases filled with fresh flowers. The convent garden has a multitude of nooks, crannies, and benches suitable for meditating or reading if that is what one wants. The garden supplies the monastery with all the necessary vegetables, wine, and fruit.
>
> As you can tell, I am fascinated by this place. It is ideal for working, and there is an extremely strong work ethic among the guests.

Most of us begin our work at 6:00 or 6:30 in the morning and continue until 8:30, when breakfast is served. At
9:15 we go back to work and continue until 1:00 in the afternoon, when we have lunch. This is the substantial meal
of the day – four courses and wine. Coffee is then served
on the terrace and we take a siesta until 3:00 in the afternoon. We then work for a couple of hours – if there are no
common activities scheduled or local festivals to attend
(there are many in October). We go to bed early, between
10:00 and 11:00. It is pitch-dark at 6:00 and the monastery has no television.

This is one of the best things I have done in many years.
I can highly recommend it for anyone who wants to accomplish a piece of work that has been neglected for a long
time.«

The outcome of my stay at San Cataldo was a typology that operated on
two dimensions: a personal dimension and a dimension reflecting the
individual's connection with various social subcultures. The personal
dimension concerns degree of social isolation, which we divided into
two categories: the extrovert and the introvert (borrowed from Jung's
psychoanalytical personality typology). For the second dimension, social grouping, we operated with the drug addict's degree of connection
with the drug environment and with conventional society.

The choice of these rather than several other potential dimensions
was grounded partly in our empirical data and partly in our hypotheses
on their strong connection with the effectiveness of various types of
treatment. We recognized the two personality types in our material and
could operationalize them fairly easily. Furthermore, it was our opinion
that the two personality types demonstrated different requirements for
treatment. The introvert would benefit more from individual therapy
than the extrovert who, on the other hand, would benefit more from
group therapy. To mix the two types at an institutional treatment centre
that used primarily group therapy (the most prevalent type of therapy at
that time) would, in our opinion, be directly problematic. The other dimension, degree of connection with the drug environment and conventional society, was chosen because our data revealed that this dimension
was decisive for the eventual path their life took. The more the drug addicts isolated themselves from the conventional and became swallowed
up by the drug environment, the more they resembled one another –

and this was the same force that maintained a state of addiction and tied them to the associated lifestyle.

When I returned from Italy, I continued working on the final framework of the typology. In the following year, 1981, I worked primarily on the dynamic aspects of the life paths. As mentioned, we were interested in identifying the factors that pushed and pulled the drug addicts back and forth between the drug environment and the conventional world. It appeared that the introvert and extrovert types (here to be perceived as ideal types) were affected by different push and pull factors. In other phases, identical factors pushed and pulled the addicts back and forth in the course of development. We could see from the interviews that the drug addicts were actors on several different stages during their course of development. Thus we needed to construct a phase model that took into consideration characteristic phases in the development process within which certain types of explanations were predominant. We divided the development process into the following phases:

- the introduction phase
- the double phase
- the drug phase
- the treatment phase
- the conventional phase.

Our assumption was that specific pushes and pulls can be found within each phase, and that these pushes and pulls are crucial for reaching an understanding of where the drug addict finds him- or herself in the development process. We also assumed that various push and pull factors affect the various personality types. This particularly applied to the first and the last phase and, to a lesser degree, to the drug phase. Our assumptions were empirically grounded with a point of departure in the various life histories.

The result of the above considerations was that explanations as to why an individual's development takes a certain path depend in part on the drug addict's personality and in part on his or her situation at the time.

In the spring of 1982, I submitted the unfinished rough draft of our manuscript to Gyldendal Publishing, asking whether they would be interested in publishing it. Their reaction was positive. They were very interested in seeing our work as it progressed. We promised to submit a final manuscript no later than February 1, 1983. This agreement succeeded in giving us further impetus: a definite deadline significantly encourages one's creativity and work discipline.

Preben West Hansen and I organized a 3-day working seminar at a hotel away from our offices. Here we planned the final manuscript in detail and divided the work between us. We then got to work. The manuscript was produced without further problems, although I admittedly experienced periods during which I simply had to force myself to write.

Strategies for Research in Deviant Behaviour

We continued our work. Among other things we reviewed literature on deviant behaviour and the methods for doing research in that field. In the majority of the studies in which research attempted to find explanations for drug addiction, it was the norm to take a point of departure in psychodynamic explanations. As we worked our way through the material, we found these explanations increasingly inadequate. As we searched for a more comprehensively theoretical explanation, inspiration was found in Albert K. Cohen (1966).

Cohen has outlined various strategies for research in deviant behaviour at the psychological level. He distinguishes between theories that primarily emphasize the agent (the individual), or the situation, or attempt to combine the two strategies. Emphasizing agents, Cohen suggests two types of theories:

- The theory of personality type attempts to set up a personality typology and, based on this, to explain behavioural differences.
- The theory of biography also operates with human personality typology, but here the emergence of a specific personality type is conceived as the outcome of a certain history of development (biography). Thus this theory attempts to answer the question: »Why have these individuals developed the way they have?« If heritage or other forms of early biological events are unable to provide an adequate answer, the personality type must be explained in terms of a theory of personality development or learning.

If situational factors are emphasized, one does not assume that deviant actions are committed by a specific type of individual. On the contrary, given the same situational factors, anyone might react in the same way. Such situational factors may take the shape of provocation, temptation, extreme pressure, opportunity, or mentoring.

Conjunctive theories, as indicated by the terminology, combine the above-mentioned theories (theories of the agent and of situational factors). Here emphasis is put on the fact that deviant behaviour is a result of one or several specific combinations, partly the conditions to which the agent is subject and partly conditions in the situation itself.

Finally, Cohen mentions yet another research strategy based on what one could call a dynamic conjunctive theory that emphasizes the interplay between the agent's conditions and the situations viewed in a developmental perspective. According to these theories, a deviant action develops over time and goes through different stages. The choice of a deviant or nondeviant action is determined by the situation and the agent's condition.

We used Cohen's typology to help guide the focus of our description and analysis. Furthermore, it was used to produce an outline for the book. In describing the drug addicts' conditions during childhood and adolescence, we wanted to emphasize the agent and his or her psychological background. This was the first part of the book. When focusing on the individual's first experimentation with drugs, we wanted to combine this model with theories that stressed situationally determined conditions as well as a series of social interrelations. This was the second part of the book. In addition to this anchoring in a psychological framework, we also wanted to emphasize a sociopsychological and a sociological level of explanation. This particularly applied when we had to explain why the individual made certain decisions in various, situationally determined occasions: why he or she chose, for example, to become a drug addict and not an alcoholic, a stamp collector or a sociologist. This was the third part of the book in which we intended to develop a theory of situational dynamics. The final part of the book was to draw theoretically based conclusions and implications for preventive actions and treatment of drug addicts.

Results of the Study

The most important results of the study were the successful discrediting of the myths that all drug addicts are alike, that they share the same life paths, and that they, by and large, all require the same type of treatment. Apart from this, the study proved that psychodynamic explanations do not work. Conditions during childhood and adolescence are not the sole determinants for the individual's subsequent development into a drug addict. Several of the individuals in our study population had no noteworthy problems in childhood and adolescence. Based on the results, we suggested a series of changes in the treatment of drug addicts and methods for intervening in the life paths of drug addicts.

Budget and Resources

The original budget on which we based our application for funding from the Danish Social Science Research Council proved to be far too conservative. Twice we found it necessary to apply for additional funding, which we received. We thus ended up spending twice as much as originally estimated. A number of the subsequent follow-up studies were financed by the National Board of Social Welfare.

Publications and Other Means for the Releasing the Results of the Study

During the project we produced a number of status reports, which were forwarded to various institutions: the Ministry of Social Affairs, Højbjerggård, the Danish Social Science Research Council, institutional treatment centres, etc. Throughout the project we collaborated closely with Højbjerggård, and the project team participated in a large number of meetings at the centre. Encouraged by Højbjerggård to do so, we wrote articles for newspapers and participated directly in activities as (nonsalaried) consultants. The final report was forwarded to the Danish Social Science Research Council in 1982 and an edited version of it was later published by Gyldendal (Andersen & Hansen 1984).

A student at the University of Copenhagen's Institute of Psychology conducted a follow-up study on our clients and wrote a dissertation on the subject (Lassen 1983).

Jørn Daugaard Pedersen, the sociology student who participated in the project, also wrote a dissertation (1980) on the organization of drug addiction treatment in Denmark and compared it with the results of our study.

The fact that the project stretched over a long period of time caused great problems, some of which have already been mentioned. By the time our study was finally published, some of our conclusions had become obsolete – in relation to the treatment centres in the Copenhagen area. The centres had adapted new forms of treatment or abandoned treatment altogether. The nature of drug addiction had changed to a very mixed abuse of intoxicants, of which alcohol played a significant role, and the Copenhagen treatment centres had begun to focus their scarce resources on traditional, societal dropouts. Also, there seemed to be too little direct, subsequent contact with policy-makers in this area, with treatment centres and with the Ministry of Social Affairs and the counties and municipalities responsible for treating and helping drug addicts. Furthermore, the centres had been subject to a series of changes. The counties were expanding and improving their youth centres, which gradually took over many of the treatment tasks that had previously been handled by (more or less) private organizations.

On the other hand, our book contained a number of general conclusions that could be used by the established treatment system as well as by a broader circle of individuals, among others, general practitioners. Anders Groth, a psychiatrist who has treated drug addicts and done research in the field for many years, reviewed our book in a Danish medical journal. He wrote, among other things:

> »It [the book] is...a well-written, easily read, and very pedagogic presentation of the »the social dynamics of drug addiction«,...and it is specifically aimed at producing applicable results in relation to treatment and preventive actions. ...physicians who work with the problems of drug addiction should acquaint themselves with and begin to use the psychological and sociological approaches to this problem. The book makes it easy to understand the authors' conceptual framework and the more fundamental theories that lie behind it.« (Groth 1984, our translation).

However, Anders Groth was also critical of the book. His criticism lay in our scientific position, or lack of it (according to Groth):

> »The subtitle of the book is »A study on the causes of drug addiction, its course of development, and the options available for intervention«, but it is not a scientific account of a study, despite the fact that it has been funded by the Danish Social Science Research Council and the National Board of Social Welfare.« (Groth 1984, our translation)

Groth did not specify what he meant by the study not being scientific. It is my guess that Groth probably did not feel that we complied with traditional, scientific medical standards for conducting research with the attendant quantifying of variables, statistical analyses, and experimental design. But, as I said, it is only a guess.

We exchanged information with employees at Copenhagen treatment centres right up to the last few days before submission of the manuscript to Gyldendal. I discussed the manuscript and results with them, from which both parties gained. A ripple effect occurred in the spreading of the ideas and results contained in our comprehensive study.

The manuscript was submitted to Gyldendal on February 1, 1983, and the book was published on March 1, 1984.

3. The Unprepared Journey Into the Hospital World

Finn Borum

In Search of Lost Times

In 1971 I received a Ph.D. scholarship at the Institute of Organization and Industrial Sociology, Copenhagen Business School. At that time scholars were responsible for the same amount of teaching as associate professors. I had a Master's degree which, in those days, was attained by combining a Bachelor of Science in Business Economics and Administration (a 3-year day programme) with a Bachelor of Commerce in Organization or another specialization (a 2-year evening course that followed the B.Sc.). After having become a Bachelor of Science, I worked for 7 years in the private sector as a systems planner – most of the time in a management position. From an initial fascination with information technology, my interest gradually shifted to the human and organizational aspects of this technology. This shift in interest was not surprising. As information technology developed, the bottleneck for administrative rationalization turned out to be the interaction with users in terms of design and implementation of systems.

Thus, further studies in organization theory would be a natural way to gain better knowledge about the issues that caused me originally to follow the Bachelor of Commerce studies. By the time I graduated, I was tired of my work as a systems planner. This was greatly due to the fact that urgent daily tasks constantly superseded long-term planning, which was where my interests primarily lay. Teaching and research seemed to be more attractive – even though the salary was not.

The Institute of Organization at the Copenhagen Business School was looking for a scholar who knew something about information technology. Combined with a subsequent grant, this made me fairly confident of having a job for the next 6 years. I contracted for a wage that was half of what I made in the private sector at that time – and even less when viewed in terms of my expected future earnings. However, as I was single, I felt that I could afford the privilege of prioritizing my subject interests over finances, and I took a plunge into academe, which I have never since regretted.

The subject of my Bachelor of Commerce dissertation was an analysis of the interaction between information systems developers and information technology users by means of communication theory. Naturally, I planned to continue to conduct research on the planning of information systems based on the perspective of communication and decision-making theory. However, I never seemed to get anywhere with this plan. No doubt, this was due to the influence of new colleagues who gradually steered my interest from information technology towards organizational theory. Thus, information technology lost its status as my primary field of interest and became merely an inspiring empirical field. Furthermore, my application of communication and decision-making theory by and large resulted in only slight modifications of the dominant approximated, rational planning model, and it did not treat important issues related to information technology tasks and their structural consequences.

After half a year, I was ready to challenge these self-imposed constraints. In this situation, a project turned up. The founder of the Institute, Professor Torben Agersnap, became involved in an organizational development project at the (at that time) largest hospital in the City of Copenhagen – Bispebjerg Hospital. The project was initiated by both the city hospital directorate and Bispebjerg Hospital with the purpose of drawing up a proposal for more efficient work procedures for both the overall management of the hospital and management of the departments. The project was in fact an early effort to begin a change process aimed at solving financial, structural, and motivational problems. It marked the start of the comprehensive restructuring process necessitated by the construction of new hospitals in the Copenhagen area (Organisationsudvalget 1974).

A project steering committee was established with representatives from the various occupational groups, the hospital management, and the hospital directorate with Torben Agersnap functioning as an external consultant. The steering committee needed both information and premises on which it could base its recommendations for restructuring and the organization of the development process and therefore ordered three separate organizational studies. Apart from the project in question, the studies comprised analyses of the administrative systems and the work milieu. The latter study was conducted in terms of interviews with all the employees who had left the hospital during the previous 6 months.

The subprojects required staffing. Three »junior researchers« – I was included in this group – embarked with varying degrees of commitment on the least well-defined sub-project: an investigation of the systems of management and collaboration systems at hospital departmental level.

I was attracted to the project as I viewed it as a possibility for gaining a more basic knowledge about the empirical and methodological aspects of organizational sociology. My approach to working with information technology had been normative, and I had been deeply involved in designing the world. I had never seriously tried to analyse and understand a social system. Neither of my previous studies had provided me with knowledge appropriate for filling this methodological vacuum. Therefore, before starting on »my« research project, I felt a need for further training. Thus, my involvement in somebody else's project as project assistant was a sort of personally designed Ph.D. course. As far as I remember, my plans were to design a research project on the organizational aspects of information systems after completing the above-mentioned hospital project within an anticipated short 6 months.

The hospital project seemed to offer good opportunities for individual development: the project leader delegated responsibility for the sub-projects to the research assistants and devoted himself to the discussions with the steering committee and associated political processes. Additionally, both the problem and the methodological approach were so ill-defined that the project provided great opportunities for floundering in deep waters.

In this context, it should be borne in mind that the project was anchored in the aftermath of the events of 1968 in Denmark: rebellion against positivism, rebellion against authorities (or the search for new ones?), the abolition of professorial power, etc. At the Institute of Organization, participation and democracy were central values and focal research issues. In this context, the project was legitimized and at the same time provided me with suitable conditions for enacting my own youthful rebellion – albeit slightly delayed.

Thus, I committed myself to participation in the first phase of the project – a preliminary investigation running for half a year. Shortly after its start in 1972, it became clear that no project group would be established. After half a year, I was the only one who was still intrigued by the project. Five years later, I ultimately concluded the project by publishing my Ph.D. dissertation. During those years, my interest shifted from information technology and methodology to general organization theory and action research, and several times I was tempted to leave the project, the Institute, and research altogether. Only the backing of a support group of good colleagues, a patient wife, coincidences, and a fair share of stubbornness helped me cling to a complicated and vacillating path.

The project thus proved to be my greatest expedition into the nature of organizations, couplings between organization and society, organization theory and analysis, change processes – and my own temperament.

The First Design

The official title of the subproject was »A Problem-oriented, Explorative Investigation of Managerial and Collaborative Conditions at Selected Hospital Departments«. The purpose of the study was to examine how the hospital departments functioned – emphasizing the aspects of the system that functioned less satisfactorily. In one way or another, this had to be translated into a specific design for the study. The possibilities were legion and further multiplied by the size of the organization and its complexity: all medical specialties were represented; the number of departments was tremendous, with numerous service departments included; 35 different occupational groups were represented at the hospital; the organization functioned 24 hours a day, etc.

Any idea of designing an all-encompassing or representative study was immediately excluded by two factors: a very low budget (as far as I recall, we had DKK 35,000 to cover all costs) and the short duration of the project. Furthermore, the possibility of conducting a survey was excluded, as the steering committee wanted to get a better idea of how the departments really functioned managerially and collaboratively.

During those turbulent times, any authority or institution was subject to criticism. At the Institute, we were engaged in the criticism of bureaucracy and focused on participation research, action research, and phenomenology. The qualitative interview played a major role methodologically as a means of disclosing the experiences of actors.

The logical outcome of the steering committee's wish for insight into the functioning of the departments versus the research system's orientation towards »the man or woman on the shop floor« was to select a limited number of departments to investigate. The number ended at two departments: one surgical and one medical. Many stories could be told about the process leading to the choice of these two departments. However, in the interest of space, I will leave this part of the story to the reader's imagination.

Various imaginative ways of conducting the study were discussed, including hospitalizing the researcher, letting the researcher act as a physician, nurse, etc. We did a great deal of reading, as we had access to abundant literature in English on the sociology of hospitals. Hospital research was a well-established school within organizational sociology in the United States and, to a lesser extent, in the United Kingdom. Occupational sociology was also to a large extent rooted in hospital research. Hence, one possibility was to construct a deductive project design based on existing knowledge. However, at that time the only Danish studies in existence were a couple of studies on the work climate, one of which was being conducted by the Institute of Mental Health. Everyone agreed that a concrete study based on reality was needed.

We ended up opting for an interview survey that would begin with participant observation in the departments. Having reached this conclusion, we started. The first step was a given: get out and look at the field! The project leader hurried to organize an information meeting with the staff of the two departments, and we were received very positively. Participant observation as a first step was chosen in view of the fact that it would be impossible to get any further before we had developed a preliminary understanding of the system. Therefore, shortly after this meeting, I found myself dressed up in a white coat and walking around in one of the departments.

Meeting the Field

I was well received – and on the whole neglected. People working in hospitals are used to seeing many strange individuals circulating – and knowing only a few of them. Housemen (interns), trainees, students, orderlies, assistants, laboratory technicians, physiotherapists, you name it drifted through the units: the association of a central train station during rush hour often came to mind. Everyone was dressed in white and, in the name of democracy, titles on name tags had been abolished. My appearance more or less resembled that of a befuddled bumpkin who awkwardly and constantly managed to get in the way. Thus, in this female world I was perceived not as an orderly but as a medical student.

Apart from hanging around, I talked to whoever happened to be nearby – including a few patients. However, I stopped this practice very quickly when it became obvious that they expected some type of hospital treatment when confronted by anyone dressed in white: in view of these expectations, patients interpreted an organization analysis as an organ examination. That was more than I had bargained for, so I joined the rounds, the conferences, and the meetings, all three of which were a great experience. The ward rounds were headed by the chief surgeons or physicians or the senior registrar. Second in command were the head nurse and the secretary. Staff nurses, trainees, junior registrars, and stray dogs, such as organizational researchers, brought up the rear. The vanguard recorded patient status and coordinated future treatment, diligently consulting and discussing the case record across the patient's eiderdown. The rear troops generally ended up in the hallway and were not able to make much sense out of the bits and pieces of the discussions that filtered out from the front lines.

The conferences were fairly large gatherings of physicians, nurses, secretaries, and in some cases physiotherapists, social workers, etc. Of the 15-20 people gathered, it was generally only the chief surgeons or physicians – sometimes only the head nurses – who spoke. The agenda was set by the physicians. There was general frustration with these conferences: to what purpose were they intended? Education, exchange of information, coordination, decision-making? On the whole, everyone agreed that none of these issues were satisfactorily addressed.

During the day each department had a number of scheduled meetings: meetings in the morning and in the afternoon served to pass information to and from the day shift and often marked the beginning and end of the working day. Time schedules, however, often made it difficult for day, evening, and night shifts to be present at the same time and pass on the baton. To amend this problem, there were other types of meetings that I no longer recall. But the endless coffee drinking made it difficult to find out whether a meeting was going on or whether the staff were merely taking a break.

I spent a fair amount of time on these gatherings. But it was in quite different situations that I felt the system start to talk:

- Spontaneous talks occurred in private or in small groups in connection with work situations or during short breaks. Dissatisfaction bubbled to the surface and was, in terms of specific examples, tangible and traceable to work situations causing frustration that resulted in less efficient task performance.
- Talks occurred late in the evening when tiredness and exhaustion broke down defence mechanisms. Problems with the career, the boss, and the family were then allowed to flow freely.
- Emergency situations with the unexpected arrival of a patient sud-

denly mobilized all available competencies in the organization or forced the staff to handle defects in the formal system.

The impressions were multiple and overwhelming. A month of more-or-less intensive participant observation (I also had to attend to my teaching) left the hopeful researcher confused on a higher plane.

Have Experience – Data Wanted

During the study, a Danish journalist wrote a series of articles on hospitals focusing on tyrannical physicians, oppressed nurse's aides, overtime, and neglected patients. It was necessary that our organizational analysis somehow dissociated itself from a journalistic approach – which otherwise seemed a natural continuation of the phase of participant observation. Also, the steering committee clearly expected a scientific report on which they could base their claims for change in relation to the physicians.

This situation represented an insoluble problem: the study was expected to meet the type of scientific criteria as defined by the natural scientific paradigm of medical science. This was quite different from the scientific paradigm of the Institute of Organization at that time with its elements of phenomenology, hermeneutics, and critical theory. The scientific tradition of my own research was thus in outright opposition to positivist-oriented medical science. At this point in the process, I suddenly realized the seriousness of the problem that had been there all along – it was embedded in the contract for the study.

The fact that the study was defined as explorative provided me with a straw to grasp: slender data and interpretations could be justified by stressing that they would be tested in a subsequent main study. And, incidentally, surgeons talk about explorative surgery when they are unable to diagnose a disease based on diverse symptoms and therefore have to look into the patient without necessarily performing an actual, ultimate surgical operation.

Here I was – filled with personal experiences and impressions from the participant observation phase that simply could not be used as data...merely as background for designing the collection and interpretation of genuine data. The steering committee would undoubtedly define my first impressions as far too subjective and questionable.

Right from the beginning, however, I was aware that most data from the preliminary study would inevitably have to be subjective since the data would comprise the experiences of the hospital staff recorded in qualitative, taped interviews. My choice of approach could also be interpreted as an expression of the methodological stereotype by which organizational research had responded to the positivist surveys for several years (Broch, Krarup, Larsen & Rieper 1979; Enderud 1984).

But who was I to interview and about what? The first observations provided a certain insight into the hospital system, but this also created new problems. The system's complexity and degree of institutionalization were even more comprehensive than I had expected and made it necessary to set definite limits. The functioning of the departments was affected by external factors (such as hospitalization of long-term patients in the medical department, staffing, grants, etc.) and by internal structures and forms of management – which, however, were also exogenously shaped by the current educational system, negotiated division of labour, agreements, and established standards for how to organize and manage the division of labour in a hospital.

The solution to the first crisis was to focus on the internal structure of the hospital and its management system and to view the selected departments as exemplary. This approach was most in line with the commissioned task, and any excursion into the political system in which the hospital was embedded would be akin to opening Pandora's box.

A hospital department proved, however, not to be the most appropriate unit of analysis. First, the structures of the departments were very different due to their differing specialties and varying degrees of interaction with other departments. An analysis of the two departments might be rejected as too singular and irrelevant in relation to other departments. Second, a department was identified with the chief administrative physician. Thus, identified problems or strengths might easily be attributed to the form of management exercised by the chief physician in question. Third, a department was simply too complex to constitute an appropriate unit of analysis.

So, instead we chose the ward unit as the unit of analysis. One of the reasons, as far as I remember, was that with this choice we could get close to the patients. Even though we were in no position to assess the treatment of patients, we could identify connections between structure and the milieu surrounding the patients. Second, we would be close to the shop floor and hence to the attitudes and problems that normally were suppressed. Third, the nursing staff identified themselves with the unit. Finally, a unit was an elementary part of the hospital structure: it could be identified unambiguously, there were a great number of units, and they were immediately recognizable. Figure 3.1 illustrates the ward unit in terms of a systems model.

Figure 3.1. Systems Model of the Ward Unit

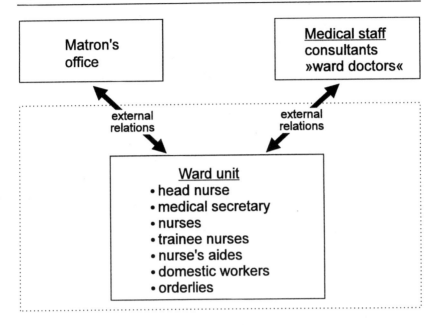

This delimitation implies some drastic choices. The physicians are identified as belonging to the environment of the unit. Their offices were located elsewhere, and from a sociometric perspective their interaction with the nursing staff and the patients was limited. Furthermore, the study viewed management and collaboration from the perspective of the nursing staff. Looking back, it is not surprising that this simple systems model later gave rise to intense criticism, especially from the physicians.

However, choosing the ward unit as the unit of analysis solved several problems. First of all it provided a reason for selecting interviewees and for excluding many of the occupational groups that we could have interviewed. Second, it portrayed the unit as composed of certain roles and positions. This simple description points further towards a structural analysis of individual experiences: how did individuals experience their role or position and their relationships to that of others?

Now I was able to generate data, and I returned to the field with a list of the selected roles that had to be covered, a quickly designed, role-oriented interview guide, and a tape recorder stuck into one of the pockets of my white coat.

Generating Data

The first thing that struck me on my return to the field were the dramatic consequences that resulted when shifting roles from that of a participant observer to that of an interviewer. Suddenly the relationship between researcher and informant became considerably more formal: you made an appointment for an interview, usually met at the scheduled hour, and the interviewer asked a number of questions. This situation was repeated over and over. Usually the interview took place in a conference room; only high-status individuals could be interviewed in their offices. In the middle of the table was the tape recorder, quietly reminding those present that this was not just a chat.

Contrary to the first phase, during which data in the form of statements and impressions were produced without any effort and as mere byproducts of both the system's everyday life and the presence of an observer, the current situation demanded hard work. The interviews had to be prepared and the production of a successful interview situation demanded great effort. The best interviews were produced when I forgot all about the interview guide and used it as merely as a kind of checklist at the end of the interview.

But how was I to decide who to interview and how many to interview? I had to hear from at least 11 roles and to cover four ward units. In principle, the minimum number was 44 interviews. I only did 43 interviews, 15 of which involved nurses and head nurses. I had no intention of making a comparative analysis of the ward units. My intention was to outline an ideal type of ward unit based on the preliminary investigation. The question of which people should put life into the roles was solved during the process. I had already made a number of preliminary interview appointments during my first sojourn in the field, and there were also a number of high-status individuals whom I simply had to interview. Consequently, I already had so many prior appointments that it was superfluous to make any additional.

My own impressions and sympathies, as well as advice from people with whom I had fruitful discussions, guided my selection of the last interviewees that were needed to cover the role system fully. In principle, a role was sufficiently identified when the last interview did not add any new aspects. This principle could not, however, be strictly enforced. The list of interviews was long, and ahead of me was the threatening task of writing the report; the clock not only ticked – it raced. Some of the interviews were very good and very enlightening; others were poor – some to the extent of uselessness. I found it was actually possible for an interviewer and his interviewee to produce 45 minutes of empty conversation.

The hospital is, and was, characterized by great differences in status that the interviews clearly reflected. At the top of the system (the physicians), people were accustomed to expressing themselves, but their statements were also more strategic in relation to knowing what they wanted to discuss. I clearly remember how frustrated I felt after an interview with a registrar who, after a heart-to-heart talk during one night shift, got cold feet and gave me nothing but empty words during the formal interview. Why risk your career for an organizational analysis? I have the same clear memory of the interviews with the chief surgeons and physicians. During the interviews, none of us at any time forgot that the interview concerned a leader. I asked politely. They answered politely.

Then there were the head nurses who, at that time, were stuck between the consultant surgeons and physicians and the nursing staff, and who had chosen, as a main strategy, confrontation avoidance with the chief surgeons and physicians. This attitude was disclosed by a series of interviews with individuals who had left the hospital – interviews that were conducted simultaneously with the preliminary study. With one exception – the leader of a completely burned-out surgical unit – my interviews with the head nurses were devoid of content.

From the women in the middle, I proceeded to the women at the bottom: the cleaning woman who spoke with everyone and with whom the patients felt safe talking. One interview ended in a disaster – »physician« tries to interview »female employee«. I was rescued by the coffee break – during which I tried to make an appointment for the next interview. The cleaning team felt that it would be much better if we all talked together at the same time. We did so and the result was a brilliant group discussion during which they supplemented, corrected, and commented on one another's statements. My role was reduced to holding the microphone.

Distilling Data

At a point in time I finished my data collection. The role positions had all been covered, and time for additional interviewing had passed. If data proved incapable of providing me with the necessary information for my report, I would have to catch up with it later. This is how you always reason with yourself and others, but do you really have the energy to follow-up on data collection? Since the study was explorative, I did not have the energy to do so. I felt I had enough data, and the feeling of having collected all the pieces for my puzzle was very comforting.

However, this comfortable belief came to an abrupt end when I started to listen to the tapes. The recording quality of tapes was rather poor at that time, and sometimes the primitive on-location recordings resulted in so much background noise (anything from chatting and rustling paper to shouting and the rattling of garbage cans) that it was extremely difficult to decipher the recordings unless you knew the context in which they had been produced. Handing over the transcription of the tapes to someone else was unthinkable; the only way out of the situation was to sit down and listen carefully to all of them and write down quotations or take notes. These data were actually data scraps that had to be subjected to further engineering.

It takes quite some time to process one 45-minute interview. Usually I did not get started until late in the evening:

> »It's three o'clock in the morning. The table is an organic pile of cups, bottles, overflowing ashtrays, tapes, bits and pieces of interviews, and notes that nobody understands. The noise of the tape recorder running out just woke me. In short, qualitative methods are being applied in organizational analysis.« (Borum 1979: 297)

It was outright gruesome. I was caught in a trap I had constructed myself. I was keen on getting started on the analysis and synthesis but was forced to transcribe the interviews in order to make data accessible. I panicked and lost myself in details. I lost all the knowledge and insight generated through participant observation in the first phase. I had not thought of writing down my impressions at the time, and they were completely overridden by the acute problem of processing the raw data. I was totally bewildered. And it lasted some time.

After a while I had worked my way through all the tapes, and this resulted in files filled with quotations, key words, and references to the tape sequences of interest. Now I was prepared to get started with the serious business of analysis. However, I soon discovered that I, due to panic and tiredness, had not been consistent enough when producing the transcripts. Therefore, in this phase, too, I had to spend quite some time listening to the tapes again. The process was, however, somewhat easier this time since I had transcribed parts of the interviews.

Nevertheless, there was one bright light at the end of the tunnel: the data were good. They pointed toward a wealth of problems in terms of: dissatisfaction with the coordination between the departments; frustrations about work processes, meetings, and staffing; the existence of a pecking order and lack of understanding between occupational groups; stress, etc. Most of the interviewees talked about topics that were important to them. These were serious problems that revealed the difficulties of surviving as a human being in a system that was inhuman at times. The interviewees were not discussing some remote system, but one in which they had a part. The statements revealed emotions and attitudes, joy and distress. It was worth struggling with such data.

Have Data – Problem Formulation Wanted

And it was indeed a struggle. Where could I find a framework of interpretation that both was capable of containing the many different types of statements – thereby allowing the actors to make themselves heard in detail – and capable of suggesting a pattern in the statements, that is, a potential structural explanation behind the statements. Ideally, I would want, like the sculptor, to be able to make the stone talk – it was a matter of removing as little as possible and allowing the possibilities embedded in the material to reveal themselves through simple means.

I went through several abortive attempts at writing. I started with the roles that seemed to be a natural continuation of the interviews, but the result turned out to be too rigid and uninteresting. A sequential presentation of the content of each role, expectations of others, experienced expectations from others, attitudes towards others, etc. resulted in a detailed, but non-focused description. Furthermore, the data were awkward in relation to a consistent role analysis. The interviews contained statements about anything and everything, and many of the most telling sequences had nothing to do with roles. I needed a framework of analysis that was more problem-oriented. The analysis came to a standstill. My early problem formulation had not been clear, and I was now receiving the punishment. I had to define a research issue that was consistent with the data.

The solution came unexpectedly through one of my colleagues, Tore Jacob Hegland, who had written an article on the properties and problems of bureaucracy and alternatives to bureaucracy (1971). The article contained a section on »the problem of alienation in bureaucracy«, in which Tore Jacob claimed that bureaucracy resulted in feelings of powerlessness, meaninglessness, social isolation, and self-alienation among employees.

This was the solution! The dimensions of alienation proved to be extremely suitable for encompassing the major part of the actors' statements on experienced organizational problems. The structural dimensions could be used to describe significant characteristics of the internal structure and management form of the hospital. Finally, it became possible, based on the actors' explanations and my own interpretations, to tell a coherent story about the structure producing alienation. Well, I still had a lot of work to do, but my mind was at peace. Not only had I found an analytical anchor but a social one as well. At that time Tore Jacob Hegland was the standard-bearer of the criticism of bureaucracy and institutions at the Institute.

As to the dimensions of structure and alienation, there was still a great deal of work to be done in terms of adaptation, operationalization, and selection. The very framework of interpretation raised the problem of to what extent alienation could be explained as a consequence of internal or external factors in the system or as a combination thereof. The final explanatory framework is illustrated in Figure 3.2.

Figure 3.2. Alienation at a Ward Unit

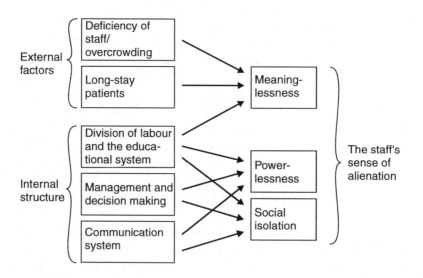

Within this explanatory framework the different roles had to be brought to life. A colleague of mine, Bjarne Herskin, provided me with the solution to this level of the analysis.

And finally, sorting out quotations along the dimensions of structure and alienation was quite a puzzle. During this process several dimensions had to be redefined or abandoned or new ones had to be added. But the pieces of the puzzle fell into place, and the final report utilized a large share of the interview quotations glued together in terms of explanatory and interpretative text based on the theoretical structure.

Figure 3.3. Communication Pattern Between Occupational Groups

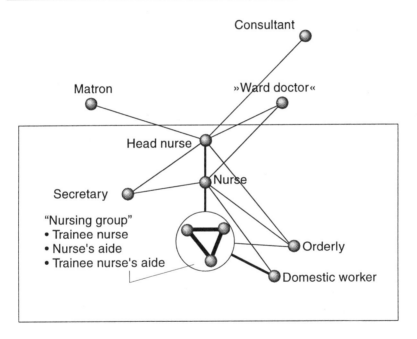

Consequently, it became possible to further develop the original systems model of the ward unit. This model stemmed from the attempt to summarize the observed patterns of interaction among role holders. The phenomenon was complex and data diffuse (interview quotations, observations, and attempts to summarize). I started to draw a figure. I showed the figure to my contact persons – without much explanation. They asked questions and commented on it. I made corrections and showed it to them again. After a few attempts, the figure was okayed. The reaction was »This is the general picture, but naturally it is a bit different here.« And the picture was in keeping with data from the study (Figures 3.3, 3.4).

Figure 3.4. Communication Pattern Between Patient and Staff

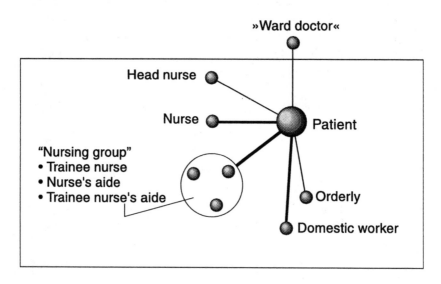

It should be borne in mind that the figures contains the following dimensions: status (position in the hierarchy), social distance (the linear distance between two role positions), intensity of interaction (boldness of lines), and centrality in relation to patient milieu (the nursing group indicates the centre).

Feedback to the Field

Proud and relieved, I delivered the report on the preliminary study to the steering committee with only a few months delay. They were not very pleased with it. It was also fairly provocative, with its main message being that the hospital staff was alienated and that this situation was brought about primarily by an inappropriate internal structure. In addition to this, statements from the staff interviews were printed in italics, which might have created unintended associations with newspaper headlines and sensational articles. Finally, the report was probably characterized more by youthful daring than by the wisdom of age. Thus, at some points the report contained unnecessarily provocative statements and easy formulations. The committee judged the report unfit for distribution to the departments – which we had promised the interviewees throughout the study. It was stamped *confidential* and regarded as a useful, internal working paper for the committee.

The form of the report is not immaterial as an explanation of this and subsequent reactions. Compared with contemporary journalistic reports from the hospital world, the report's use of quotations might cause the unexpecting reader to interpret it as a journalistic essay. Added to this, the fact that the report was written about and to an organization dominated by the research paradigm of natural science was akin to asking for a fight.

Expulsion from the Field

Confidentiality increases market value, and somehow the newspaper *Information* got hold of the story and printed a half-page article that gave a reasonably fair summary of the report. Consequently, the steering committee could no longer withhold the report from the units.

By now, however, the committee had become accustomed to the report and considered it in a more favourable light. The committee felt subjected to pressure and agreed to submit the report to the chief physicians and chiefs of nursing and thereafter discuss it with them at a meeting.

At this meeting the physicians strongly criticized the report and tore it to pieces scientifically. Neither the interview method nor the method of analysis was acceptable as a way of producing valid knowledge. The latent conflict between what the hospitals and my research environment defined as science now unfolded in full. Furthermore, the report was interpreted as a massive criticism of the specific departments – and hence their management – and not as an effort to identify more general, systemic problems based on four hospital units. Naturally, the critical statements came from the chief surgeons and physicians, and, quite understandably, none of the head nurses felt inclined to put themselves on the line and disagree with the physicians with whom they worked every day.

The process of witnessing that report torn to pieces was one of the most horrible emotional experiences I have ever had. I did not quite understand my reaction and still don't, but I can identify certain elements of an explanation. The simplest one is that I had put a great deal of work and commitment into an analysis that was rejected. On the other hand, others, who were not in a tight spot, had commented very favourably on it. Perhaps the problem was rather one of wanting to be on good terms with everyone although the report revealed a system of strongly divergent interests and assessments. The logical consequence of the study's perspectives and interpretations would be to continue the study based on a ward unit or on a group of the nursing staff. It was naive to think that the department heads would be interested in using the results from the preliminary study as a basis for an organizational development.

The preliminary study's methodology of viewing the hospital from the bottom was inconsistent with submitting the report to the top of the hospital. It would have been more consistent if I, during the study, had produced preliminary analyses that I had discussed with the interviewees and had provided information about findings at unit meetings. I did not do this, partly due to project crises and partly due to the lack of insight and consideration as mentioned earlier.

As a result, it was not I but the steering committee who was in control of what kind of feedback the interviewees received. But there was a discrepancy between generated knowledge and subsequent action, which could be traced back to my own anxiety in choosing a path and too little reflection. Both explanations gave rise to a guilty conscience, which was a waste of time and distressed me greatly and which even caused me to refrain from discussing the problem with others. Good colleagues had earlier rendered substantial support in critical situations, but now I shut myself off.

Returning to the Field

In spite of being stamped confidential, the report gradually found its way out. I discussed it with the staff at other hospitals and units and received mainly positive reactions that confirmed both the analysis and the need for changing the internal structure. I had little confidence that the overall organizational development project could relieve the problems at the departmental level. For this reason I was strongly motivated to initiate a concrete organizational change project.

Coincidences are not to be sneezed at. A head nurse's skiing holiday (and her subsequent absence when the steering committee met with the department managers) contributed to assuring the continuation of the study as an action research project. During her interview, she had expressed great dissatisfaction with the current working conditions and the lack of coordination between the departments. For several years she had tried to do something about the problems and was now facing a run-down and burned-out unit. Furthermore, the nursing staff of the surgical unit was also interested in participating in a concrete change project. We established a contract for a joint venture after having analysed the practical and political possibilities for launching a change project that involved neither the steering committee, the physicians, the consultant surgeons and physicians nor the central management.

The nursing staff was burned out to such an extent that something had to be done. Among themselves, they had discussed the possibility of collectively resigning. Together we agreed that it actually would be possible to initiate a change project from the bottom of the organization since:

● The surgical unit was an autonomous unit that was not formally subordinate to the chief physicians and, therefore, was in a position to act.
● The objectives of the change project were justifiable and legitimate: better coordination between departments, better handling of patients and a better working climate and productivity in the unit.
● It was possible to establish hard indicators for the unit's problems.

The latter element was important. It would be possible to produce argumentation that was acceptable to the natural scientific line of thought dominating the hospital system. The surgical unit's resemblance to a workshop made it possible to design detailed statistics on productivity that would not have been possible for a normal ward unit. By supplementing with other quantitative indicators (the well-being of the staff, absenteeism, and staff turnover), it would be possible to produce argumentation based on hard data and not soft experiences.

Naturally incorporating this perspective into the project was not without its problems, as there was the danger that it might result in the participants and/or myself tending to adopt a more mechanical view of the organization and its staff.

From Analysis to Action
(with a Little Help from My Friends)

Starting on the action research phase required dissolving the inconsistencies between analysis and fieldwork. This required reading, thorough and in depth, of theories on organizational change: their major components, demands on change processes, and especially the basic conceptions of an organization.

The key solution was to view the hospital organization from a conflict perspective rather than a consensual perspective. This was basically in keeping with the preliminary study's diagnosis of the hospital as a hierarchical system strongly characterized by alienation especially among the lower status strata. Inspired by Dahrendorf (1959: 161-162), this resulted in the two conceptions of an organization illustrated in Figure 3.5.

Figure 3.5. The Harmony and Conflict Model of an Organization

---

TWO MODELS OF AN ORGANIZATION:

CONSENSUS

- An organisation is a stable structure.

- An organization is composed of well-integrated elements.

- All elements of an organization are functional elements, that is, they contribute to maintain the organization.

- An efficient organization is based on consensus among the members about mutual values.

CONFLICT

- An organisation is always undergoing change.

- An organization always contains disagreement and conflict.

- Any element of an organization contributes to dissolve and change the organization.

- An organization is based on some members imposing control on others.

But this did not solve another crucial problem: how was it possible, through internal action, for a low-status group (the nursing staff) to implement organizational changes against the will of a high-status group (chief physicians). The problem became even more critical as theories on organization development by nature assumed that the acceptance of top management was a decisive condition for initiating organizational change.

A conception of organizations as pluralist, political systems led to power theory. The more traditional school of power theory contained, in terms of powerbase theory, an operational understanding of power relationships. Indeed, the more traditional version sought to explain the outcome of zero-sum games. However, nothing seemed to eliminate the possibility of making the power-base dimensions more dynamic and action-oriented.

Six power bases emerged as central for the understanding of a group's power position in the hospital:

- group cohesion
- energy
- expertise
- autonomy
- political connections   .
- strategic competence.

These dimensions made it possible to assess the power bases of the nursing staff and the chief physicians and to identify the possibilities for strengthening the position of the nursing staff. Based on identified possibilities of action, activities were initiated that aimed to create conditions that would later enable the nursing staff to demand that their wishes for change be discussed and implemented.

Now, I was both theoretically and morally equipped for working in and with the field. Once again I found help among colleagues – this time not among scholars I had met, but among scholars whose works I had read.

The remaining part of the action research project was not altogether easy, but it was at least consistent with a clearly defined path that facilitated the necessary strategic thinking, the necessary division of labour between the participants, and the utilization of the participants' different skills. A student aide and I functioned as theoretical and analytical resource persons, whereas the nursing staff that would have to live with the change process and its consequences were the only participants who knew enough about the field to make the critical decisions about specific actions.

The action research project is analysed in detail in Borum (1976, 1995). The project itself took 9 months to conduct, and analysing the results took 18 months. The important objectives of improved coordination and planning of work were both attained as a result of the project. An important byproduct of the project was, however, that several of the participants – including myself – learned a great deal from it.

A follow-up on the project 18 months later not only proved once more how difficult it is to change complex systems but also contributed to the implementation of new actions aimed at preserving some of the results previously achieved.

4. The Long and Tortuous Journey of the Ph.D. Candidate: From Theorizing on Industrial Policy to Innovation Practices at the Company Level

Peter Karnøe

Introduction

My journey into the role of a research fellow began in the autumn of 1985 after having graduated from the University of Copenhagen with an M.Sc. in Political Science in the summer of 1985. I was hired as a research assistant for the Dynamic Specialization Project, a newly launched research project at the Copenhagen Business School. My career continued from 1987 to 1990 as a Ph.D. candidate at the University of Copenhagen. During this 5-year period, which was a blend of creativity, persistent effort, and being at the right place at the right time, I was subject to a fundamental theoretical and methodological re-education – the outcome of which was a Ph.D. in innovation economics and technology from Pol. Science department. Thematically, the two research processes were closely related, but they turned out very differently both in terms of the theories and the empirical methods applied. Methodologically, my re-education resulted in a new perspective on how to conduct empirical inquiry. My own research process was an emancipation manoeuvre that freed me from the chains embodied in my project work and master's thesis. Theoretically I shifted from the perspectives of political science to those of the economics of innovation at company level: the historical development of Denmark's wind turbine industry with a focus on the process of innovation and learning.

Master's Thesis and Choice of Career

I was recruited for the job as research assistant for the above-mentioned project while collaborating with a fellow student on the last phase of our master's thesis. Our topic was the interplay between Denmark's energy policy and industrial policy. We were interested in the industrial effects arising from the various energy policy priorities and investments in nuclear power, district heating, and wind turbine technology. We concerned ourselves with the industrial basis for each of these types of energy technology, but as students of political science we focused on a power analysis of the corporatist-type actors and their ability to influence governmental policies.

Our power analysis was intended to demonstrate how the specific policies and the institutional forms of regulation differed for the three types of energy technologies due to different actor setups and traditions.

The political economic debate of the early 1980s was an important source of inspiration for us. At that time, both Denmark's academic environment and the Folketing (parliament) were divided into two mainstreams of very differing opinions as to the causes of and solutions to the serious economic crisis that included rising unemployment and a worsening trade deficit. The Liberals, Conservatives, and others introduced a neoliberal strategy: reduction of public expenditures, lower taxes, and »more room for market mechanisms«. The Socialist People's Party and the Social Democrats, on the contrary, adhered to a neoreformist strategy: a far more active, governmental role in »getting the ball rolling«. My political inclinations fell in line with the neoreformists' economic policy, as I was strongly in favour of an active industrial policy that stimulated industrial development in order to reduce unemployment and improve industrial competitiveness.

Being trained in Marxist analysis, we were aware of the importance of elucidating the historical process, for example the political, technological, and industrial aspects of the development of nuclear power from 1953 to 1984. In the years from 1955 until the early 1980s, government subsidies for scientific and technological rearmament in preparation for the use of nuclear power were based on the idea that Danish industry should be in a position to exploit the future national and international market for nuclear power plants. But why didn't the government, in view of the potential technological and industrial opportunities, introduce similar schemes for subsidizing the wind turbine industry? Furthermore, the construction of nuclear power plants had virtually ceased after the Three Mile Island catastrophe. This accident had led to greater demands for security and hence rapidly increasing construction costs and (particularly in Denmark) public resistance. Based on an analysis of the position of relevant actors in government councils and committees, attempts were made to draw an empirical picture in two areas: which strengths did the various actors use in attempting to promote certain interests, and which coalitions lay behind the particular energy policies?

The empirical data on which we based our analysis consisted, by and large, of anything but interviews. Historical data and industrial statistics, newspaper clippings, professional journals, and other sources provided information on which companies produced the various types of energy technology. In identifying these companies' affiliation with corporations and/or industrial interest organizations, a picture of their socioeconomic strengths gradually emerged. In combination, these methods provided us with good material, and it did not occur to us that it might be a good idea to supplement it with interviews with key individuals. This was not a research tradition at the Department of Political Science.

Up until the early spring of 1985, I tried to get a position in one of the fascinating ministries such as the Ministry of Finance, Energy, or Industry. However, I changed my mind while working with a professor on his project concerning the welfare state. Discussions with him opened my eyes to other job opportunities. He was certain of a future need for studying the problems with which I was working. I had never perceived of projects and research as a viable occupational alternative. It sounded exciting, and I decided to give myself 2 years outside the ministerial employment system.

Research Assistant

Where does one find a research project? At that time I was hardly aware of the existence of the Danish Social Science Research Council. In mid-May 1985 I mentioned this choice of career to my university supervisor and asked him whether he knew of any projects. The following weekend he attended a conference in Nyborg. At this conference he spoke with a colleague who was looking for a research assistant for a project on industrial development and industrial policy (Dynamic Specialization Project, hereafter known as DYS). The following Wednesday I sat down with my little brown bag and ate lunch with the two project leaders; they hired me as a research assistant for an 8- to 10-month period starting September 1. This made me speed up the work on my master's thesis, and after final exams in June, I finished the thesis during July, August, and in the evenings of September.

Even though DYS was scheduled to run for 30 months, I could not count on being employed for more than 6-8 months. The plan was to hire two research assistants, one of whom was already employed. The other one, a »real« economist, could not start until December 1. This, combined with the somewhat lower wage scales to which we were entitled, meant that the project had resources available.

The Paradigm of the Dynamic Specialization Project (DYS) Study

The DYS study was an explorative project. The aim was to reach a more profound understanding of the potential of small and medium-sized enterprises in Denmark for technological development and competitive strength on the global market for niche products. This theme should, among other things, be viewed in the light of the debate occurring at that time on competitiveness and potential industrial policy measures. A more profound understanding of these companies would facilitate the development of more appropriate industrial and technological policy measures for the strengthening of the international competitiveness of Denmark's economy. This was very close to the issues with which I had been working – although it placed far greater emphasis on the economic and technological conditions.

The project focused on successful small and medium companies that had implemented significant industrial innovation of products and achieved economic success by investing relatively large amounts of resources and systematic development in the last 5 years. The unit of analysis was not the company itself but the development of the individual product.

The idea was to unravel this development and thus determine the underlying conditions for its materialization. By unravelling the process, we hoped to be able to describe the structural characteristics and »behavioral« categories behind the companies' success. The DYS project operated with the companies' competitiveness being based on (Frøslev & Valentin 1986):

- research and development, in the traditional critical mass perspective held by engineers and scientists;
- flexible production technology; or
- commercialization of knowledge in terms of services.

The following issues were to be highlighted:

- basic information on the company, the nature of the product, and a description of the employees according to education;
- information on product development focusing on opportunities arising for initiating the product development, a description of methods of work and investment of resources during product development as well as of which networks the company was part; and
- a description of the company's parameters of competition.

The emerging innovation economics was the theoretical basis for the DYS analysis. One source of inspiration was the IC (International Competitiveness) group at Aalborg University Centre. They found sustained relationships between producers and users in industrial markets to be a central mechanism determining whether or not the users' specific needs for technological solutions became known to the producer (Andersen, Lundvall & Johnson. 1978; Lundvall, Olsen & Aaen 1984). The DYS project took this network perspective further, as it focused on the network relations of the product-developing companies to uncover network patterns as input-output systems in terms of product and knowledge.

The second source of inspiration was Schumpeterian innovation economics (Freeman 1982; Rothwell & Zegveld 1985), which focused on companies that, via major investment and in close collaboration with scientific research and development, had developed a radically new product and made a true technological leap.

As to the correlation between scientific research and technological development, we implicitly assumed that the increased importance of the company's internal research and development activities implied that the core input of knowledge can be described rather simply as an injection of scientific knowledge. Product groups with a great deal of research and development behind them demonstrated the highest value added and growth rate. This interpretation by and large corresponds to the linear model illustrated in Figure 4.1.

The project shared this linear model interpretation with the dominant macroeconomic theories, the recommendations of the Organisation for Economic Co-operation and Development (OECD) for economic policy, national whiz kids, and government bureaucrats (it was a rationalized myth and dominant mental model). Another prevailing idea was that

Figure 4.1. The Linear Model

small, high-technology and research-intensive companies would materialize and save Denmark's economy. In the wake of the microelectronic and biotechnological revolution, several OECD studies as well as other studies on innovation were tracking this type of company.

We contacted some of them to make some that they suited our purpose. One consequense was that our picture of product leaps was somewhat modified after I talked to a few of the companies and soon understood that their success was not brought about by quantum leaps in product technology. On the contrary. Over a number of years, they had gradually improved and refined a basic product design. This picture of gradual, incremental technological development was added to the questionnaire as a third method of work. »Incremental« was now placed next to »systematic with necessary investment of resources« and »goal-oriented without investment of large amounts of resources«.

The collection of data was divided into three phases: phase 1, identification of approximately 40 companies; phase 2, conducting a survey via questionnaire; and phase 3, intensive interviews with approximately ten of the companies. For all of us, this was our first practical encounter with reality. None of us had previously carried out empirical work of this type. My task was to begin identification of the companies, contribute with input to the questionnaire and later to make the preliminary analyses.

It soon proved that statistics were of no use in identifying companies that had recently developed distinctive products (Karnøe 1986). Therefore, we chose to let a number of people with significant knowledge of Danish industry identify the companies for us. We worked with approximately 100 informants that were representatives of technological institutes, chambers of commerce, and trade associations. Simultaneously, we went through numerous newspapers and journals and ultimately identified 350 companies. The large number of companies changed our methodological approach as it now became possible to work out statistical analyses.

The comprehensive questionnaire (20 pages) was mailed to the companies in March 1986. Apart from constituting the basis for an independent data analysis, the survey was to be used to select the 40 companies (the original number had been ten) that we wanted to subject to intensive interviews, that is, 2-hour interviews with the companies' heads of development. The issue was not organizational analysis. Nevertheless, the interview was methodologically important, supplementing information from the questionnaire.

Formulating a Ph.D. Project

I felt extremely comfortable with the DYS project. Everyone was very enthusiastic, and we were looking forward to sending out the questionnaires. But I also knew that DYS's resources were scarce. In March 1986, I applied for a research fellowship at my old institute at the University of Copenhagen but did not get the position. It would soon become difficult to continue financing my position on the DYS project, but my desire to become a ministerial civil servant had dried up in the interim. As the summer of 1986 approached, we began receiving the first returned questionnaires and now had to embark on the tremendous task of distilling data, encoding data, and starting on the statistical analyses. But what did we have here?

It was at this point that my luck began to improve. My old supervisor offered to employ me part time on a comparative, Nordic labour market project from August 1986 until February 1987. This meant that I could continue to work part time on the DYS project. In the autumn of 1986, another unspecified research fellowship at my old institute was advertised. This time I was hired.

I thus became a research fellow on a project of a fairly broad description. It was rooted in the general discussion on industrial and

technology policies. The aim was to analyse the relationship between
the need for political control mechanisms – hopefully based on identified market failures occurring in industrial reality – and the political-
administrative ability and will to develop adequate policies. The
project description thus combined my old interest in actors, interests,
and industrial policy with (the expectation of) new results from the
DYS project.

I did not start on the research fellowship until July 1987, as the DYS
project was able to pay me until then and we were just about to start the
series of in-depth interviews in the winter and spring of 1987. I wanted
to finish this task before starting on my own project.

Preparing Interviews
– Tracking an Empirical Anomaly in the Observations

The paradigm of the DYS project, the process of collecting data, and the
preliminary analyses played an important role in my own research process. During the winter of 1986-1987 the wind turbine industry as an industrial network complex became increasingly interesting. The newspapers reported ever-increasing exports to California. Among the companies that had returned the DYS questionnaire were four wind turbine
producers, a tower producer, a producer of electronic control systems,
and two producers of blades: an industrial network. They represented
the structural outline of the roots of a new Danish production complex,
which had successfully gained ground on the international market up to
1986-1987. The industrial success was largely conditioned by a national
energy policy that had created a kind of incubator for the wind turbine
industry through subsidies and the establishment of research centres –
that is, an active and selective industrial policy.

Since I had previously been sniffing around in the field of energy and
wind turbine industries, wind turbines became my turf.

Based on the information from the survey I wrote a note to the
project team describing the wind turbine industry according to our selection criteria:

- development costs (high)
- method of work (systematic and incremental)
- contact with research institutions (high)
- contact with customers and suppliers (high)
- commercial success (immense).

The wind turbine industries thus accumulated a high score in relation to our primary selection criteria.

The first interview was to take place in February 1987. I did not have much time to prepare myself theoretically prior to my actual meeting with the real wind turbine enterprises.

In general the DYS project did not include much specific literature studies or analyses of the specific technological aspects of product development – or of the pattern of interaction between research (associated with new scientific knowledge) and technology.

During the winter of 1986-1987 I became aware of a Ph.D. course on newer economic theory of the firm and the theory of science at the Copenhagen Business School. The course was a confrontation with the optimizing, rational actor and the neoclassical economists' ahistorical concepts of economic processes. The new, evolutionary economic theory was in and offered a frame of reference for a historical perspective on the development of companies and their behaviour by applying the concept of routines. Routines are a general expression of the organizational rules, norms, and cultural conditions that form companies' behaviour. The routines underlying a certain type of behaviour are not static and thus imply that the company may learn from its actions over time.

Neither then nor later did I explicitly formulate the problem nor operationalize product development behaviour in view of the evolutionary perspective. It seemed too far removed from the structural categories related to industrial policy. Nevertheless, intuitively it seemed like a useful theoretical focus for the world views I subsequently developed when analysing the interviews with the wind turbine industries.

Having no precise theoretical guidance, the specific character of my research project emerged from working concretely with the wind turbine enterprises. I carefully studied both their completed questionnaires and brochures in order to get some ideas for which questions to ask them about their development work. The empirical analyses of the industries' development activities and the development of the wind turbine technology led to the discovery of some inconsistencies – or rather »my« anomaly. That is, »anomaly« in the sense of deviations from the DYS project's and my own more or less explicit assumptions that the interplay between research and technological development could be described in terms of the linear model.

There seemed to be a messy mixture of the DYS project's three methods« of product development mentioned earlier: »incremental«,

»goal-oriented«, and »systematic« combined with large investments in resources. Several firms indicated that they applied all three methods simultaneously. However, the larger firms' research and development costs were fairly high, which made me expect that they engaged in the kind of science-based product development we were seeking. The output, however, seemed to indicate that they were merely upscaling earlier product designs. No new wind turbine was produced – merely a larger one. Was the product an advanced technological development when it did not represent a radical technological leap? Why would it be more difficult and more expensive to produce an improved upscaled version after having produced the first one? I kept returning to this anomaly during the remaining part of my project, and it finally led me to my unit of analysis.

The idea of simple upscaling was combined with empirical observations dating back to the time when I was writing my master's thesis: there were a first and second generation of companies and wind turbine technology. Based on this, I was of the opinion that the wind turbines produced in the mid-1980s were second-generation technology based on 5 years of development and production of first-generation wind turbines. Perhaps they were just about to introduce their third generation. From this perspective it was easy to identify the technological trajectories of development and a continuity in the firms' developmental behaviour.

I still did not feel that I knew enough about wind turbines. First of all (seen in retrospective) I did not, at that point of the analysis, have any questions that could guide my data collection. Second, I had to be able to talk to those developing the wind turbines. Without specific knowledge about the technology behind wind turbines, I would be unable to ask relevant questions and hence describe and understand the problems and working methods used to develop the technology.

From the brochures I knew that wind turbines consisted of various components (blades, transmission (hubs and gears), a generator, brakes, an electronic control system, and the yaw system). But which parts had been most intensively developed? Why hadn't they solved all the problems when they built the first one? We did not discuss this important question, since our perspective on technological development and its underlying knowledge formation was not procedural. Describing a structural relationship between research and industry does not say much about its content of knowledge or causal relationship.

Words the Redeemer – The Importance of Milieu

Until the interviews started in February 1987, I was confused by the mixture of working methods, resources invested and the incremental technological change and by the wind turbine as a system of subsystems. As a political scientist I was dealing with problems I had little thechnical background to understand and formulate propely

On several occasions I sat thinking aloud in the office I shared with a colleague, and one day my contemplations struck a chord. My colleague, our real economist on technology, suddenly recalled something he had used in his master's thesis. It was an article written by the economic historian Nathan Rosenberg (1982c) in which he contemplated similar ideas in relation to complex technological systems (aerospace). After reading Rosenberg's articles, some of the pieces fell into place. I felt more safe and was particularly struck by one central point: scientific methods alone could not predict the performance qualities of complex technological systems. Such methods had to be supplemented with a quite different kind of knowledge generated through learning by using, that is, operational experience beyond the test period that could be incorporated into the next design. This allowed for inclusion of a great deal of nonscientific knowledge.

Rosenberg's concepts of technological system and learning by using made sense. Now the wind turbine industry could be described as a particular type of technology characterized by a particular development and (generation of knowledge).

A couple of weeks later I was thinking aloud again. Again my colleague reacted. He recalled something about an article describing how a technology can run through the technological avenues of development almost unchanged but with strongly improved performance qualities (Sahal 1985). After all, an aeroplane still has two wings and an automobile still has four wheels.

Similarly, to describe the production capacity of a wind turbine in terms of figures was to describe its performance qualities. It did not say anything about the underlying generation of knowledge and the technological learning process. To describe this was to capture the invisible generation of knowledge behind a technological development. This approach to knowledge made it possible to elucidate the role of research-based scientific knowledge as opposed to more experience-based technological knowledge. This was what I was looking for, but it took me quite some time to recognize this knowledge aspect of the development of wind turbines. Neither I, nor the DYS project, had formulated this as a specific issue. However, working with the empirical material the issue emerged.

In a later phase of the project, the very generation of knowledge about the product technology became a cornerstone (cf. Valentin 1990; Frøslev Christensen 1992).

I might have traced the anomaly had I paused and allowed myself to become absorbed in the two articles and related literature. However, reading and conceptual discussions on these issues always took second priority, since the interviews had to be conducted during the spring of 1987, and other issues and tasks related to the project kept me occupied. I failed to realize that this was the very clue that could persuade me to abandon the linear research and development line of thought.

Thus, the idea of focusing the analysis on mapping out the generation of technological knowledge did not occur to me. However, I felt sufficiently equipped – with basic insight into the field – for visiting the wind turbine enterprises.

Visiting the Field for the First Time:
The First Interviews

The first interviews took place at a renewable energy test centre. Since the mid-1970s, the manager had been one of the grassroots pioneers in Denmark's wind turbine industry, and he was a member of the steering committee for renewable energy appointed by the Council of Technology. He provided us with an outline of the wind turbine industry's grassroots phase from 1974 to 1980. But he did not share my concept of the wind turbine as a complex technological system that is difficult to develop. He found the technology fairly simple. Why then did it take so much resource investment and time to develop the next generation of wind turbines? He could not answer.

For me it became an exciting encounter with reality. A series of company interviews provided us with a wealth of data. The interview guide governed the questions. We got the impression of a very high level of product development activity of various degrees of product novelty and redesign. The industries were working on their third-generation technology. Furthermore, we learned much about the background and development of the companies and their way of establishing a formal organization of product development. There was information on the importance of the domestic market, network collaboration on the development of new components (blades and electronic control systems), and topical problems facing the industry.

However, we learned very little about the specific – the technological change and the nature of knowledge formation. We gathered important information on changes in the organizing of product development work, methods of work and new expertise in terms of recruiting new engineers. The companies had changed routines and organizational structure. The data were evidence of experience-based technological development and gradual upscaling, even though the industry at this point tried to do it at a faster pace than earlier. But we were still unable to say anything about the connection between engineering science, technological knowledge, and technical progress.

Leaving the DYS project and starting on my Ph.D. project, I brought along this preliminary data and a paradigm. I clearly perceived of my own project as an extension of the DYS project.

Outlining the Framework of My Ph.D. Dissertation

Shortly after starting on my own project, the DYS project was asked to write a memorandum to the Council of Technology: *The State of the Wind Turbine Industry*. Since I had transcribed all the interviews and knew the story, I wrote the memorandum in collaboration with one of the project leaders.

From 1978 to 1987, the wind turbine enterprises and technology had changed dramatically. I tried to demonstrate that, technologically, the current enterprises were radically different from the image of smithies with which I was often confronted when discussing the industry. Product development units had been established; the high development costs were recorded in the industrial statistics as true research and development.

The memorandum provided a useful basic insight into the dynamics of the development of the wind turbine complex. It could be related to either industrial and technological policy, trade development, networks of industries, production complexes, or the industries' innovation or product development processes. There were several units of analysis or levels to choose among.

Chains of the Past and Lack
of a Specific Problem Formulation

For a long time my own project was strongly influenced by the DYS project, sharing the same data, paradigm, and interests. At the general level, I did not then feel that there was any discrepancy between my Ph.D. project on market and policy failures and working with the wind turbine industry. I expected that emphasizing the indus trial and technological aspects would make me better equipped for evaluating the need for new industrial and technological political measures.

I had read Rosenberg but did not find the technological learning process or the generation of technological knowledge particularly interesting. I could not shake off the DYS project's and my own project's broad approaches and the fact that they rested on the »correct« innovation economics. Also, their issues of industrial policy, trade development, and the establishment of a new production complex within Denmark's industrial structure were stimulating.

No one asked me to define the problem clearly, and I did not worry about it. I felt that I was getting somewhere. However, my previous (master thesis) supervisor came up with some somewhat disappointing comments on my work with the wind turbine industry. He strongly doubted that the project would result in any new thinking, and as far as he knew the wind turbine industry was facing declining exports (which was actually true). But old love dies hard. I had made many interesting observations, and the DYS project focused on the same type of analyses. So it could not be completely wrong.

Formally, I stopped working on the DYS project and started my Ph.D. project on July 1, 1987. However, in reality I spent most of my time working on the DYS project until May 1988. But I had made an agreement with the project to exchange favours. In return for my work, I got access to the complete DYS data base.

Due to a deficient problem formulation, my own research process had a very broad orientation. Actually, the memorandum to the Council of Technology contained an embryo in its description of the total historical development dynamics of the wind turbine industry. The subsequent work was characterized by a balance between two different points of orientation: on the one hand, to analyse layer by layer the construction and development of the industry and the technology (the wind turbine technology, the establishment of the industry, market development, the production network complex, and the industrial policy); on the other hand, the growing focus on the formation of technological knowledge.

Some Decisive Interviews – on the Track of a Common Thread That Was Not Picked Up

During the autumn of 1987, I gradually approached a specific problem formulation and unit of analysis. This was more the result of a muddling-through process than of rational or systematic contemplations based on relevant theory. The problem emerged when I continued to work with the apparent anomaly between input (method of work and resources invested) and output (the incremental technological development) I had observed.

After completing the first series of DYS interviews in the spring of 1987, I mailed a questionnaire to companies within the wind turbine industry in order to collect more complete data for my analysis. However, any contact with the companies was limited to the heads of development. Prior to the autumn's two wind turbine interviews, I forwarded a copy of my memorandum to the Council of Technology. These two interviews proved to be of decisive importance to the further process.

The interview with an engineering firm TRIPOD that had specialized in services to wind turbines producers proved to be particularly decisive. During the interview, I gradually realized a dual change in the product development process: a change in methods of work and a change in the underlying basis of knowledge. The method of work had changed from a trial-and-error search process to more systematic development work.

I abandoned the DYS interview guide and asked my own questions in order to get closer to the generation of knowledge, and during the interview I succeeded in groping my way to something about the technical uncertainties and the relationship between engineering science calculations and practical experience.

As the interviewee put it: »The brilliant graduates from the Technical University of Denmark are not terribly useful here. All they learn is how to calculate according to standard formulas. They don't learn how to interpret and work out those problems that don't fit into their formulas.« In his opinion, the body of knowledge of wind turbine technology was still so immature that it was impossible to calculate the solution to all problems. This represented a qualified approach to looking further into the relationship between theories of engineering and the relevance of practical experience.

For the first time I felt that I was slowly approaching an understanding of the anomaly. Retrospectively I realize, however, that I was not even handling the information properly. Had I been more concentrated and less distracted by the competing problems, I might have stuck to this theme.

However, the interview opened several doors to the technological development process of wind turbines. There arose different, technological development strategies such as:

- the Tvind wind turbine
- Denmark's wind turbine industry
- the United States wind turbine industry
- the large Nibe wind turbines initiated by Denmark's Ministry of Energy.

This interview prompted me to engage in a comparative analysis of the types of technology development applied by modern wind turbine enterprises. The technological policies of top-down and bottom-up strategies were not introduced until much later (see Figure 4.2). However, I was not yet ready to pursue this central, comparative perspective.

Figure 4.2. The project's analytical dimensions

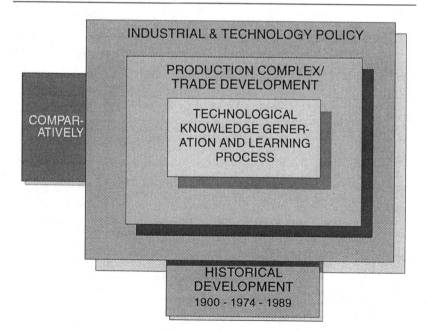

The other important interview took place in Jutland in December 1987. The interviewees, the technical manager and the sales manager of Vestas, had been working within the wind turbine industry since 1978 and thus belonged to the pioneers, possessing a wealth of knowledge about the field. We were picked up in the small local airport and had set aside 2 hours for the interview. Instead, we stayed there from 9 in the morning until 2:30 in the afternoon, discussing the wind turbine industry and its technology. Here, I gathered additional information on the early establishment of enterprises, the experience-based muddling through approach, and the technological learning process. I also learned that the reason for the success of Danish wind turbines on the Californian market was that the clumsy, heavy Danish wind turbines were much more reliable than the sophisticated wind turbines produced in the United States. But I still felt that I needed more information, and I revisited the company several times. They were actually interested in answering my questions since they were interested in having the history of Denmark's wind turbine industry written. This attitude made me comfortable and allowed me to ask naive questions, since I did not have to put on the façade of an expert.

Both these interviews furnished me with information significant for my understanding of the background of the industry and its problems, and they opened the doors to the formation of technological knowledge, but I was not in a position to concentrate on this knowledge at that time. I was preoccupied with the DYS project and other related tasks and did not have the time to contemplate the Vestas interview before the spring of 1989.

The Start of 1988:
Where Is My Project Heading?

The final interview in the autumn of 1987 put me on a high. Mildly stated, I was rather hooked on the wind turbine industry. Gradually, I had collected more or less complete data on the wind turbine industry within the framework of the DYS project and expanded these to comprise the historical dynamics from 1974 to 1987.

There were many pieces to hold together, and I still had not formulated the problem clearly. What was the unit of analysis – the enterprises, the industry, the wind turbine technology, the technological learning process, the industrial and technological policies? A bit of everything. To what should I devote myself? I wanted to write the history of a newly established Danish industry. But what history? And what was the common thread or the theoretical point? I had not yet decided.

Through the autumn of 1987 and until May 1988 I primarily worked on the DYS project and thus lost the continuity of my own work process. Perhaps I was not aware of how far I had actually come at that time. I was inexperienced in doing studies on enterprises, industries, and technology. On the other hand, it is also possible that my observations and impressions were given time to mature. Otherwise I may never have been able to free myself of the chains of thinking in terms of industrial network structure and industrial policy and instead delve into the sociology of technological learning processes. I was also moving away from the original Ph. D. project and my formal supervision in political science. In practice I did not discuss this with him.

Retrospectively, I think that I avoided panic by telling myself that, if I was able to produce a fairly complete, empirical and historical account of the industry's development, I was well on my way to producing a good report. After all, only a few analyses of this type had been conducted thus far in Denmark, my supervisor supported me (he thought I was taken care of in the DYS-group), and the DYS project had received positive feedback on my memorandum on the wind turbine industry. Sooner or later, I would find the precise problem formulation and the common thread. I was not quite certain whether or not this would meet the requirements of a Ph.D. dissertation, but I still had lots of time, and my supervisor had not yet tightened the thumbscrews.

1988: A Work Process Governed by Occasions As the Project Grows Historically and Comparatively

I started the year producing the statistical material for the DYS report and preparing the course I was to teach at the university (industrial and technological policy – somewhere between politics and economics). This was new to me and it did not leave me much time for my own project.

Nevertheless, 1988 offered a series of important occasions that kept the pot boiling, that is, writing down some of my ideas and starting to expand the project with an historical and a comparative dimension.

The first occasion was writing an abstract for an international conference on wind turbine technology. It took place in Hawaii and was organized by the American Wind Energy Association. I was going to present a paper on the connection between technological learning processes and the importance of the domestic market changing character in Denmark.

The second occasion was a request from Aalborg University Centre to give two lectures on the development of wind turbine technology since 1974. From my visit to *Folkecentret for Vedvarende Energi* (the National Centre for Renewable Energy), I knew that the modern wind turbine industry had a past. I tracked down some more information and concocted a story about the works of early pioneers such as La Cour (1891-1908), F.L. Smith (1940-1947), and Juul (1947-1962). I wanted to be well equipped for the lectures. It turned out to be a paper of thirty pages. Denmark's wind turbine technology rested on a certain tradition, but I was not at all sure about the nature of this technological heritage. Unfortunately, no one benefited from my pearls of wisdom – the course was cancelled the day before it was scheduled to start.

In the spring I received an important breakthrough by mail. I subscribed to *Windpower Monthly*, and the March and April issues brought two articles that answered my prayers. The engineer and mathematician A. Garrad (1988) wrote about the necessity and possibility of now improving the formalized model development to encompass the basis for calculating and designing future wind turbines. His point was that due to the lack of scientific engineering knowledge about aerodynamics and structural dynamics, the development strategy of trial and error (understood between the lines to be the Danish strategy) had proven most adequate until 1988. This was almost an authoritative proof that it had made sense to use experience as an avenue to development at least until 1988. Garrad formulated more explicitly what I had tried to extract from my Tripod interview half a year earlier. Combining Garrad's point with Rosenberg's ideas, I was able to characterize the wind turbine as a complex technological system whose behaviour cannot be predicted scientifically and not at all when the underlying scientific engineering knowledge is immature. This proved to be the key in making the wind turbine engineers talk and to draw on their experiences.

The third occasion was the DYS report on product development activities and the generation of technological knowledge, which I was expected to present at a conference in early May 1988. This was the first important step towards focusing on the major issues of knowledge generation. The important distinction between the three elements method of work, organizational structure and generation of technological knowledge was gradually becoming useful analytically. The learning process may be characterized by trial and error, that is, new problem definitions and solutions are rather based on experience than on the results of scientific engineering. Organizationally, it may all take place in the product development department, and the costs may be entered as research and development. The incremental aspect both referred to the technological learning process and to the technological development. The anomaly was about to be described but not yet as sharply as it has been done here.

I tried to compare this experience-based learning process of the wind turbine industry with the more analytical-theoretical strategy behind the costly Nibe wind turbines developed by Denmark's Ministry of Energy and the electric utilities in collaboration with researchers from the Technical University of Denmark. The turbine never functioned satisfactorily. Here, I tried to operate with one comparative dimension: the development strategies based on theoretical research (top-down) against the experience-based strategy (bottom-up) as methods of work and ways of generating technological knowledge.

At the conference, I did not feel that the participants found particular relevance in my perspectives on theoretical research versus experience-based knowledge and systematic work methods. On the other hand, there was much talk about the political climate when subsidies were introduced in 1979 and about the crises within the wind turbine industry. Exports had almost come to a standstill, and wind turbine production still depended on government subsidies. I certainly did not feel encouraged. Was the problem of theoretical research as a slow generator of theoretical knowledge irrelevant? No – it was relevant to me and to the practitioners. It was more likely that I had made a poor presentation of my ideas. I knew too little about theory and concepts and had not worked with it enough. This was the first time I presented my ideas about the technological learning process.

I felt somewhat discouraged after the conference but soon recovered when I unexpectedly came into contact with someone from the world of technology who understood what I meant. He had graduated as a mechanical engineer from a technical university. He was currently working at the Test Station for Wind Turbines and had just received a Bachelor of Commerce in Organization at the Copenhagen Business School. His major interest was organizational innovation processes. In his opinion my project was the right approach to understanding and formulating the process of Danish technological development. I reminded him of the stories told in the Test Station for Wind Turbines. I was very encouraged, and he provided me with more factual knowledge about the wind turbine technology. Furthermore, he prepared the engineers at the Test Station for my visit in the autumn of 1989.

In May-June I finished teaching at the university. My abstract for the Hawaiian conference on wind turbine technology was accepted, and I finished this paper during August 1988.

During the interview with the two Vestas pioneers, they had handed me an article by the United States wind turbine engineer Stoddard (1986) that concerned 10 years' experience with the development of wind turbines in the United States. Since I was going to the United States, I decided to read the article. His analysis showed that the Danish design philosophy had resulted in clumsy and heavy wind turbines. He also demonstrated that this development strategy unintentionally had reduced the effects of the unsolved or unknown theoretical problems that the more theoretically oriented wind turbine engineers from the United States could not handle – theoretically or practically. These results later became an important part of my own wind turbine history. The comparison proved that Denmark's presentation and innovation practice is even more unique.

Participating in the Hawaii conference in September 1988 was important. It was my first international presentation. Here, I gathered information on the costly top-down strategy in the United States (the US National Aeronautics and Space Administration and Boeing Engineering) and on the problems that United States wind turbines and wind turbine producers were facing.

During the autumn of 1988, I felt that I needed better and supplementary data. I designed a short questionnaire that, apart from updating some information on the companies, focused on the generation of technological knowledge. Among other things, I asked the companies to indicate the importance of four sources of technological progress:

- internal development work
- operational experiences from the market (learning by using)
- contributions from research institutions
- input from suppliers.

In November 1988, one of my colleagues from the DYS project saw an advertisement in a weekly journal. The Technical University of Denmark had arranged a competition on the history of technology. This became the fourth occasion for writing. During November I compiled the Aalborg lectures and the Hawaii paper to a report with the title: *The Development of Danish Wind Turbine Technology from 1891 to 1988. A Case of Technological Response to the Needs of Society.*

I received the first questionnaires containing information on the technical progress. They looked very promising, demonstrating that the most important input to technological improvements of products was the company's internal generation of knowledge combined with operational experiences (learning by using). Research institutions and suppliers were important but not to the same extent.

In the late autumn of 1988, Peer Hull Kristensen and Finn Borum from the Copenhagen Business School invited me to write a chapter in their text on *Technological innovation and organizational change* in Denmark (Borum & Kristensen 1990). This fifth occasion for writing was an important encouragement. The subtitle of the text was *Danish patterns of knowledge, networks and culture.* However, I didn't start to write until the spring of 1989.

The Project at the Beginning of 1989: More Comprehensive Than in 1988 but Not Yet a Final Focus

At the start of 1989, two incidents became decisive in not only holding my project in limbo between different issues and covering several levels of analysis, but also expanding it with comparative breadth and historical depth (Figure 4.2).

The first incident was that in January 1989 the Copenhagen Business School announced the Tietgen competition (with a prize involved) for a Ph.D. dissertation that was to be submitted by September 1990: »Desired is an analysis of how the development of new product areas are affected by industrial network relations and instruments of industrial and technology policy. The analysis may be based on the establishment of a new industry.« This hit close to home on the issues with which I was working and could by and large be written based on the data I had collected to date. But it did not fit in with my increasing focus on the generation of technological knowledge. This, however, didn't become obvious to me as, at that time, my wheels were doing a great deal of spinning, and my mind spun accordingly. No doubt, the ambition to submit an award-winning dissertation contributed to maintaining the breadth of my project.

The other important incident was the feedback I received on the competitive paper submitted to the Technical University of Denmark. I did not receive the award, since the paper did not apparently satisfy the demands required for a Ph.D.-level paper. On the other hand, I got very fine feedback, including some questions that contributed to the final profile. The conclusion of the comments was that I had tried to sit on two chairs simultaneously – the perspective of the history of technology and that of industrial policy. Furthermore, that paper was found to be deficient in information on and proof of the competitiveness of Denmark's wind turbine industry. At that time, the industry was in crisis and there was much talk about when the various companies would merge into »Danish Wind Turbine Technology Ltd«. Wagering on the small wind turbine producers had, perhaps, been a waste of money.

I was going to prove them wrong. These were the prejudices of the establishment being served to me in black and white. If I had not been aware of it earlier, I knew now that the technology and the industrial performance of the wind turbine industry was something unique from which we could learn – even though the process was not in keeping with theory or with the linear research and development model.

I turned this into my driving force and means of survival in order to avoid making a fool of myself on account of a stupid dissertation on these idiotic wind turbines. In view of my story and points of industrial policy, I desperately hoped the wind turbine would survive at least until I had submitted my dissertation. Thus, any hostile attacks on energy and industrial policy were interpreted as a direct, personal attack. I wrote a feature for *Børsen* (a Danish, daily business newspaper) discussing the unreasonableness of forbidding, from one day to the next, wind turbine export financed by the investments of private taxpayers without making room for transitional or alternative arrangements (Karnøe 1989). Ships, for example, were financed in this way. Why the prejudice against wind turbines?

Feedback on the paper submitted to the Technical University of Denmark pushed me into providing more adequate documentation of the technological development environments behind the recent top-down and bottom-up strategies. I was especially searching for data on the financial resources allocated and the link to more formal technical and scientific development environments. I also needed information about the wind turbine tradition in the United States in the twentieth century, the establishment of companies during the last fifty years, the market shares of the wind turbine industries in Denmark and the United States, the level of product technology of producers in Denmark and the United States, the types of industrial and technological policies used to support the industry, and the dimensions of these schemes. Eighteen months before the project was scheduled to conclude, this represented a considerable expansion of the project in terms of issues, time, and data. But that didn't worry me. I thought that I had the time. Time proved me wrong, as I had completely underestimated how time-consuming it was to formulate the theory related to my anomaly.

Embedded in the core of the history of the industrial network complex and the wind turbine technology that I wanted to describe was this anomaly that still intrigued me but which I could not grasp precisely. At the same time, I did not want to let go of the opportunity to write the multifaceted story about modern wind turbine technology – a story about companies and measures of industrial policy, not to forget the political aspects of grassroots movements, energy movements, and visionary and stressed politicians. I had a great deal of solid data on the dynamics between industry, technology, the market, and the industrial and technological political measures. And I still wanted to nourish my old interest in industrial policies by producing something with implications for industrial and technological policy. As a result, my project comprised several levels of analysis and issues, of which only the generation of technological knowledge was treated in depth (Figure 4.2).

The project was gradually expanded as the comparative and the historical aspects began to sneak in. I did not realize then that, as a result, the project was becoming (too) comprehensive and perhaps ambiguous as well.

I had no doubt that I was going to write the story of modern wind turbine technology in a way that had implications for the design of industrial and technological policies. This choice was confirmed by two Ph.D. dissertations on industrial and technological policy published in 1987 and 1988. One viewed the development from an economic perspective (Kristensen 1987), and another viewed it from the perspective of political science (Christensen 1988). They were interesting, but did not reveal much of anything new in relation to my teaching and ideas. I was convinced that the discussion on industrial and technological policy could not be taken any further until a deeper understanding had been achieved on what was going on out there in the economy.

Thus, I found it easier to tell my supervisor that I was not going to elucidate the political aspects in this project. (This was, of course, the basis on which I had been granted a scholarship.) In relation to my institute, it had become a problem that, until the final year of my scholarship, I only spent half of my time there and had devoted much more attention to the economic problems of innovation than to those related to political science. However, in my teaching on Denmark's industrial and technological policies, I had combined these two perspectives. Finally, I felt free. There were three other Ph.D. candidates at the institute, and during 1988 we had been told that due to the budget and job situation we should not expect subsequent employment as assistant professors or the like. Another argument was that the aim of the new Ph.D. policy was to educate a greater proportion of Ph.D.'s who would be employable as specialists outside the research and educational system.

In early 1989, I was still operating with my original, broad approach (and the inherited knowledge from the DYS project), which had been further elaborated through the papers in 1987 and 1988. At this time the work process was characterized by a tension between broad aspects and analytical dimensions, historical depth and a growing focus on the generation of technological knowledge. The latter turned out to be the final unit of analysis or the pivotal point of the whole thing, though I was unable to formulate this explicitly before the very last phase. Even though my mind was reeling, my work process was not completely chaotic. I knew when I was working with industrial policy, industrial development, technological development, competitiveness, networks, etc.

Towards a Productive Connection between Empirical Data and Theory

The road to discovering a connection between theory and empirical data was tortuous. My strong empirical orientation had furnished me with a concrete insight into the technological development and the underlying process of generating knowledge. But what I discovered did not have anything in common with the linear model. Rosenberg's concepts of learning by using and technological complexes were a beginning but far from adequate. It was very comforting to have my empirical impressions confirmed but difficult to find other analytical concepts that could be used to couple these observations to a more general, theoretical discussion. I could not build on one chapter in a book! Therefore, I had to continue to work with this specific problem until I found concepts and models in support of my empirical data. I was determined not to reject them as accidental incidents.

I wanted to give colour to my assertions:

- that it may take a longer time to generate knowledge through scientific research than through the experience gained from local, technological search processes; and

- that the technological knowledge in wind turbines (and in a number of other technologies) far outweighs the scientific knowledge.

For my teaching in the autumn term (1988) I had selected a book on technology policy and industrial change (Rothwell & Zegweld 1985) viewed from the perspective of the theory of innovation. This book also treated the relationship between scientific break-through and technological innovations. The book contained two quotes: one about the technological innovation process and one about technological development, which was not based on any theoretical understanding of why it worked. Well I never! They were both quotes from Rosenberg. I had just never read all the chapters in his book from 1982 (Rosenberg 1982a). As early as 1987 I had an applicable approach that I did not use, since I had no clue about what in the world a technology-oriented, economic historian would discuss in a chapter on »How Exogenous is Science?« (Rosenberg 1982d).

During this period of searching, I found great moral support in a Ph.D. course at the Copenhagen Business School on the theory of technology (February 1989). Presenting my project, I spread it a little thick, saying that I worked with Denmark's wind turbine industry and talking about the low-tech industry's triumphs over the far more research-based development strategies. The professor in charge of the course, a technology historian, fully agreed. It was time to explode the myth about technology being applied science. I left the course revitalized.

I now turned to Rosenberg's chapter. It hit home. It demonstrated that, from an historical perspective, much scientific research activity derived from technological problems; the effect of new scientific research on technological development was often of secondary importance. This was almost contrary to the linear model according to which new research initiates technological development. The most famous examples are the steam engine, which worked for fifty years before Carnot formulated the theory of thermodynamics in an attempt to understand (and increase) its efficiency. Pasteur discovered microorganisms and founded microbiology when working on resolving some fermentation problems for the French wine industry. Rosenberg did not refute the importance of scientific research, concluding that the subsequent technological development has much to gain from the interaction with scientific research. This made sense in relation to the wind turbine technology and the new image I had formed.

The Final Phase

For the first time during my project I did not have to involve myself in other projects or teaching. I felt that I was just on the brink of having sufficient data to write my grand narrative about the wind turbine industry and its technology and to describe the generation of technological knowledge.

I was well into the work of constructing an analytical hook for my anomaly. I still had a year left and wanted to start working on the theoretical part systematically; I had to fit in some theory in order to have the work accepted as a Ph.D. dissertation. I only needed to collect data on the historical and comparative aspect of the wind turbine technology. It proved to be time-consuming to collect reliable data on the development of the California market in regard to competitors, Danish market shares, etc.

Now the laboratory seriously started to work overtime. On several occasions I found myself sitting next to my wife in the cinema with not a clue about the film rolling across the screen, but fully absorbed by a project that had gradually invaded my mind.

Theoretically I started out by pursuing several paths within the Schumpeterian theory of innovation. The first was Pavitt's (1984) attempt to design a taxonomy of the nature of technological development within various industrial and technological fields. This showed, among other things, that machine industries such as the wind turbine enterprises primarily base their generation of technological knowledge on internal development work. Their link to scientific research is much weaker and different from that of chemistry and electronics. This supported my assumptions.

The other path was the evolutionary, economic paradigm focusing on an industry's routines, search processes, and heuristics of solving problems (Nelson & Winter 1982; Dosi 1982). In a theoretical sense, technological innovation processes could be perceived as problem solving activities and the company as a knowledge base. Dosi's article (1982) strongly inspired the coupling of organization, technological change, and generation of technological knowledge. However, I did not agree with his focus on scientific research. It did not fit into the wind turbine technology, which primarily was based on some technological design principles that were gradually supported and improved by science.

This made me pursue a third path more closely: the scrutinizing of Rosenberg's early articles and books. Here I finally found an anchor. I was surprised by the depth and clarity of his analyses of technological development and his assertion that the economists of this century had not been able to contribute to our understanding of technological change (Rosenberg 1976, 1982a). After all, I did not need to be an engineer to make technological analyses. Furthermore, he emphasized the methodological point that:

> »the social and economic history of technology can only be properly written by people possessing a close familiarity with the technology itself.« (Rosenberg 1982b: 56).

All the time I had spent on understanding the technology of wind turbines had thus not been in vain.

Kline & Rosenberg's (1986) explicit rejection of the linear model was just what I needed. They tried – like I – to formulate a constructive alternative to the linear model. They launched new concepts to verbalize it. For example, a technological search process can be characterized by empirical guidance if no adequate scientific basis exists, and »basic research into technological systems may be as pure research as basic science«.

I wanted to continue my documentation of the independent position of technology and technological knowledge. I therefore turned to some of Rosenberg's references. I was introduced to the research tradition of technology history and its problems related to the connection between technology and science. I found the concrete analyses and concepts very encouraging. They much resembled my own work. Rosenberg's strength was that he combined technology history with Schumpeter's economic perspective. However, I also pursued a reference in Kline & Rosenberg's article treating »an important technological innovation in aerospace without science«.

This led me to an historian of technology who suggested characterizing technological search processes as doing or »knowing how«, in contrast to »knowing why« search processes tied to scientific activities (Vincenti 1984). That is, the construction of scientific and technological knowledge could be viewed as two essentially different cognitive processes. This fit well with wind turbines and supported my distinction between top-down and bottom-up strategies. Now I was able to explain and understand – albeit somewhat simplistically – that the stronger strain of knowing of top-down strategies may generate knowledge more slowly than the more action-oriented technological learning process. It was often more time-consuming to try to understand a problem than to solve it through empirical search processes: make it work.

When technology is not applied science, when mechanical technology is less tied to scientific research than chemistry and electronics and when action search processes may be a faster way of arriving at technological solutions, explanations may exist for the competitive strength of Danish wind turbines. This clearly had implications for Denmark's technology policy. Focusing exclusively on educating a larger number of scientifically oriented engineers would not strengthen Denmark's technological competitiveness.

My dissertation was progressing, and I felt that I had time to fit in the necessary theory. I continued to work with the current and historical empirical data. Wind turbine export was growing, two large Danish wind turbine producers merged, and I had to look into a number of other issues.

I went to Turkey with my wife on summer vacation – in a relaxed frame of mind.

I resumed work by the end of August 1989 – strongly motivated. The Tietgen paper was to be submitted on August 1, 1990 and our first child was due to arrive in April 1990 – Made in Turkey.

At the end of September, I participated in a Ph.D. seminar in Jutland with scholars from the Copenhagen Business School, Aalborg University Centre, and the Technical University of Denmark. For this occasion I had designed a table (Figure 4.3) combining the companies' type of knowledge generation (research-based as opposed to experience-based) and their technology bases and heuristics (the United States aerospace technology versus Denmark's machine technology). I had now launched the comparative aspect of my project.

One dimension characterizes the technological policy: a top-down research and science-based (science-push) strategy as opposed to a market-driven bottom-up and experience-based development strategy. The other dimension illustrates the technology base (heuristics of problem-solving) on which new industries based their development. The industries are characterized by either an aerospace or a machine technology base of knowledge. The combination of technology base and development strategy provides a certain approach to generating knowledge. For example, comparing B and D indicates that the knowledge generation and innovation practice of the United States tradition was based on aerospace technology, whereas Denmark's was based on machine technology. During the 1980s, Denmark's companies in Field D devel-

Figure 4.3. Comparative Dimensions of the Project

STRATEGY FOR TECHNOLOGICAL DEVELOPMENT

		TOP-DOWN Research-based large-scale turbines	BOTTOM-UP Market-driven small-scale turbines
TECHNOLOGY BASE	KNOWLEDGE BASE: AEROSPACE TECHNOLOGY	A: NASA/Boeing Eng. Lockheed British Aerospace	B: (examples of U.S. industries) U.S. Windpower Carter Enertech
	KNOWLEDGE BASE: MACHINE TECHNOLOGY	C: Danish Nibe Wind turbines Westinghouse (USA) German M.A.N.	D: Danish Wind turbine Industry

oped a leading world position in market share and product performance.

I received positive feedback from individuals doing innovation research at Aalborg University Centre who were in closer contact with various international research environments than the DYS people. Thus, I
felt encouraged to pursue this path.

I continued to read and spent much time in the library. I wanted to
track down any research apart from Rosenberg's that dealt with the construction of technological knowledge. An on-line search at the Royal Library resulted in one reference, *The Nature of Technological Knowledge*
(Laudan 1984), a newer anthology with a number of exciting contributions. Once more my theoretical framework crumbled when I included
a combination of technology history and the sociology of knowledge that
attempted to describe both the generation of knowledge in and of itself
and the practitioners who created technology. The point was that the
two aspects were inseparable.

Therefore, »communities of practitioners« was a pivotal concept, that
is, human beings working within a field of technology and developing
their own solutions to problems based on their own value system. Working my way through various references, I came across an historian of
technology who had studied the difference between the construction of
water turbines in France and the United States in the nineteenth centu-

ry – the former science-based and the latter experience-based. He emphasized the difference in both the technological and the subsequent scientific tradition.

I found the »community of practitioners« an exciting approach – different from that of traditional innovation economics and complementary to Rosenberg's. It represented a concrete anchoring of abstract concepts such as routines and heuristics. These sociologists of knowledge also applied the concept of heuristics, and I realized that there was a connection between the theories of evolution and economics, technology history and the sociology of knowledge. The technological learning processes in companies in Denmark and the United States could be analysed in terms of the concept of a »community of practitioners« representing certain value systems and behaviour. This also clarified a colleague's comment that the strong production culture in Denmark's machine industry forced the engineers to work with a more practical orientation.

I realized that this perhaps represented a new and more interesting theory. But I did not have the luxury of the extra time needed to start a new round of data collection from my population. I had to finish the dissertation and convinced myself that I had enough data to produce an adequate analysis. Nevertheless, I used the »community of practitioners« concept to demonstrate that the generation of knowledge is not confined to the individual company. This made sense knowing that there is a high level of informal collaboration activity between engineers working in the various wind turbine companies in Denmark.

In November 1989, I conducted a final, important interview with three engineers at the Test Station for Wind Turbines. It was late in the process, but now I had a number of specific hypotheses I wanted to test. The interviews provided me with new data and enabled me to test one of my hypothesis: Had the practical technology been far in advance of the more scientifically oriented development in Denmark? How had technology and science been integrated, and what did the engineers know about the development of wind turbine technology in the United States?

At the same time two important things happened. The Copenhagen Business School advertised a vacant position for assistant professor within the field of »technological innovation« and learning processes«. The deadline for applications was January 8, 1990. I wanted to apply for that position. I had to speed up my process of writing and thinking. I succeeded in incorporating almost all the empirical data in a working paper even though the theoretical analysis was fairly incomplete. During this process much fell into place for me, but I found it very difficult to formulate my points in a way that made it possible for the reader to follow my reasoning. Second, through the internal mail at the University of Copenhagen, I learned about a number of foreign researchers who wanted to get into contact with Danish researchers. Among them was a professor from PREST (Policy Research in Engineering Science and Technology) at Manchester University. I wrote to him, briefly describing my project, and he reacted immediately. He was coming to Denmark (Aalborg University Centre) in December and suggested that we meet. Together with the DYS team, I went to Aalborg. A number of mutual interests appeared between PREST, the DYS team, and the Aalborg University Centre team in the research they were working on in innovations, strategies, and technological learning processes. We decided to organize a joint workshop in Denmark in May 1990.

I realized that I was running out of time. In the beginning of 1990, I negotiated with my institute so that they received one month of my salary, thus enabling them to employ an external instructor to handle my teaching obligations in the spring term. I was now working simultaneously with the empirical data and the theoretical framework, depending on my mood. Many ends needed to be tied up. Then there was about a week's preparation for a paper to be presented at a conference on Technology Management in Miami in mid-March. In April our first child was due, and the nest had to be prepared. A great deal of my concentration was devoted to that in the month of March.

After spending 4 weeks adapting to our new family situation, I started to work full time in May, having promised the family that I would submit the dissertation on August 1, 1990. I had scarcely 3 months left and a lot of loose ends.

Preparing for the workshop with the PREST group in May, I continued work with my two by two matrix but collected my theoretical bits and pieces under one theme of technology, science, and the generation of knowledge in various industrial environments. I was coming to a showdown with the linear model: if companies in their innovation activities primarily use engineers who are too oriented towards knowing why and it takes a longer time to develop an understanding than to get something to work (knowing how), this may explain why Denmark won the first round in the world market for electricity-producing wind turbines. At the same time, the innovation practice in Denmark's wind turbine industry, made up of practical engineers and skilled workers, could represent an alternative way of developing technology. Feedback was positive.

After the workshop, I spent 3 weeks on elaborating and improving my ideas. I tried to link my point to a more general discussion: engineers in the United States are far less practically oriented than their colleagues in Denmark, and this had affected their innovative capabilities. In other words, I tried to take the discussion beyond a generation of knowledge itself and instead focused on how this was the result of different innovation practices in Denmark and the United States. I forwarded a copy of this paper to Professor Rosenberg at Stanford University in June and received a wonderfully positive response just when I needed it. I had less than 2 months to go... Even though I had completed the overall structure of the dissertation, I still had a lot of work to do in relation to the structural aspects before I could formulate my points satisfactorily. These last points on innovation practices were especially incomplete.

Nevertheless, I kept my promise to my family and submitted my dissertation to the Tietgen Prize Committee on August 1 – and went on a 7-week holiday to rediscover myself and my family again. I was awarded the Tietgen Prize.

It Was Completed But Not Quite

Back from vacation, I faced new commitments in the shape of my appointment as assistant professor as of June 1990. In November I received a letter from a publisher agreeing to publish my dissertation (Karnøe 1991). I agreed to submit the manuscript around February 1, 1991. But I had frighteningly miscalculated my teaching load. The job involved teaching new subjects that required much preparation time, and I was simultaneously to rewrite my dissertation, incorporating new data into the manuscript. The aim was to produce a coherent perspective on science and technology intervention, technological learning processes, and national innovation practices. The task of rewriting my dissertation was comprehensive, and I was always short of time. As a result, I first submitted the manuscript in October 1991. It was a satisfactory result, but one that could be improved on. And there are still ideas wrapped up in this that pave the way for my future research, although they have been transformed into a more sociological and institutional approach.

5. Production Life in Denmark: Discoveries Meet the Prepared Mind

Peer Hull Kristensen

Introduction

This is the story of a successful field study and its process. The ambition is to provide the reader with an insight into the measures and techniques and, in particular, the couplings between the individual phases that strengthened the project.

The field study was not successful in the sense that I found what I expected to find – on the contrary. The results of the field study – or rather the series of field studies – were a number of surprises. Surprises are strange things. They only exist in relation to something else. In this field study, some observations and phenomena were in direct conflict with much of the social science theory I had been studying and that, according to social science academics in Denmark, had been verified by empirical research in Denmark.

Since then much of my research has been governed by a desire to understand how these surprises were possible: which aspects of Denmark's social structure, its processes and history, made it possible to find something quite different from what I expected to find within Denmark's industrial enterprises?

In other words, my field studies were successful in the sense that they upset much of my previously established picture of the world.

Many scholars, students, and others who read a book like this do it in order to improve, plan, and implement their own field studies. They hope to get some tips straight from the horse's mouth that will enable them to handle a confusing and chaotic phase in their research and studies rapidly and easily. This was the way I felt in the summer of 1985 when preparing the project. I wished that the series of field studies I was about to conduct were over and done with so that I could get back to my desk at the institute and start my real work: reading serious and weighty literature, topical reports, and articles and then writing similar things. In my opinion, the field studies were an interruption to concrete, serious, and efficient work. I just wanted to get them over and done with – fast and with no more trouble than necessary. This feeling was reinforced by the fact that since field studies are perceived as unpleasant interruptions, they are always postponed until the very last moment when one is inevitably pressed for time.

Viewed in this perspective, a field study is bound to fail if it leads to surprises. However, my conditions were different. I was lucky to have been brought up to believe that unpleasant tasks should not be postponed but handled right away to allow more time to do the pleasant things. Thus, my feeling of being pressed for time was rooted in something else.

Therefore, my first tip straight-from-the-horse's-mouth is that most researchers look for the wrong tips when preparing themselves for doing field studies. It is very important that you start out enthusiastically and look forward to the fabulous opportunity of meeting a community of people, companies, institutions, and organizations with which you are only indirectly acquainted from your daily work. If my experience can be generalized, the researcher preparing a field study can be in the process of creating for herself a new, intellectual anchor that may change her future perspective on research.

Don't misunderstand me. I know very well that people are different and use different criteria for assessing field studies as successes or failures. Some people feel most confident if their field studies function trouble-free and produce exactly the type of data that the database has been prepared to handle. Many of the ideas and methods characterizing this smooth process are about living undisturbed – and a variety of techniques have been developed for this purpose. However, they are not the subject here.

Background of the Project

In 1985, it was not an inexperienced researcher who embarked on the field studies I describe here. However, at that time I had little more than theoretical conceptions and expectations related to the nature of industrial companies. I had been working with the need for re-enforcing technological innovation and technology and industrial policy. As a student at Roskilde University Centre, I had been working on a number of projects. In collaboration with a fellow student, I had submitted a research report to a research institute in Sweden: *The Small Country Squeeze*. For a number of years I exploited my knowledge of this field. I worked for the Economic Council of the Labour Movement as its representative in the Technology Council and on a number of other committees dealing with industrial and technology policy. Later, when I worked as an assistant professor at Roskilde University Centre, I gained the chance to study industrial and technological institutionalization in the Scandinavian countries in connection with writing a research report on the innovative capabilities of these countries. No doubt, these works and changing occupational positions provided me with a certain degree of acceptance among the narrow circle of structural economists and technology theorists who were the prime movers discussing industrial policy in Denmark. This narrow community affected me in two ways. On the one hand, my research was oriented towards technocratic and instrumental problems. On the other hand, in this narrow circle, we had been through so many discussions about industry, technology, and politics that I often amused myself by (mentally) attempting to finish any sentence one of these scholars began. In other words, my line of thinking was becoming greatly uninspired and was neither surprised nor stimulated by new ideas presented by other Danish scholars within the field.

In this perspective, my year at the Massachusetts Institute of Technology as a visiting professor came to play an important role. Naturally, I had gone to the United States hoping to find new buttresses for my instrumental, technocratic research tradition. I was lucky to get in contact with a number of scholars within the field of industry and technology whose perspective was far more exciting. Somehow, they had succeeded in preserving a small island where the best of the classic European tradition within sociology and humanities lived on and was used to understand some of the significant questions related to the development of industrialized society.

One of the island's natives was the direct cause for my change in orientation toward field studies. Professor Charles Sabel at the Massachusetts Institute of Technology and I came up with the idea that Denmark ought to be an ideal, experimental laboratory for studying the transition from mass production to flexible specialization (small batches with frequent switch-overs facilitated by flexible production factors), a change the industrialized world was facing, according to Sabel's theories (Sabel 1982; Piore & Sabel 1984).

Since Denmark's industrial structure was characterized by an abundance of small companies, we expected that large parts of the industrial community had already embarked on this restructuring. However, we assumed that these companies had to struggle with great structural problems, as we felt that the labour market had adapted to mass production since the Second World War. Therefore, this might prove to consti-

tute an obstacle to the labour force's ability to develop the flexibility necessary for the companies' restructuring to flexible production – a flexibility that had been further facilitated by new computer-based technologies. On the other hand, the conditions for developing this flexibility
might have been destroyed during the 1970s and the early 1980s, when
the mutual trust relationships between Denmark's workers and employ-
ers had deteriorated severely.

With so many forces at work – supportive as well as obstructive –
Denmark constituted the ideal laboratory for studying how a country
and a whole society experimented with finding a new rationality or model for its development. We did not expect to find a well-planned restructuring process. Quite the contrary, we assumed that the drift towards
flexible specialization was not the result of one or several actors' conscious strategy but rather the result of a compromise between various
actors' conflicting strategies governed by an unconscious drift towards
flexible specialization.

Preparing the Field Studies

However, I realized that this frame of understanding might make it impossible for me to structure my research when returning to Denmark.
Suddenly anything that happened in Denmark became interesting.
Could rifts between various interest organizations strengthen or weaken
the drift towards flexible specialization? Do the banks take actions that
cause a backlash in the financial patterns? Do increasing interest rates
push towards short-term rationalization that discourages the development of flexibility? Does the government's introduction of fixed wages
and salaries create such ill-feelings at the workplace that the trust required to develop flexible specialization is blown apart? In short, all the
news of the day became potentially important and had to be considered
to understand possible effects on the process of restructuring.

Even though it was evident that I could not fulfil this ambition, my
dream was to ingest everything, and I consumed a vast number of newspapers, reports, and books about the historical, political, and organizational conditions. I read about what was going on within the various industrial sectors and preferably about restructuring in the individual
company. For better or for worse, I became completely immersed in the
image of Denmark as reflected by the various media. My hungry curiosity reached such dimensions that it began to appear that it could only
be satiated if the Danes, their companies, institutions, conflicts, and

compromises sauntered in and presented the titbits of their lives to my voracious mind. It was a very open mind that digested anything – in short, a mental situation quite different from the one I had experienced before I went to the United States. Indeed, I had formed a clear picture of which effect to look for (flexible specialization); however, I had only a few ideas about the specific Danish causes capable of provoking this effect. At the same time, flexible specialization was a heuristic concept suitable for stimulating an open search process; but flexible specialization might be organized in many ways, which is why the search concerned an indefinite phenomenon that had been given a definite name.

Had all things been equal, I might still be sitting there feeding my insatiable brain with all the food for thought that was generated by my searching. However, all things were not equal. Fortunately, my mind was forced to structure its digestion and search process, since I had committed myself to trying to raise financial support for the project. It would be possible to sell the project to deep pockets in Denmark and the European Union by overemphasizing the aspects of introducing and applying computer-based production technologies: NC (numerically controlled) and CNC (computer numerically controlled) machines, robots, computer-aided transportation and stock systems, flexible manufacturing systems (FMS), computer-aided design (CAD) and manufacturing (CAM) and computer-integrated manufacturing (CIM). Giving the project this perhaps slightly opportunistic twist created the feeling of having some very substantial points for measuring the companies' restructuring towards flexible specialization: why did the companies introduce new technologies? Was the primary goal automation or did they want to reduce the time required to set up and switch-over production? Was new technology introduced to automate production, whereupon the companies realized that it could be used to reduce the time required to set up and switch-over production – to expand the production programme without increasing production costs? Did the technology challenge the skills of a labour force characterized by narrow, special competencies tailored to fit the repetitive rate of work of mass production? These questions led to other questions. Which types of conflict arose among the various unions? Had the demands for broader qualifications started the debate on the need for renewal in the labour movement? What were the conflicts at company level related to the division of work between the various occupational groups, the specialist workers, and the unskilled, female workers? Did the new technology involving a layer of salaried programming staff lead to increased bureaucratization of production? Or would the programming functions be carried out on the shop floor and thus become a lever to the creation of a broadly qualified, flexible machine worker? Was this the background for the Danish Metal Workers' Union talking about securing their workers' status as salaried workers? Which strategies had the companies developed towards the workers? Could management successfully reorganize production from a division of labour that made it easy to replace one hourly paid worker with another in jobs requiring very little training? Did managers dare at all to become dependent on competent workers? And on and on.

In writing the applications for grants, I was forced to formulate the study's focus, and this provided the project with a more appropriate start. Fortunately, the project did not have to wait for my mind to come to grips with itself. We could start working immediately.

Some of my students at Roskilde University Centre did a pilot study on small iron and metal firms in the Roskilde area. Their data were very promising. For many good and bad reasons, the small companies introduced CNC machines, but none of them used the technology to obtain rationalization advantages in a typical mass-production perspective. On the contrary, after some time during which the workers experimented with the machines, most companies used the equipment to improve their profile. They started to target production areas that required greater precision, high quality, and frequent modifications. This change in the company's market profile was directly shouldered by the workers using this technology. Apparently these small companies were not burdened with any type of occupational rigidity. There were people – a confectioner, many skilled metal workers and unskilled workers – who were crazy about computers, and through their work they found an outlet for their hobby. The owners did not seem to notice that gradually they, and the continued survival of the company, became dependent on their workers' special skills. On the contrary, this seemed to have been the situation as well before the introduction of computer-based technologies. The introduction and application of CNC technologies happened without much fuss in the companies that, before the introduction of these technologies, had been managed along principles close to those we associated with flexible specialization. Rather than being in the process of restructuring, these companies were in the process of renewing their flexible specialization strategy technologically.

These observations created somewhat of a schizophrenic crisis in the project. On the one hand, they seemed to indicate that Denmark was much more of an experimental laboratory than expected. On the other hand, studying the small companies would not enable me to fulfil the expectations that I had created among the institutions that had granted funds for the project: to provide reports elucidating the applications of integrated computer technologies (for example flexible manufacturing systems and computer-integrated manufacturing). Normally I would have chosen a one-sided solution to this problem, that is, been true to my friend and colleague Charles Sabel. However, at that time the grantors constituted a complex construction of three Danish research councils and two European institutions, the latter implying a commitment to collaborate with a French and a German team. As a result, I had to find a solution that felt like the equivalent of trying to be accepted into the Zen Buddhist monastic order.

I succeeded and started to develop micro-theories on the situation characterizing Denmark's business community and its various companies. One reasoning was that even though small companies played a significant role in the restructuring of Denmark's industry to flexible specialization, these companies could not be used to study and test the restructuring at a general level. However, the medium-sized companies were suitable for this purpose (that is, companies with between 200 and 500 employees). Why? For several reasons: first, the size of these companies allowed for functional specialization between units and employees. Consequently, they might gradually have moved towards exploiting the advantages of large-scale production within relatively small market domains. In short, the companies might have developed a kind of mini-Fordism during the 1960s. On the other hand, they might have been unable to lift themselves out of this mini-Fordism, because they were not large enough to finance the development projects that enabled large companies to jump from one market to another by developing new products. Thus, in medium-sized companies, flexible specialization represented a radical shift that was much more difficult to implement and much more in conflict with the company's previous orientation than was the case in small companies. On the other hand, a shift towards flexible specialization in medium-sized companies would have a great impact on the remaining industrial structure. Frequent shifts in and restructuring of production in the medium-sized companies would inherently spread to the small companies that often functioned as subcontractors of semi-products, production equipment, or other types of technology. If the medium-sized companies were in the process of implementing comprehensive restructuring towards flexible specialization, studying these companies would furnish us with a fairly good picture of the situation.

Furthermore, I also expected the medium-sized companies to provide us with data on integrating ways of applying computer technology, which we needed for the report.

If the medium-sized companies were in the midst of such restructuring, it would be a good idea to talk to the production managers to get a picture of these changes. I assumed that they were familiar with developing production towards ever-increasing efficiency and high-capacity utilization of machines and personnel. Therefore, if the restructuring had started, they would be in the midst of an incalculable change in connection with which they would have to replace most of their previous rules of thumb. In short, they would probably find themselves in a considerable identity crisis. By going for the production managers as respondents and getting them to tell how they personally experienced the situation and their role, we would be able to collect significant evidence of the companies' situation. Finding themselves in the midst of restructuring, the production managers would be very interested in speaking to someone who had a perspective on the restructuring and change that they probably found very confusing. One way of approaching the subject could be to discuss the restructuring of the company in general, the factory layout, and the production flow, considering the interplay with sales and the development department. This would make it possible for us to get an overall picture of the company; in addition, we would learn how the production managers experienced the demands on machine operators – currently compared with previously.

In the final preparatory phase, Christian Lisberg – an engineer with expertise in computer-based production technology – joined the project team.

The preparatory phase consisted of creating and developing a series of coherent expectations of what we would find in the companies and interviewees' situations. In short, we developed contingent micro-theories based on the project's macro-theory about the restructuring problems facing medium-sized companies in Denmark in 1985. Mentally, we had developed a very distinct and simple way of reasoning and did not feel any need for developing an interview guide to govern these interviews.

An important point of the project was not only to capture the restructuring towards flexible specialization but also the reasoning – the logic – applied by the staff to comprehend this development. If the interviewer incessantly interrupts the flow of the interviewee's thoughts in order to stick to the logic of the interview guide, the interviewee's logic is bound to crumble. Such an approach obscures the general understanding that places the respondent's answers in a context. It is imperative that the researcher be mentally prepared to reason in specific situations if she wants to capture surprises in the proper sense of the word. Interview guides may, for many practical reasons, be necessary, but in principle they represent mental laxity, and they prevent the researcher from identifying herself with the logic of the company. If, during the field study, the researcher follows the interview guide, she is not very likely to discover anything but that which was anticipated. On the other hand, the ability to capture the logic of the company creates a competitive, contextual understanding that is a challenge to the researcher's logic. But if she finds it so difficult to manage this logic that she needs a reminder in terms of an interview guide, she is very unlikely to discover that the two forms of logic have begun to diverge. And therefore the ability to realize that something has been discovered – or uncovered – is minimal.

However, researchers are rarely that well prepared at the start of their field study. What forces them to find such a level of clarification in normal circumstances? They still have ample resources and time. In our case, it was a matter of eradicating a dilemma by constructing a theory that could combine two different projects. However, I confess that the reason why I did not resort to constructing an interview guide was that it simply did not occur to me. I had been indoctrinated in a research tradition that normally did not conduct field studies.

The Selection Phase

We had no trouble determining the criteria for selecting interesting companies for the study. The target group was a natural consequence of the project formulation that had furnished the project with the necessary grants. We had committed ourselves to investigating the importance of integrated computer-based production systems, that is, flexible manufacturing systems and computer-integrated manufacturing (or elements of these) for the companies' preconception and administration of such systems. Urged on by my greedy curiosity, I had, for several years prior to the study, generated comprehensive files of newspaper articles, research reports, and much other information on companies introducing these technologies. Thus, the task was easy: I merely had to go through the files and select the companies that were likely to have introduced such technologies or were in the midst of doing so.

However, we had yet another criterion. We wanted to avoid the most fashionable companies that, for some reason, were assumed to be in the lead technologically or economically. To secure some kind of representation, we endeavoured to get into contact with companies that could be viewed as undistinguished representatives of the population of medium-sized companies. Also we wanted to delve into companies that were fairly unknown to the public. Another aspect of the selection criterion was regional. A number of large companies in Greater Copenhagen and on Sjælland (the island on which Copenhagen is located) had been subjected to several studies, and they had become trend-setters for what researchers believed was happening in Danish companies. These famous companies were largely atypical, if only for the reason that a typical company in Denmark is characterized by having a name only known to a few people. The unknown, undistinguished companies in Jutland had been characterized by powerful dynamics; however, we knew very little about these companies (apart from a few important exceptions).

On the other hand, various articles and reports put us on the track of the specific companies. These articles were important for continuing the process launched during the preparatory phase: by generating data from articles, reports, etc., we could improve on the micro-theories. We could take the concretization of the micro-theories a step further and adapt them to a specific company that had been running certain projects.

Going over the material, we selected 18 medium-sized companies (within the iron and metal industry) that seemed to represent different aspects of the reaction of the industrial structure to the demands of the market and to the technological potential for moving towards flexible specialization.

The Contact Phase

Our plan was to contact these 18 companies, persuade them to open their doors to us, interview the production managers, and get a guided tour of the factory. Each visit was scheduled to last half a day. After this phase we hoped to do in-depth field studies in three of the companies. We planned to study each company for a week, which would make it possible for us to gain a deeper understanding of the organizational phenomena characterizing the restructuring towards flexible specialization.

However, Christian Lisberg and I were afraid that the companies would turn us down. This feeling was reinforced by the fact that the project was located at Roskilde University Centre, which was perceived to be a »red« university at that time. Frankly, on that hot, August afternoon when we were discussing how to make contact, we were afraid that all 18 companies would turn us down. We felt an urgent need to develop a strategy before we started to contact them. Since then, I have seen many field study projects that failed to administer this phase properly. That is, the researchers had not started to develop a contact strategy until all the companies they wanted to participate in the study had turned them down.

The strategy was based on the following considerations. First, the project had to be presented as relevant to the overall company and in particular to the person – the production manager – whom we intended to use to get access to the company. Christian came up with the brilliant idea to rename the project the 3F Project (Future Flexible Factories) and, in a very short presentation of the project (two pages), to describe the ongoing restructuring and the technological, organizational, managerial, and cultural problems characterizing this process.

In a letter to the individual company accompanying the project description, we briefly referred to what we already knew about the company, explained why it was important to our study, and indicated the types of problems that we expected were being experienced during the process of restructuring.

In other words, the contact strategy was based on and exploited our experiences from the preparation and selection phase. Without having been through these phases, we would not have been able to appeal to the hearts of the production managers.

Another key phrase was *talked with*. Before mailing the letter and the project description, we called the companies' production managers, told them about the project, and explained why we were particularly interested in including their company in our project. In this way, we obtained a general impression of the company's current situation and of issues related to our project. Consequently, we were able to focus the subsequent letter with the project description on issues that we knew were important to the companies and thus make them interested in participating in the study. However, the telephone conversation had yet another effect – we got to know these production managers more intimately and felt that they would plead our cause when our letter arrived.

The strategy was successful. Even though we were forced to visit all the companies within a period of 2 weeks for financial reasons (hotel accommodation and transport), we succeeded in visiting 14 of the 18 possible companies during the first round.

The 2 weeks turned out to be a celebration. All the companies visited were deeply involved in finding ways of handling the extreme demands for flexibility, and they had a broad spectrum of experiences on which they drew. We had expected our role in these interviews to be that of a consultant – to make the production managers realize why they experienced the problems the way they did; but during the interviews, the topic shifted to the comprehensive and complex problems of moving towards flexibility. At this point, our micro-theories proved their strength as they were submitted to the most severe tests. To our surprise, some of our theories didn't hold: the production managers whom we interviewed were not a bunch of confused, stressed, and frustrated individuals but were people who, for several years, had been working on reorganizing the company towards a structure about which we didn't think they had a clue. The factories were not moving towards flexible specialization simply because they had invested in computer-aided and -controlled machines for the purpose of rationalizing production and only later discovered that this machinery could be used for other purposes. In fact, none of the companies we visited had anything that met the international definitions of flexible manufacturing systems, even though we had chosen them based on articles, and during the telephone conversation they had confirmed that they were well into flexible production systems and computer-controlled machines. In this sense, the project seemed to be falling apart in terms of fulfilling our expectations and promises to those who had provided us with money for the project.

However, viewed from the perspective of flexible specialization, this phenomenon almost seemed to be more interesting. The companies had long been experimenting with production teams and team technology also in relation to individual CNC machines, and they experimented in many ways with flexible production systems; but it had nothing to do with flexible manufacturing systems. Also, at the level of the company, some of our assumptions proved wrong. Many of the companies were quite familiar with the demand for flexibility. In several cases, the size of the companies was determined by the fact that they produced a large number of products in an extremely large number of varieties. In other words, these companies had as early as the 1960s broken with the rigid specialization in which we expected they had been trapped. During the 1960s, they had succeeded in fitting this flexibility into the philosophies of control springing from the scientific management of mass production. Changing market conditions and high interest rates (and consequently soaring storage expenses) had forced even companies with decades of experience with flexibility to find new ways of flexibly organizing production. Many of the production managers were on very good terms with the workers on the shop floor, whom they perceived as their best allies in their efforts to make the new production philosophies function, whereas they expected strong resistance from other departments and top management. Only a few felt that they, in collaboration with the rest of management, had to combat reactionary workers and stubborn shop stewards and union representatives. Years back, they had started as apprentices and had reached their current position after having worked for a long period as skilled workers and gone through intensive, continuous training. Deeply rooted in this typical artisan way of life, they knew one another across company borders, and it was evident that the people we talked with knew one another from different stages in their careers. The fact that we were able to travel from company to company, bringing regards from one colleague to another, eased our way into the hearts of these people. Gradually, we were able to tell discreet stories about how their colleagues understood the problems facing the iron and metal industry.

During the interviews we benefited greatly from the preparation and selection phases. We had specific knowledge about the industry and its situation, which enabled us to illustrate the theoretical perspectives with practical examples. This translation was incredibly important in making the production managers understand our considerations and relating them to their situation. Also, the practical examples of the factories' restructuring problems enabled us to highlight the individual company's problems. In this way, we could create something that resembled a general, yet non-theoretical conception of the problems, which they thought were unique to the company whose production they managed. We felt that we became valuable sparring partners with whom they could openly discuss their problems and count on a worthy response. The fact that we virtually assumed the role of a priest to whom they confessed their problems was more than we had ever bargained for. We established a number of very friendly relationships during these two hectic weeks in the autumn of 1985.

I have since learned that many field studies are concluded after this phase. Nevertheless, I have chosen to label this period the contact phase, as it proved to be a good way of establishing the relationships necessary for the actual field studies we had planned to do in three companies that were scheduled to run for a week each.

Had we started out by asking three companies whether they would agree to let us study them for a week, I am sure that our request would have been generally denied. Now, however, the first three companies that we asked agreed to participate. And I am sure that the reason why it went so easily was that we had established friendships in the companies, and these friends pleaded our cause. These were friends who did their utmost to convince their peers and superiors that it was a good idea; who told the shop stewards that our work would not be used against anyone. In my opinion, a company gives a very generous gift when it opens its doors to be studied for a whole week. The labour costs of the people involved in interviews and assisting the study team during the process amount to almost 2 weeks' wages, and it causes a great deal of disturbance in the factory and in the offices. As a result, you can't help feeling that you have been given a gift when you are granted permission to walk around in the company as you please for a whole week – a gift that, according to the rules of reciprocity, implies that the company, or at least the friends who have helped, are owed a gift: to do a proper piece of work from which the company can benefit one way or the other. This feeling of being harnessed by an obligation is very appropriate when you proceed to the intensive phase of the field study.

The Intensive Research Phase

Retrospectively, researchers inevitably attempt to justify intensive field studies by referring to the effect rather than to the initiating motives and ideas. Frankly, I felt that the results of the 14 explorative and short-term field studies mentioned above were excellent – that I had gathered enough information. The studies had proven that Denmark's iron and metal companies more than fulfilled the requirements of restructuring towards flexible specialization. They had had to tackle a series of problems, but they seemed to be well on the way to completing the process. Restructuring involved a series of thematic problems, but on the whole it could be implemented in Denmark. I strongly felt that I had acquainted myself with the reality of the companies. I knew what ideas occupied the minds of the key actors in this restructuring process – the production managers. So, to be truthful, I must admit that my motivation for subjecting myself to 3 weeks of hard field studies was certainly not overwhelming.

Again, I was rescued by the commitments I was obliged to fulfil according to the project description. In the application for funds, I had promised to do a series of in-depth, intensive field studies, and now I had to fulfil my promise. I wanted to get it over and done with as fast as possible in order to be able to devote myself to the normal pursuits of a scholar.

This proved to be a good push. Not until I started on the intensive field studies did I really understand the significance of a company being composed of many conflicting drives or interests and strategies. Companies moved towards flexible specialization as an inadvertent result of various interested parties' strategies, rather than as a result of well-coordinated strategies.

Getting Behind the Rationalized Façade

I soon realized that what we had captured during the preceding series of interviews was a rationalized façade, or story, in which the interviewed production managers played the lead role as the heroes and administrators of the new rationality. This role soon started to crumble when we moved around in the company and talked to all kinds of people about what was going on and acquired the stories behind the present situation. First of all, the story and the main characters changed according to whom we interviewed. But this was not the only thing. The overall problem of restructuring towards flexible specialization also changed from person to person. Sometimes I even doubted whether restructuring towards flexible specialization presented a problem at all. I was surprised to discover that in this social system – the factory – the occupants were operating with a great number of projects, interpretations, and policies. My conception of the factory changed from one of a well-organized, technical system to a mysterious, secretive human drama. I was seized by the same urge to pursue the truth as William was in his attempt to unravel the mysteries of the monastery in Umberto Eco's (1984) *The Name of The Rose*. I increasingly felt that I might risk repeating William's laconic reflection to Adso: »There was no plot...and I discovered it by mistake«.

Getting a Feel for the Company's Own Logic

This lament strongly indicated that I was about to identify with the way in which the employees experienced the situation and handled their everyday life, their aspirations, and their formulations of the company's problems. One of the field researcher's tasks is to get a feel for these conflicting aspirations and interpretations and, from those, to attempt to create a whole by allowing the apparently conflicting aspirations to unite into one dynamic process.

Nevertheless, it was surprising to find that all the interviewees were profoundly committed to the process. Each had his or her own interpretation and opinion of the company, which disproves the presence of passivity that managers profess prevails among subordinates. When numerous interpretations and opinions are at work, the interpretations and strategies of management have to win authority when competing with a vortex of other interpretations and strategies. This competition between many interpretations and strategies decides the company's logic. This was our assumption, which is why we started to talk with employees at all levels in these companies, but we were surprised to find that we were right in our assumption.

Coming across such a vortex of opinions, ideas, and information, you have to watch your step as a field researcher. On the one hand, you have to hold on to your own project: what am I here to investigate (in this case the restructuring process towards flexible specialization)? On the other hand, you must not be tempted to form an alliance with those who understand the problems of the company from your perspective (a question of flexible specialization). I was able to escape this vortex since I was interested in gaining a holistic conception of the many unknown aspects of restructuring a whole company made up of widely different interests and world views.

For that reason alone, I stuck to my plan of visiting all parts of the company, which implied talking to witnesses with differing opinions on what the problems were, how they could be resolved, the glue that held the company together, and why things were as they were.

Finding Witnesses

Not all witnesses are equally good. Managers, for example, often know very little about what is going on in the company. Certain roles seem to set certain limits for which information the environment communicates; likewise the roles produce certain ways of perceiving the surrounding realities. A company's social system is often developed to perfection to give a manager the feeling of managing while ridding her of the insight that makes management effective. Similarly, the workers on the shop floor, for instance, usually identify themselves with their institutional roles to the extent that they are unable to view things in a broader perspective. They are often so absorbed in their roles that they are incapable of identifying their own personality.

However, there are exceptions. Some of the best witnesses in my search for a holistic understanding of the problems of restructuring were the apprentices. They demonstrated a rare ability to dissociate themselves in an ironic way from the company. They were able to caricature the system's roles and to see through behavioural relations, such as the vicious circles created by the company's way of functioning. Apprentices are good witnesses for several reasons: (1) they move around in the system and experience the company from different angles; (2) they have not yet become true members of the company and, due to their outsider status, they have therefore retained a certain amount of perspective; (3) they have not yet been socialized to see the life of the specific company as the most natural thing in the world.

As a field researcher, it is wise to get hold of people possessing one or more of these characteristics. They are important witnesses and should be interviewed early in the process; however, most of them will occupy a status in the hierarchy which, unfortunately, either can cause you to wait until the very last phase to talk to them or perhaps ignore them altogether. Such witnesses must never stand alone. Naturally, all the usual witnesses must be involved. Nevertheless, it is often these institutional outsiders who shed fresh light on the statements of traditional witnesses.

Speaking of institutional roles: the field researcher, too, has a tendency to play an institutional role. Many, and I emphasize *many*, field researchers are extremely concerned with being taken seriously by management who granted them access to the company. Their interviews are often governed by this fact. Too often the researcher will talk incessantly in order to convince the VIP that he is indeed sitting in the presence of a researcher with exceptional abilities. It is a poisonous, institutional role that thus emerges. First of all, because the field researcher now starts to search for interpretations of the field that will ensure the survival of this role. But also because the researcher starts to measure progress in terms of the ability to get access to people at the top of the hierarchy. Bearing in mind what we have said thus far, this is the safest short-cut not to discover anything of interest to write in the report, which the very same managers whom the researcher has tried to please will read as a faint echo of their own words and find profoundly uninteresting. The most important secret about the art of doing field studies is, perhaps, to break with the institutional role surrounding the field researcher.

Finding Clues and Solving Mysteries

In the field study phase, I played a game with myself. I imagined –
without losing but rather reinforcing my own sense of self-irony – that I
was a detective unravelling a mystery, a case, and therefore looking for
clues.

The nature of the mystery was known – theoretically – prior to embarking on the individual field study. My simple task was to unravel the
plot of the mystery in each of the companies. Theoretically, I claimed
the companies to be schizophrenic, simultaneously pursuing flexibility
and the ideas of efficiency connected to mass production. In my opinion, they were bound to find themselves in a dilemma, which might be
experienced in the form of seeing the company torn to shreds. At best,
the individual employee would experience the same feeling of being torn
to shreds – of being suspended between different behavioural norms,
each pulling in their own direction.

As the workers had previously been forced to perform monotonous
and tedious jobs in an efficient manner and were now suddenly confronted with the demand for flexibility and adjustability, it struck me
that, in my pursuit to understand the nature of the forces at work in the
company, I might as well talk with the workers about their work and everyday life in the company.

In order to learn about these issues, it was important that I left it to
the respondents to talk about whatever they felt like talking discussing.
I collected a large number of life stories, learned about their experiences
from other workplaces and how the work had changed and got meticulous descriptions of the current work. Consequently, I gradually
changed my perception of the people with whom I had spoken, the work
they performed, their motives for being with the company, and their way
of approaching problems.

The interviewees revealed an opinion on most issues that broke with
the theoretical and conventional perception of workers and managers,
industrial organization, and class division: the baggage I carried from
my days at the university. In fact, many of them did and always had performed a complex and varied job in which they drew on their life-long
experience. Therefore, they were proud of themselves as craftspeople.
As a result of this pride, their position in the company was far from one
resembling structural suppression. Quite the contrary. They were, depending on the behaviour of the company and its various management

types, able to develop a large variety of counterstrategies that could completely change the management's expected effect of a certain wage system, a way of organizing work or reorganizing it.

As a result, the systems implemented by management rarely had the desired effect. They had an effect, of course, but not the desired effect of structuring behaviour. Drawing on their experiences, skilfulness, and professional pride, the workers developed counterstrategies not only to protect themselves but also because they took pride in developing strategies that enabled them to escape and restructure the structural power of managerial systems. For example, clever workers were fully capable of undermining a wage system meant to improve productivity.

In order to understand a certain company's specific efforts to move in a certain direction, I had expected to study the schizophrenic situation of two conflicting managerial systems. But I soon realized that I was confronted with studying a system of two managerial systems and a multitude of strategies counteracting these systems and their combined effects on behaviour, etc. And I would have to study this if I wanted to understand the contradictory endeavours that pushed a distinct company in a distinct direction.

This is impossible and brings us back to William: »There was no plot...and I discovered it by mistake«.

Clues are strange. During an interview with a machine worker, I thought, for instance, that I had found evidence of an inappropriate lack of influence when he complained that his 3-month-old suggestion to invest in some cables and computers for his work place, which comprised two CNC machines, had not yet been considered (the costs involved amounted to approximately USD 36,000). In his opinion, the management was insensitive to alternative solutions, and the workers lacked influence.

In the context when the statement occurred during an interview, it seemed to be a clue signifying the workers' lack of joint influence. However, after I had worked my way through the whole company and talked to various people, I gradually began to grasp the complexity of the company, which changed my interpretation of the interview. This company had established a comprehensive system of joint influence. What the workers complained about was that they were not in a position to make decisions about investments overnight. Therefore, the statement was not a clue, and the mystery was something quite different.

The Mystery and Craft of the Field Study

What has been said thus far leads to some significant reflections on the techniques used for field studies, reflections that contrast sharply with most of the advice I had received on how to approach field studies.

As I emphasized earlier, in order to identify yourself with the company studied, you have to listen carefully to what the witnesses say without imposing your own logic on them. In this way, you can gather information that can put you on the track of quite a different mystery plot than originally expected. The more you allow yourself to identify with the respondents' logic, the more you can use their contrasting explanations and perceptions to ask questions that come closer to the company's motives.

Instead of operating with the company's theoretical inconsistencies, you start to play off, one against another, the inconsistent explanations of what goes on in a specific company. Consequently, the respondents are faced with increasingly demanding and specific questions about life in the company as you proceed to ask questions.

Thus, you gradually learn more and more about the logic governing a certain company and, as it appears from the example above, it is not until you realize this logic that you begin to understand fully the meaning of earlier statements that contributed to an understanding at that stage.

This touches on a crucial problem of the technique applied during the explorative phase. Many field researchers are strongly opposed to taping interviews and prefer to take notes from the field. There are many good reasons for this attitude. First of all, using a tape recorder makes the respondent more careful about what he or she says and thus yields less information. Second, when coming back from the field you are unavoidably confronted with an information overload problem when you have to edit the tapes. I fully agree with these reasons for not taping interviews.

The problem of taking notes during the field study is, however, that you always tend to note what you find important at a given time. As a result, it becomes difficult to compose the context or company logic on which to base your understanding of the individual statements in any gradual fashion. It becomes almost impossible to dissociate yourself from your own logic and identify with the company's logic. If you succeed, you usually fail to catch statements from the first interviews that could have been used to support and understand this company logic.

We chose to tape all the interviews except when it was technically impossible, for example, when interviewing a machinist while he is operating his machinery. Consequently, the material that had gradually allowed us to identify the company's logic could now, after the explorative phase, be subject to renewed scrutiny from a different perspective. When listening to the interviews later, you realize that quite different statements become important than those originally remembered as being important.

The Phase of Analysis

I admit, and thus confirm for the sceptics of the recorded interview, that when I returned from 14 extensive interviews and three intensive field studies and realized that I had more than 200 hours of listening ahead of me, my feelings were somewhat ambivalent, to say the least. It is impossible to listen to all of it just to generate ideas. Some researchers are in the lucky position of having a secretary to transcribe the tapes. I made the mistake of spending the funds I had been allocated for a secretary on a PC, which was an expensive investment at that time.

However, even this seemingly insurmountable obstacle of getting started on the analysis proved advantageous, as the only feasible method was to keep a cool head: to think carefully. This was quite easy due to the path the project had taken. The strength of the preparation, selection, contact, and intensive research phases fully materialized. Because the expectations had been formulated very clearly in terms of major and minor theories, they had been disconfirmed on a number of points. Therefore, we had avoided the inevitable self-affirmation that characterizes much social science research. The generally self-affirming nature of Danish social science research is quite fascinating. For example, researchers rarely operate with hypotheses that are formulated clearly enough that they may be negated by subsequent empirical evidence. Unfortunately, this attitude is also reflected in writing. Formulations are vague and much in keeping with what has been conceived to be true. It is hard to tell what the message actually is and thus difficult to contradict it. The fascinating aspect of trying to avoid criticism from others is that one's perception becomes blurred due to obscure thinking.

We had avoided falling into this trap due to the very process of the field study, which meant that we actually had something to write about. For example:

- The restructuring process: Denmark's industry was in the process of implementing a comprehensive restructuring, but not the type we had expected: going from mass production to flexible specialization. It was a restructuring process from one type of flexible specialization to another.
- Flexibility was not impeded by the qualification structure among Danish workers but had always been present as a part of it. For some reason, the skilled workers had succeeded in maintaining a role on the shop floor during the post-war period of professed Taylorization.
- There was no evidence of the professed rigidity of Denmark's labour market if rigidity means resistance to introducing new technology. On the shop floor, the various unions and groups of workers competed for the ability to use the technology. As a result, they pressured management to introduce new technology rather than resisting it.
- In general, technology was not introduced top-down in terms of investments in large, optimizing solutions. On the contrary, it was introduced in increments and, to a certain extent, not coordinated for a variety of reasons – often due to influence from the individual workshops rather than because of something that resembled a company strategy.
- Managers and workers did not constitute separate worlds but were part of a continuum in which they could float during their career and in which it was not only possible but actually the norm that an apprentice could end up as, for example, a technical or administrative director.
- Consequently, there was no need to develop relationships of trust across class distinctions but merely to integrate workers of various ages and career stages, ranging from apprentice to journeyman to supervisor. Once a smith, for example, has served his apprenticeship, he becomes and stays a member of a community regardless of whether he is a machinist or a managing director. Whereas workers who have not served their apprenticeship have a rough road to travel before they can develop relationships of trust and can be included into the community, whether they are civil engineers, labourers (unskilled or semiskilled workers) or merchants (for example business school graduates).

I felt it would be impossible to write a paper that revealed these surprising findings. They could not be documented – or rather would require that the reader was willing to follow my line of thought and thus change his perception of Denmark's manufacturing enterprises based on these findings that had pulled the rug out from under my previous perception of these enterprises.

However, a quite different and more specific demand became decisive in determining how I started to process the material. As I stressed earlier, the companies I had inconvenienced for a whole week deserved a gift. I sensed that they were primarily interested in a comprehensive, descriptive analysis of their own company and nothing more. During the preparatory phase, I had read numerous field study reports and knew that there was quite a need for this type of analytical descriptions of the life in Danish companies.

This fact decided the general outline of my subsequent text on the study (Kristensen 1986). However, my original intention was not to devote so much space to the three companies that had been subject to intensive field studies.

The section describing the intensive field studies was analytically fairly easy to write. During the week I had spent in each of the companies, I had developed a clear notion of the nature or placement of the clue that existed in each company, wherein each of the companies' schizophrenic dual efforts (operative efficiency versus flexibility) would interact. Thus, the clue in each company was given and now I merely had to compose the drama, demonstrating the correlation of many factors, players, units, groups, and systems. I started to listen to the tapes in order to place the schizophrenic clue on stage, and the tapes proved to be a rich source of information. They were actually exciting to listen to – one by one – and I slowly began to construct and write the individual field study on my new PC. The block and move functions were very useful, to this novice PC user, for gradually changing the structure of the analysis as I listened to the tapes. I was able to develop an increasingly fine-meshed construction of the company studied – a construction that was built much more solidly than I would have imagined possible before listening to the tapes. Even today, I find that these stories ably illustrate the aspects of life in some of Denmark's iron and metal firms.

In this way, the phase of field analysis and documentation became a pleasant process. This does not, however, imply that it was easy. For approximately 5 months I spent day and night listening to the tapes: listening, thinking, writing, and then listening again. Often one interview suddenly enabled me to make sense of another interview and place it in its proper context. Then I had to listen to the first interview again, searching for statements to combine the two interviews in the construction of the field study. Naturally, listening to the tapes also refreshed my memories of the visit. I want to stress that while working with and constructing the individual intensive field study, I did not engage in any other activities. The task demanded my continuous, undivided attention in order to materialize. My personal perception of what it means to identify yourself with the company's logic stems from this period in particular.

I experienced the period as pleasurable. But viewed from the outside, my behaviour looked rather perverse. I chose to ignore this. An institute that wanted to find out whether they should recruit me had offered me an office. During the 5 months I spent there, a set of earphones was permanently attached to my head. I was rather offensive if someone dared to interrupt my listening odyssey. It became obvious that potential, future colleagues gradually grew annoyed with me, which in turn made me stick to my work even more persistently, because I wanted to get it over and done with as fast as possible. As far as I remember, I had calculated a period of 6 weeks as being adequate for finishing this task. I did finish it – after working virtually night and day for 5 months.

And then I turned to my future, potential colleagues for inspired conversation. They had, however, in the meantime turned their backs on me (it later proved to be a temporary condition that lasted only 2 years) and did not feel inclined to talk to someone whom they had ample time to agree was thoroughly antisocial.

I should have felt miserable, abandoned, lost, and in a true crisis. Frankly, I was very happy, feeling that I had found a soul, a tone, or a logic in Denmark's manufacturing firms that was worth continuing to work with. The study furnished me with a quite new and powerful stronghold (in the Archimedean sense) for relating both to my colleagues in the United States and to the Danish and European research funds that had financed the project. The nature of this stronghold was a very preliminary cross-analysis of the tales from the field. Having completed it, I had run out of time for this phase of the project. The resulting book was on the whole composed of a series of working papers, but I was quite satisfied with it.

Each of the companies that had participated in the intensive part of the study received an 80-page report on their specific company. On a number of dimensions it cut deeply, enabling the company to see itself in a new light since a field researcher, particularly if he or she aspires to do a holistic study, is able to see correlations that are concealed from the individuals who occupy institutionalized roles. Thus, I had reciprocated the companies' gifts.

For a short, blissful period of time, I was in the situation of having paid everyone his due in relation to the project. On the other hand, I was probably the loneliest researcher in all of Denmark. However, I don't think I was aware of it at the time, and I happily proceeded to the next phase.

The Phase of Reflection

Those who claim that the phase of analysis is rather insubstantial are correct, when judging from the traditional field study perspective. Viewed from this perspective, the phase of analysis and documentation conclude a project. However, in my opinion it is a misconception to think that a field study is ever concluded. On the contrary, it changes the researcher's life.

I have previously pointed out a number of conditions that surprised me by being quite different from what I had expected. Read these passages again. They show that companies seem to be quite different from what we expect, that the people operating the machines are not the kind of workers we expect to find based on the theories and previous descriptions. Nor do those managing the factories fit with what we have been told, and their interrelationships are quite different from what we thought they would be.

As an effect of this series of surprises, my previous understanding of social science largely collapsed. I could have chosen to neglect these surprises and continued to try to be at peace with myself. I could have accepted the facts. But wouldn't that require that I totally abandon the theories on which I based my research?

I am a man of compromise. So I chose a third path: to try to explain how Denmark's social development had produced different types of managers, workers, and companies than those prescribed by global social science theory. In my search for reasons to explain why Denmark's enterprises might be different (compared with the theories – perhaps not compared with those of other countries), I gradually became caught up in a fascinating game. The game consisted of demonstrating that those forces that will produce a certain development according to theory will also produce a certain development in Danish society. Thus, I had to look for conditions in Danish society that invalidated the theoretical forces and were capable of turning the development in other directions. By extracting the conditions specifically characterizing Danish society, a pattern or system gradually emerged that made me realize the inner coherence of the specific type of social development in Denmark in which the meaning of concepts such as company, manager, and worker is quite different from that derived from global social science.

This task primarily involved working my way through stacks of literature on the history of Denmark that could provide me with the information I needed to construct new explanations. Thus, my isolated position in Denmark's research environment could be exploited. However, looking back on this period in my life, I think that I was near the end of my rope in terms of coping with my role as the lone wolf while I devoured stacks of historical works on all sorts of peculiar subjects.

I have gradually developed an idea about the specific type of industrial development in Denmark, which implies that a series of the anomalies that other social scientists have indicated exist in Danish society can be explained by reasoning in this developmental logic. In short, gradually one develops a way of reasoning that is a theory about the developmental dynamics of Denmark's industry. In my continuous test of this grand theory of Denmark, I constantly draw on my field studies. Is it possible to build a theory that complies with these field studies? Will my most recent version of the grand theory of Denmark create a better understanding for what I discovered in the companies studied? Is the logic compatible with the people I met in the companies I studied?

In this way the phase of analysis and documentation is never concluded. I sometimes call some of the people in these companies to hear how certain conditions have developed, when I need new input for the continuous development of my grand theory of Denmark – or if I learn about events in these companies that seem to contradict my grand theory of Denmark. I recently revisited one of the companies for 10 days and conducted a series of interviews.

In addition, my field studies have furnished me with a frame of reference that makes it possible for me, by arguing based on the studies, to ask questions that may upset some of the conclusions that colleagues undertaking field studies have taken the liberty of drawing. However, conclusions that are rejected often point to discoveries that are worth paying attention to in one's future research.

In other words, my research practice has changed radically, and I do not refrain from using my new research practice to influence others for a very good reason: to create a practice within social science research for developing theories capable of explaining specific phenomena and developmental processes characterizing specific societies. General, universal theories merely constitute the framework for starting the game.

Part 3:
Elements for a
Research Practice

6. Research Environment and Research Practice: Analysis of an Art and its Social Context

What is the Message of these Tales?

First, a departure from the norm of how research projects ought to progress is the norm for all four tales in Part 2. Second, the field in question in all four studies made a lasting impression on the researchers who conducted the projects. Third, the researchers passed the test and maintained membership and positions in the academic field.

On the other hand, none of us has been able to change the agenda of international research through our projects. Each of the projects fall within the golden mean of research. Nor are we able to provide an analysis of the four tales which provides us, or the reader, with a recipe for how to find international fame or receive the Nobel prize. The following considerations and advice spring from far more modest aspirations.

The reader has no doubt also noticed differences between the four tales. Let us, for a moment, stick to the traditional idea that projects that include field studies pass through three phases:

- preparatory phase
- explorative phase
- analysis and writing phase.

Looking at each of the three phases, we cannot find any common characteristics in terms of either mistakes made in the projects or in solutions. On the contrary, each project is characterized by internal coherence between theirs phases. The conclusion could be that each project is a function of its own dynamics, which, among other things, depend on the personality of the researcher and the conditions of research – both those of the academic field and those of the social field studied. We must appease ourselves with normative and rational theorizing.

This conclusion would bring us back to the situation characterizing Danish social science research today. All Ph.D. candidates are introduced to methodology in terms of literature and lectures that present the technology and techniques of the rational research process as ideals. But real training happens in quite a different manner. Most students learn to formulate a project and implement it by trial-and-error as apprentices supervised by journeymen (associate professors) and master journeymen (professors) who themselves thrive on these projects. The problem is that journeymen and master journeymen run projects routinely. What Bourdieu (1987; 1990: 59) calls »habitus« or »feel for the game« has usually been turned into »tacit knowledge« (Polanyi 1969: 123-211) embedded in the spinal cord or flowing in the blood of these journeymen. Such skills are difficult to communicate in the usual academic way. Many hardened (or experienced) researchers are often not aware of what they do when conducting research. When they attempt to communicate this knowledge to colleagues or students, the yawning void is filled with statements from well-read methodological literature rather than statements from gained experience.

Any researcher can find inspiration for the different phases of her project in traditional, rationalist, methodological literature. But there is often disparity between the books' advice and recipes and the troubles experienced by the researcher. This disparity cannot be eliminated; however, the following analysis of the tales contained in Part 2 is an attempt to lessen it. We will try to disclose some of the »secrets of the spinal cord«.

Thorough Theoretical Preparation

There is one specific, important reason for helping one another create an experiential methodology for field studies. If the researcher follows the advice of rational methodology too closely, she may go out into the field and not learn anything new. As teachers and tutors, we have seen field studies in which the theoretical thought processes by and large eliminated the field effect. Figure 6.1 illustrates the process of such a project.

Caricatured, the process can be described by the following sequences: in the preparatory phase, the researcher takes a point of departure in a theory, formulates hypotheses based on this theory, and reformulates these into an interview guide that steers the studies in the field. In the explorative phase, the researcher interviews representatives of the field. She attempts to hold both herself and the respondents strictly to the interview guide in an attempt to avoid giving free rein to the respondents' imagination on things and phenomena that the researcher finds irrelevant. If answers do not match the interview guide, the researcher tries to repeat the questions more explicitly. The researcher merely uncovers aspects of the field that are theoretically relevant. There are many reasons for this; however, the result is always comparable responses that ease the analysis phase.

Figure 6.1. A Rational Theory-determined Project

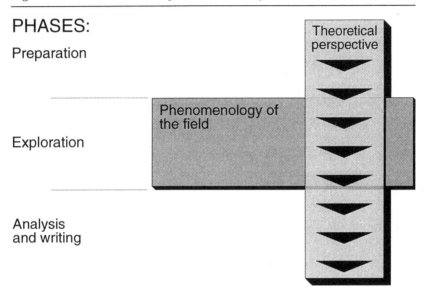

In other words, the researcher has asked the field a series of theoretically deduced questions that carefully avoided any impact on the data collection by the field in terms of the field's own, unwanted interpretation of things and phenomena. The subsequent analysis reveals to what extent the field measures up to the ideals of the researcher. At best, elements of the field are typified according to types of behaviour demonstrating differences and similarities in comparison to the theoretical ideal types. This comparison is often the most important component of the field analysis. Furthermore, when writing the report, the researcher often uses material from the field to illustrate and vitalize the theoretical ideas. The function of the latter is usually, consciously or unconsciously, to confirm the theoretical ideas.

As illustrated in Figure 6.1, the field has left no mark on the project apart from the theoretically planned path. The theory has been »as-

cribed to the field«, to use Kant's expression. This practice of social research has been criticized by historians and ethnographers. The field
study becomes nothing more than a confirmation of theory, and the first
victim of this self-confirmation is the researcher. But this type of process
makes it easy to manage the research process, and many techniques for
processing data can contribute to furnishing the subsequent report with
an air of science.

To See the World as It Is

As early as during the first discussions that led to this book, we agreed
to distance ourselves from this research practice, because such a process
does not give the researcher the chance of going through the learning
process that the field study offers. The learning process can only be realized when the researcher allows herself to empathize with the field.
But this implies that the field is not merely viewed and treated as a subcontractor of data. The field is a field that, through symbolic interaction, ascribes meaning to things and phenomena in a community of reflexive discourse. A micro-cosmos in its own right, in which individuals
relate practically to phenomena that may overlap the theoretical phenomena in which the researcher is interested. Consequently, the researcher can learn much more from empathizing with the field's creation
of meaning than from viewing the field as a subcontractor of data.

Many field researchers, especially ethnographers and historians,
have maintained the view that the field can be made to talk. Uncondi-
tionally the researcher should identify herself with the ideas and dynamics of the field. The tale that the ethnographer is going to create
should be evoked through a dialogue with the field, and the dialogue
will determine the content of the analysis. In his search for a post-modern ethnography, Stephen A. Tyler (1986) demands that the ethnographic text be created and shaped in collaboration between ethnographer and field. Figure 6.2 illustrates the process taken by a project that
follows these ideals.

The figure illustrates that the researcher may bring along a vague idea
about a strategy (A) for establishing a certain type of dialogue (B) with
the field. The researcher may, for example, choose a strategy for entering the field and the role in which she wants the field to see her, but aside
from this she willingly empathizes with the field and is open to possibilities (C). Therefore, her ways of empathizing with the field will be much
more complicated and heterogeneous than planned. By the end of the

journey (D), her knowledge about and insight into the field are quite different from what she projected (E) based on her imagined strategy (A).

Figure 6.2. The Open Ethnographic Project

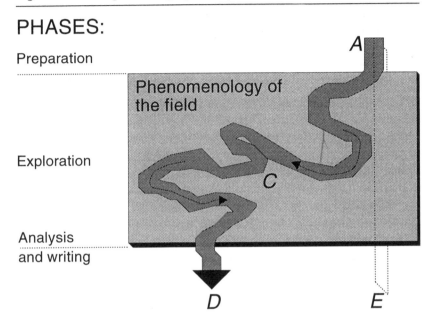

PHASES:

Preparation

Phenomenology of the field

Exploration

C

Analysis and writing

A

D   E

To the experienced researcher, who has learned the art of doing field studies, such a process is often a rewarding challenge. It calls for the researcher's total sum of experiences, habitus, empathy, and spinal reflexes for improvising her way through unforeseen situations. To the young researcher or Ph.D. candidate, this process may prove to be self-destructive.

Access to the Field

Most researchers will find that problems begin to accumulate during the preparatory phase, when knocking at the door to the field. If the door, for example, to a firm or an organization can only been opened with some kind of permit, the researcher is often asked to explain the purpose of the study. It is not enough that the researcher has a strategy for how to explore the field. The gatekeeper of the field usually demands an ex-

planation for the purpose of the exploration and why it is necessary (perspectives, questions, theories, trends, etc.) in order to demonstrate to
those in control the advantages of opening the door.

Fortunately, the young researcher who is only vaguely able to explain
the purpose, perspective, and issue will be turned away at an early stage
in the process and given the hint to be better prepared next time. It takes
more to obtain permission to evoke the desired dialogue with the field.

However, this barricade does not always function. Often the prestige
of senior researchers and their ability to improvise access to the field in
spite of unintelligible questions, theoretical expectations and perspectives is used to procure access for the young researcher. This is exactly
what happens in *the hospital project*. A professor interacts with the field
and procures access for the researcher. The young researcher grabs the
chance of implementing this open project, as well as the ideal possibility
of observing and interviewing. None of the other three projects in Part
2 come as close to the situation of the genuine ethnographic field study
as this one. But fate catches up with the researcher. How does he translate his observations into data? What should he write? Who is he after
all? The situation reaches such a deadlock that he is expelled from the
field the moment he can evoke the open ethnographic study's dialogue
with (and in) the field. As the tale shows, he finds support during this
crisis on his own ground: the institute. Other researchers provide him
with a perspective (the theory of alienation) and a theory for understanding how some of the field's actors react (the theory of power). In
the tensional sphere between his choice of theory and the completed
field study, he reaches the state that makes it possible for him to analyse
and write.

The Dialectics of Research Projects

From a rational perspective on how such projects should be planned,
you could gloatingly exclaim: »You made your bed; now lie in it.« The
hospital researcher simply treated the preparatory phase sloppily, and
this sin of omission hit him like a boomerang during the analysis and
writing phase. From an experiential point of view, the tale shows that it
is a good idea during the process to establish a tensional sphere between
empirical data and the theoretical and methodological perspectives.
Figure 6.3 is an outline of this tensional sphere.

If you question the hardened advocates of the open ethnographic

Figure 6.3. The Dialectics of Projects (I)

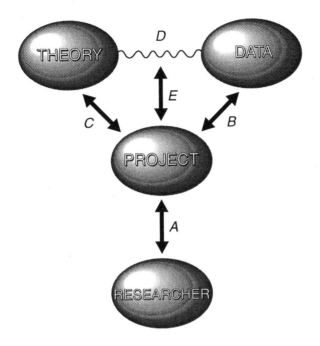

project closely, they will admit to the presence of this tensional sphere between theory and data. On the question of whether field notes more or less spontaneously organize themselves into chapters, the anthropologist Jean Leave answered:

> »It is more complicated than that. I would say that those clusters that begin to develop are constituted out of the interest and problems you come with from your years of participation in the academic field, and of course they should be issues that fascinate you. At the same time you try to understand central issues, structures and meanings in the community you study. One of the things I like about anthropologists' way of doing things is that you try to do something which you know is impossible; you say to yourself when you start, 'I want to be surprised by what happens here. I don't want to be so completely unfocused that nothing surprises me, because I am not expecting any-

thing.' You want to be somewhere in between, so that what happens can lead you to be really shocked and surprised – you didn't expect things to be the way they are – and they are really different and you learn from that. If the enterprise of doing empirical research has any purpose to it, it ought to change your theory as much as your theory informs the empirical work. And I see this as a process of going back and forth in an open-ended way so that you keep doing field research and you keep working on your theoretical understanding of the world. And hopefully, each of them makes the other better over time.« (Kvale 1992: 7).

Why should this shifting back and forth between theory and data cause problems to younger (newer) researchers in particular? Is it not merely a question of reading texts and plunging into a social field? That is much of the art, but during the process it is complicated by the fact that the researcher is subject to the influence of complex, social processes that are ignored by conventional methodological literature.

Thus, a common feature of the tales in Part 2 is that the projects emerge from social interaction. In each of the tales the narrator is merely one of many individuals interacting in a field without clearly defined roles and common interests.

In *the production project*, the first tentative features of the project emerge from a discussion between an American professor, who is interested in understanding the current restructuring of industrial society, and a Danish researcher, who primarily is interested in understanding the possibilities of pursuing industrial policies in Denmark. Later, an engineer, international agencies, French and German researchers as well as employees in many enterprises collaborate on and interact in the project.

In *the hospital project*, the scholar who felt like getting some experience with organizational sociological empirical methods jumped on the passing project initiated by a professor in collaboration with a directorate and an hospital. Thus, right from the beginning he interacts with researchers and representatives of the field. Later the circle of representatives of the research field is expanded, and he becomes part of the complex relationships of the social field he is studying.

The researcher becomes involved in *the drug addict project* while he, as a teaching assistant, teaches younger fellow students interested in investigating how a new research field (for example, research into drug abuse) emerges and develops. The dubious quality of the methodology of the study strikes him and he is critical of the help offered by the treatment centres. Years later he is contacted by one of his previous students who is now working in one of the centres treating drug addicts, and it is not until then that the project starts to develop. During the preparatory phase, several individuals representing both the research community and the field are involved in the project. The process is characterized by researchers who come and go.

The wind turbine project is the result of a young student who joins and leaves a range of student and research projects. He defines his Ph.D. project, gets it approved, commits himself to align his interests in a certain direction but is forced to stick to other projects that rob him of valuable time. The different phases of the field study are affected by third and fourth parties, accidental occasions and opportunities (ministries, evening classes, grassroots movements, many institutes, conference organizers, editors of anthologies). Not until the phase of analysis and writing does he get control of the project by formulating a question.

Instead of the very simple model for the dialectics of projects illustrated in Figure 6.3, we seem to be dealing with a much more complex process in which the researcher interacts with both an academic field and the social field studying the theoretical issues and empirical ideas of the project. Compared with Figure 6.3, which illustrates the relationships treated by traditional methodological literature, the researcher learning by experience finds herself in a much more complex situation (Figure 6.4).

The Researcher's Challenge

The researcher is faced with the challenge of learning to operate with all these relationships that mutually affect one another differently in the individual project. Therefore, it is important to recognize that a project is a learning process that implies more than exploring a social field with the aim of collecting data. The researcher also acts as participant observer in an academic field in which the choice of theory has social consequences, and the creation of social relationships has theoretical consequences. Such relationships may be decisive for the researcher's access to the social field and, at the same time, put pressure on the researcher in terms of what she ought to consider as data and what can be ignored. In other words, the researcher has to acquire habitus in many fields simultaneously. Nobody masters the art of balancing all the relationships multaneously. Nobody masters the art of balancing all the relationships of Figure 6.4 equally well, and that is why any scientific research project will always depend on the individual. Also, the figure indicates that there are many reasons for why projects might meet crisis situations.

Many classical mistakes are possible based on the relationships shown in Figure 6.4, especially if you are a young researcher. In Chapter 7, we identify some of these mistakes and see what can be done to avoid them.

Figure 6.4. The Dialectics of Projects (II)

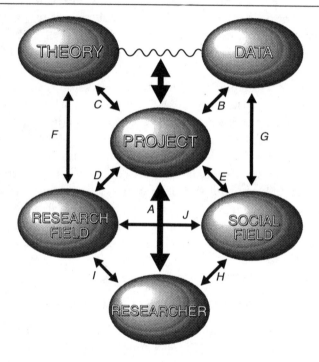

7. The Researcher, the Project and the Academic Field

Formulating the Issue and the Research Programme

Projects emerging from a system of multiple interests are subject to the common risk that no one assumes responsibility for defining the project's focal interest and issue. This is most conspicuous in *the hospital and the wind turbine projects,* although many people discuss the project and feel they understand it. However, their terminology is vague and they operate at a high level of generalization, with the result that all interested parties interpret the project in terms of their own, individual, subjective conceptualization. No one assumes the task of formulating a clear-cut research programme or issue. Why engage in this troublesome and apparently superfluous task when everyone feels that the project's objective is agreed on?

The absence of a distinct research programme is most conspicuous in *the hospital project.* The researcher perceived the sketchy project as an opportunity for individual development: »great opportunities for floundering in deep waters«. In other words: the researcher was pleased with the prospect of securing his own interests in the project, since neither a distinct theoretical perspective nor expectations of data had been formulated.

For obvious reasons it is primarily young researchers who are attracted to such vaguely formulated projects. However, they make the mistake of not defining the project's focus immediately and adequately. One of the most frequently stated reasons is that young researchers expect the senior team members to assume responsibility for defining this focus. This argument is reinforced by yet another that is connected to political interests, that is, power and status. It may be difficult to define a focused project that can encompass the interests of multiple actors. Choice of a specific focus might split the team. Therefore, young researchers in particular, feeling themselves to be in a weak position and not wanting to step on older colleagues' toes, will circle the issue – like a cat carefully pussyfooting around a hot pan. In this circular dance, everyone risks getting burned.

But in far too many cases, this dance is accepted for another reason:

»After all, you can't know what you don't know.« The argument is that it is impossible to formulate a relevant focus before you know more about the phenomenon to be studied. Having gained this knowledge, it then becomes possible to formulate relevant issues that are not distorted and relevant hypotheses that are sufficiently precise for carrying out the project. Why not postpone a possible conflict with older members of the project team and other interested parties until you know what you want with the project? Against this background, the formulation of project applications, issues, perspectives, and hypotheses is often so vague that it allows for multiple interpretations by the various interested parties and thus ensures that changes in approach and theories do not conflict with the original application.

From bitter experience, the four authors of this text know that this apparently sophisticated strategy is a dangerous procrastination mechanism. At one time or another, things catch up with you if you aren't incredibly lucky – take, for example, Don Quixote in *the wind turbine* project or the »befuddled bumpkin of a medical student« in *the hospital project.*

Be Precise When Formulating Issue, Theory and Expectations of Empirical Data

It is our experience that, regardless of the social context from which a project emerges, you ought to formulate your focal issue, theoretical perspectives, and empirical expectations as early as possible and as precisely as current knowledge allows. We think that this is the most important axiom for the researcher. Precise questions, explicit theoretical and empirical perspectives, and pointed and sharp hypotheses pave the way for clarification. The more complex the project's environments are, the greater are the demands for clarity and simplicity.

The relationship (A) between researcher and project (see Figure 6.4) is by and large the only one that the researcher controls. By investing productive energy in the project, you realize where you want to take the project. This realization returns to you in the shape of stimulating and focused curiosity. Clarified curiosity is one of the best ways of keeping the project on track when confronted with the puzzling influence of all the relationships illustrated in Figure 6.4.

Clarification produces the happiest periods of work, during which you shut yourself off from this complexity and almost automatically reach a higher level of clarification. The interaction between you and your project becomes active and pleasurable. The most illustrative example of this is *the production project*. In this case, theoretically founded questions and hypotheses about the field were clarified at an early stage. When the need for data becomes excessive, it is still possible to focus and work, even though confusion seems to govern the researcher. But luckily it does not, as things would only have been made worse. A clear project enables even a confused researcher to continue.

In the project's preparatory phase, relationships to the academic field (I, D, F and C in Figure 6.4) are generally the most important. This phase seriously involves links, the activation of which the young researcher may experience as a two-edged sword. The best means for stimulating the ability to take a position on these links include precisely formulated problems, explicit theoretical perspectives, and empirical expectations.

Taking a position on the project is the very thing the young researcher often tries to avoid. To many older researchers, who have acquired the habitus of the research field and who are experienced in the culture of critical discussions, a distinct formulation of problems, entailing evident theoretical implications and distinct empirical hypotheses, is akin to waving a red cloth in front of a bull's nose. Speaking in the heat of the moment, the issue is criticized, looked at from all angles and ridiculed rhetorically. Theoretical constructions and references are subject to testing, which is only possible due to the research colleagues' knowledge about the theoretical discourse. The project is criticized for not having taken into consideration this or that perspective or this or that author. And the empirical hypotheses? They are completely erroneous! What is to be measured and how can it be measured?

The Academic Discussion Machine

Few researchers have walked out of a heated discussion without feeling as though they just walked into a speeding truck and came away criticized to a pulp. The Ph.D. candidate, in particular, often commits the error of construing such discussions as a personal attack – rather than distancing herself from it and viewing it as merely a critique of the project. And this very lack of differentiation by the candidate makes it difficult for her colleagues to differentiate between the candidate and the project.

Many older scholars relish these duels; it is a way of keeping the ancient hunting instinct alive. James G. March (Schein 1987: 15-16) expresses this instinct with an inherent sense of irony:

One More Time

I am older
And have buried my instinct
For the delicate destruction
Of intellectual intercourse
In the clutter
Of my wrinkles

Still,
I hear your challenge
And accept it
As the way things ought to be.

Arguments
Are the arenas
In which educated men
Establish their right
To imagine themselves
Alive.

You choose the domain:
Philosophy.
Methodology.
Theory.
Politics.
And you speak first.
Choose carefully
And speak smart.

Because
If I can,
I will
Chop up your ideas
Stuff them into an old condom
And hang them in my trophy room.

Unfortunately, researchers are not always capable of not conceiving severe criticism as personal. For better or for worse, the game of the discussion machine is not only a game of insight. The game involves more than the demonstration of power and supremacy. It also involves the creation of new coalitions and the collapse of old ones; some individuals are rejected and others accepted as new members of the circle. Researchers are both saints and devils but not simultaneously. The discussion machine gives rise to friendships and animosities. For very good reasons, young researchers feel that they must pussyfoot around in this field – and it is possible that no one will ever fully understand this phenomenon. The research field seems to be populated by unpredictable individuals whose moods fluctuate concurrently with the progression or regression of the projects in which they are involved. It consists of individuals who are coupled to each of the relationships in Figure 6.4 and thus have their hands full.

It is conceivable that colleagues in the scientific community are unable to distinguish between the Ph.D. candidate and the project. Therefore, professional criticism may easily have both political and social effects. A supervisor may become lukewarm if not outright aggressive. Other researchers may view a Ph.D. candidate's failure to handle the critical discourse as an opportunity for promoting their own candidates, etc. Sometimes you can be rejected or put on ice by a project team to which you felt you belonged – until you expressed yourself clearly.

On Supervisors and Supervision

The answer to this problem is not to refrain from expressing yourself clearly. Rather, the answer is – like the fox – to make sure that you have several available exits. A young researcher should never make herself solely dependent on one single colleague's or supervisor's response to the project in construction. A supervisor may have good reasons for reacting half-heartedly if the original formulation of the issue and the theoretical and empirical interest suddenly change focus. Many things compete for supervisors' attention and limited time (see Figure 6.4), which is why supervisors may give the Ph.D. candidate or a colleague the cold shoulder when a project seems to shift focus to something he or she finds irrelevant to his or her own work. As Phillips & Pugh (1987: 22) state, supervisors have, like the Ph.D. candidate who starts on a research project, many different reasons for accepting this task. Some, for example, find it prestigious to supervise a large number of high-calibre researchers. Each time a supervised project concludes successfully, it increases their own professional status. Others do it because they are interested in the professional field the candidate has chosen to explore.

Pushed to its extremes, there are two archetypes of supervisors:

• supervisors who wish to train independent researchers; and
• supervisors who wish to train efficient research assistants.

It is not difficult to imagine the supervisory implications of these two very different goals.

Get some information on your potential supervisors!

It is important that you attempt to gather some information on the potential supervisors as well as their approach to the role as supervisor. Ask around! Which other younger researchers have they recently supervised? Get opinions about the supervisory situation and conditions.

However, you are not always in a position to pick and choose among potential supervisors. First, competent supervisors are always overburdened with students. Second, the opposite is just as often the case: supervisors choose students. This is especially the case when a supervisor »owns« an exciting research project and in this connection recruits qualified Ph.D. candidates who are expected to produce a dissertation – that is, within the framework of the supervisor's project. This was, for example, the situation of the author of *the wind turbine tale* at a certain phase of the project. He found it very difficult personally to escape the ties to his old project when his theoretical and empirical focus shifted from industrial policy to innovation practice. He was particularly troubled by his obligations of loyalty to the »owner« of the original project.

The contract between the Ph.D. candidate and the supervisor

It is imperative to bear in mind that the choice of supervisor is crucial to the Ph.D. process. It is not enough that the professional chemistry matches. It is imperative that the personal chemistry matches as well. The relationship between the Ph.D. candidate and the supervisor is a very close one. It is decisive for a successful outcome that the parties design a plan for the project and that the Ph.D. study include time schedules, etc. But it is just as important that the supervisor and the Ph.D. candidate psychologically agree on what to expect from one another –

that they each verbalize their expectations and make the necessary adjustments. This entails such questions as: what is the framework of collaboration? How often are we to meet? Which issues are we to discuss? Are we to evaluate the collaboration in an ongoing manner? Unfortunately, the Ph.D. candidate and the supervisor often neglect to discuss what they expect from one another prior to the collaboration – not necessarily due to ill will but perhaps out of sheer ignorance or because there is no tradition for doing so. But the Ph.D. candidate should insist on discussing these subjects. Having adjusted each other's expectations, it becomes easier later in the process to discuss possible changes in the collaboration, if these expectations are not met – or, if necessary, to change supervisor.

Interview your supervisor!

Official publications are not very helpful in determining the demands for and the level of the Ph.D. dissertation. However, there are two other important sources of information:

- your supervisor; and
- acknowledged dissertations within the field of your dissertation or within associated fields.

Interview your supervisor about the most common criteria for approving a Ph.D. dissertation and on what he or she personally focuses. Don't let the supervisor get away with vague, general answers. Force specific and concrete answers. Ask to see dissertations that have been assessed as good or excellent. Ask why these dissertations were assessed as first-rate. Read or skim a few of the dissertations merely to get an idea about the level. Later in the process, it may prove beneficial to read parts of them more thoroughly – for inspirational purposes when you feel stuck in the process.

It is also wise to look at the bottom end of the spectrum: make your supervisor specify the minimum demands for a dissertation – what is enough? Ask him or her to refer to dissertations that have just made it. Find out what was lacking in these projects. Use the same approach as described above.

If you apply this approach at the start of your Ph.D. process you are better equipped than most candidates who do not acquaint themselves with the qualitative demands for a Ph.D. dissertation.

If collaboration proves not to function

If you, at some point in the process, realize that the collaboration with your supervisor is disintegrating, it's time to consider changing supervisor. Approaching this problem is often complicated and painful, particularly if the relationship has been worsening for some time and you have avoided dealing with the problem. Even though you, as a Ph.D. candidate, may find it unpleasant to approach the issue, it is necessary to discuss it with your supervisor. No doubt he or she finds it equally difficult to bring up the subject and perhaps he or she will welcome your initiative. There is no other possibility than to discuss it openly. Ask directly, but in a positive and constructive frame of mind, so that your best intentions are apparent. Start out, for example, by asking your supervisor to evaluate whether you have made any progress, whether you are handling your project reasonably and whether you are following his advice. Continue to ask questions related to your collaborative relationships: whether he or she is satisfied with the way it functions or whether it could be improved, etc. In this way, the question of changing supervisors may emerge without necessarily entailing a conflict. If supervisors do not feel that they have been treated unfairly, they will be much more open. None of the parties has to resort to defensive tactics, such as hiding behind technical details (Phillips & Pugh 1987: 92-93).

The Academic Field

Fortunately, the academic field is vast. An institute harbours numerous researchers – and institutions of research and higher education harbour numerous institutes. Any country harbours more than one institution of higher education. And there are many countries in the world.

Both in order to secure your own survival and varied responses, you ought to be part of a national and international network, representing a variety of research realms. Interacting with a multitude of scientific universes allows room for independent manoeuvring. Being part of such a network will better enable you to distinguish between the field's aspects of profession and power.

The individual researcher's strategy in relation to the power aspects of the research field is one of the most neglected areas in methodological literature. We have in our own tales, either consciously or unconsciously, avoided discussing this subject. It is thought-provoking that, in *three of the four tales*, the researchers gradually moved from another institution of higher education to the one where we join in writing this book. These moves occurred simultaneously with the projects attaining focus. Our projects implied more than the exploration of a social field: except for the hospital researcher, we all encountered hostility from previous colleagues and established new friendships via the projects. In more than one sense, projects have existential consequences.

Despite the aspects of power, we maintain our advice to tighten up the project's issues continuously, no matter what the situation. Being fully aware of the risks connected to throwing your project into the discussion machine, the best insurance against unfavourable consequences is, nevertheless, to do it again and again and in as many different forums as possible. You can ponder to death the motives behind researchers' criticisms of a project and consequent rejection of a researcher. Just as you can endlessly analyse the ways in which you might be able to come in again from the cold. But this is valuable time wasted, and it is often not possible to find the answers in academic fields, pretentious as they can be.

After a few days, if you are able to rid yourself of the feeling of personal defeat and to continue your work, there is nothing more productive for further development of the project than a ride in the academic discussion machine. Here you are presented with the possibility of reconsidering the formulation of the issue. What should be preserved and which corrections should be made (also in order to get as close as possible to your own research interests)?. What are the relevant objections to the project's theoretical framework? Have some important considerations been forgotten? Did the discussion reveal unknown authors and literature? Are they relevant to your interest in the project? Which expectations for the data's ability to confirm or refute hypotheses should you abide by and how should you design the field study in order to test these hypotheses?

In short, if you are capable of using criticism constructively, the active interaction with colleagues about a precisely formulated project will reinforce active interaction with your project.

Taking several rides in the discussion machine will, therefore, hopefully not leave you dizzy, but should inevitably lead you to a refined definition of your project and investigation that is increasingly close to social scientific issues within the realm of the specific field. In this way you are able to explore what the academic field views as worthwhile to investigate in the social field. During this process, you are bound to develop and select relevant themes that can thus be subject to analysis during the final phase of writing the dissertation.

Notice how the project has already been started. Objections can be related to something formulated in writing. You can reinforce your original argumentation by arguing against the criticism or by realizing that the criticism entails changing some aspects of the issue, modifying some perspectives, and adjusting some hypotheses. Formulated in writing, the issues can be reformulated indefinitely. That is what they are for. And this very procedure may imply that the writing process starts even before the field study begins.

Formulation – Reformulation

With the continuous reformulating and sharpening of the research questions, the project attains a focused continuity. It has a focus, but it is a focus of learning. Its role is not confirmation: surprises are just as, or perhaps even more, welcome than confirmations of the original perspectives and hypotheses. However, having been through the very process of formulating the perspectives and hypotheses that are now proven wrong, you are able to register new observations. In short, by continuously reformulating the project, the process becomes one of learning.

Therefore, never throw away earlier formulations. They form invaluable and explanatory fossil layers in the project's learning process. When the results have to be explained to others at a later stage, they constitute an important fundament for selecting which results and surprises to communicate to the reader. These surprises and subsequent explanations are usually the most substantial results of a project.

However, when reformulating the project, you walk a tightrope. Don't let this get out of control. Many researchers have experienced these reformulations as jumping from one project to a second, to a third, ad infinitum, and the feeling of jumping around and wasting time soon becomes a strain. It is important to maintain some specific dimensions of the project, making sure that its nature never changes completely. Continuity is important for avoiding the feeling of having wasted a great deal of time and work when the process reaches the final writing phase.

Even though the nature of this continuous reformulation process is primarily cognitive, the social aspect of it is unavoidable. During the process, some colleagues in the research world will inevitably feel that the project is taking a direction that causes it to be unimportant to them, while other colleagues begin to see interesting dimensions and possibilities. As a consequence, you must reposition yourself in relation to the research field. During this process, it is very important not only to define yourself within some specific social contexts but also simultaneously to define yourself within possible new ones. Nothing has a more productive and disciplining effect than committing yourself to social contexts. Expectations of and agreements with colleagues, supervisors, grant allocating authorities, individuals in the field, and partners in other countries give the project the necessary push.

Viewed in this light, it is difficult to understand that *the wind turbine project* succeeded. By no means does the researcher succeed in clarifying his formulation early on in the process. Throughout the whole process, relationship A (in Figure 6.4) is very thin. It is a story of a stream of incidents. The project is realized though a multitude of small agreements that commit the researcher to a limited task, while the major task – the Ph.D. dissertation – is pushed into the background for long periods of time. On the other hand, Don Quixote in the wind turbine project is true to his own strategy: to nose about in the research world before finding his niche in the bureaucracy. When our Don Quixote continues to tilt at windmills and not only pursues his strategy but also succeeds in writing his dissertation, it is due to a specific type of continuity. First of all, he sticks to a relatively narrow field related to wind turbines. This focus is not determined by his Ph.D. application, but it is there. Second, continuity arises in connection with the writing phase during which he draws theoretical and empirical lines between the many subject areas that he has explored in connection with the wind turbines (from industrial policy to the economics of innovation to the history of technology).

Projects processes of this nature sometimes succeed. It is difficult to explain why. It is usually easier to explain why they fail.

8. The Researcher and the Project

Between Two Poles

Relationship A in Figure 6.4 between the researcher and the project has deliberately been placed between two poles: the academic field and the social field to be analysed.

In Chapter 7, we analysed some of the problems and possibilities provided by the academic field. Chapter 9 discusses the problems and possibilities of the social field. The present chapter focuses on how the researcher can create tension between the two poles and, at the same time, conduct a project that is worth the bother.

It is not an easy task to capitalize on the tension between these two poles in a project. In view of this tension, Figure 6.4 illustrates that either the academic field and the theoretical issues or the social field and the empirical expectations come to dominate the project.

The pragmatic reason for operating with this tension is that field studies are difficult to analyse without a theoretical point of reference. Surprises exist in relation to expectations. On the other hand, expectations must not be used to ignore the uniqueness of the field.

But the tensional field between theoretical themes and the social field's structure, anxieties, and dynamics is precisely what it takes to create a project that is worthwhile and enables the researcher to answer the question: »Why do I want to spend 5 long years of my short life on this project?«.

Blinded by the social process that causes researchers to embark upon projects (cf. Chapter 6), many are unable to answer this question in the early phases of a project. The answers are not linked to the project itself but to the researcher's personal situation. In *the hospital project*, the researcher wanted to experiment with organizational, sociological analysis, and in *the wind turbine project*, the researcher wanted to sniff about in the research world before finding his niche among the »neoreformist public officials« (the wind turbine project). Today, with the high rate of unemployment among academics, honest answers often imply getting a job if the chance presents itself.

The Sociological Imagination

The validity of these answers is not to be contested, but they are inappropriate answers considering the project's driving force. It requires inner motivation to successfully secure a project so that it can be completed satisfactorily for all parties. In the long run, a project requires so much energy that it has to run on »articulated curiosity«.

But what is this »articulated curiosity«? C. Wright Mills' book, *The Sociological Imagination*, provides an answer. Through his sociological imagination, the researcher must establish the tension between the anxieties of the social field and the themes put on the agenda by public and scientific debate:

In Mills' own words:

> »The sociological imagination enables its possessor to understand the larger historical scene in terms of its meaning for the inner life and the external career of a variety of individuals... enables us to grasp history and biography and the relations between the two within society. That is its task and its promise. ...No social study that does not come back to the problems of biography, of history and of their intersections within a society has completed its intellectual journey... those who have been imaginatively aware of this promise of their work have consistently asked three sorts of questions:
>
> 1) What is the structure of this particular society as a whole? What are its essential components, and how are they related to one another? How does it differ from other varieties of social order? Within it, what is the meaning of any particular feature for its continuance and for its change?
> 2) Where does this society stand in human history? What are the mechanisms by which it is changing? What is its place within and its meaning for the development of humanity as a whole? How does any particular feature we are examining affect, and how is it affected by, the historical period in which it moves? And this period – what are its essential features? How does it differ from other

periods? What are its characteristic ways of history making?

3) What varieties of men and women now prevail in this society and in this period? And what varieties are coming to prevail? In what ways are they selected and formed, liberated and repressed, made sensitive and blunted? What kinds of »human nature« are revealed in the conduct and character we observe in this society in this period? And what are its meanings for »human nature« of each and every feature of the society we are examining?« (Mills 1959: 5-7).

The Problems of the Social Field and the Themes of Public Debate

The issues Mills raises are significant. They are indeed issues that require the researcher to adopt an attitude to both a public and/or theoretical debate and to the considerations of individuals and groups (a social field). The tension between these two poles, which is completely parallel with the two poles in Figure 6.4, is exactly what stimulates and calls forth the sociological imagination. Mills' book is highly recommendable. The following two quotations further elucidate what the two poles may harbour. Theory and field, structure and individual, history and biography:

> »Perhaps the most fruitful distinction with which the sociological imagination works is between 'the personal troubles of milieu' and 'the public issues of social structure'. This distinction is an essential tool of the sociological imagination and a feature of all classic work in social science.
>
> Troubles occur within the character of the individual and within the range of his immediate relations with others; they have to do with his self and with those limited areas of social life of which he is directly personally aware. Accordingly, the statement and the resolution of troubles properly lie within the individual as a biographical entity and within the scope of his immediate milieu – the social setting that is directly open to his personal experience and to some extent his wilful activity. A trouble is a private mat-

ter: values cherished by an individual are felt by him to be threatened.

Issues have to do with matters that transcend these lo-cal environments of the individual and the range of his in-ner life. They have to do with the organization of many such milieux into the institutions of an historical society as a whole, with the ways in which various milieux overlap and interpenetrate to form the large structure of social and historical life. An issue is public matter: some value cherished by publics is felt to be threatened. Often there is a debate about what that value really is and about what it is that really threatens it. This debate is often without fo-cus if only because it is the very nature of an issue, unlike even widespread trouble, that it cannot very well be de-fined in terms of the immediate and everyday environ-ments of ordinary men. An issue, in fact, often involves crisis in institutional arrangements, and often too it in-volves what Marxists call 'contradictions' or 'antago-nisms'.« (Mills 1959: 8-9).

As will be shown in the section in Chapter 10 on the process of writing, *the four projects discussed here* are all brought home by establishing dialec-tics between the social fields studied and the public debate. A tension is established between the troubles characterizing the field and the general issues of the public debate. However, in more than one of the projects, tension (or dialectics) is not established until very late in the process, which explains some of the crises experienced by the researchers. Projects that fail to establish this tension are probably the main reason why substantial crises sometimes occur that make it impossible for the researcher to remain in the academic field. In any case, this polar ten-sion is decisive for the researcher going through the possible learning process.

Based on our collective experience, but not because we have all satis-fied this demand, we advise establishing as much polar tension as pos-sible immediately – in the project's preparatory phase. Why not use the sociological imagination to put the project in high gear right from the start, when it is this imagination that will enable the researcher to com-pose the written component of the project!

The drug addict and the production project are examples of how to create this bipolar tension: with methodological discussions in the first phase of the project and with the creation of expectations of the field during the final phase.

Bridging Theory and Field

The art or secret is to construct a bridge – with help from the project – between theoretical problems and the social field prior to starting exploration of the field. The question is, how can you create this bipolar tension before it develops de facto on its own? The answer is simple. By using your sociological imagination, you can transform the theoretical issues into expectations of what is occurring in the field. Which attitudes are held by people in various positions in terms of the general themes raised by the theory? Which challenges and potential actions do they see? What are their strategies in relation to their own social field?

The sociological imagination is not a given dimension. It is neither equally distributed among researchers nor a constant quality characterizing the individual researcher. It can be developed and stimulated by being called upon and encouraged to participate. How it works thus greatly depends on the individual researcher and her pool of experience. Therefore, there are no general recipes.

Among our tales, sociological imagination is most elaborately reflected in the preparatory phase of *the production project*. This tale, in particular, is characterized by the development of theory and expectations at many different levels. At the macro-theoretical level, the issue is global development of markets, economic policies, new technologies, new organizational forms, and new types of identity among workers and leaders. At the meso-theoretical level, the issue is Denmark's conditions for handling these changes: small factories, a peaceful labour market, institutionalized relationships of trust between work and capital, but also Taylorized skills. At the micro-theoretical level, expectations are developed concerning the restructuring problems of medium-sized companies, the production managers' feeling of confusion and paradoxes and the workers' need to requalify themselves. Finally, these micro-theoretical expectations are translated into a specific theory of the firm. Information on markets, products, and technology related to the company to be studied are used to focus the other theoretical contemplations.

The researcher produces clarification and provokes curiosity through this exercise in sociological imagination. Through this, she will be able to meet the field well prepared and full of appropriate questions. Are medium-sized companies capable of utilizing the potential of flexible work organization provided by the new technology? Are production managers capable of handling their identity crises? Is it possible to develop a new type of collaboration between management and workers? Can the workers learn to do programming jobs? Which conditions in these people's lives create the resources for implementing the changes? In short, the field researcher has become thoroughly involved in understanding the people populating the field to be studied. Therefore, she is prepared to enter into the spirit of the field carrying a basket of questions that can evoke a dialogue with the field.

Even though the researcher has carefully tried to predict, as precisely as possible, what she is going to encounter in the field, both the fact that there are detailed expectations and the fact that there also is an entire system of expectations will increase the probability that she will be taken by surprise on numerous occasions.

Therefore, the process of the project will diverge from the other two processes outlined in Figure 6.1 and Figure 6.2 in Chapter 6. It becomes extremely dialectic, as illustrated in Figure 8.1.

Figure 8.1. The Dialectic Process of Projects

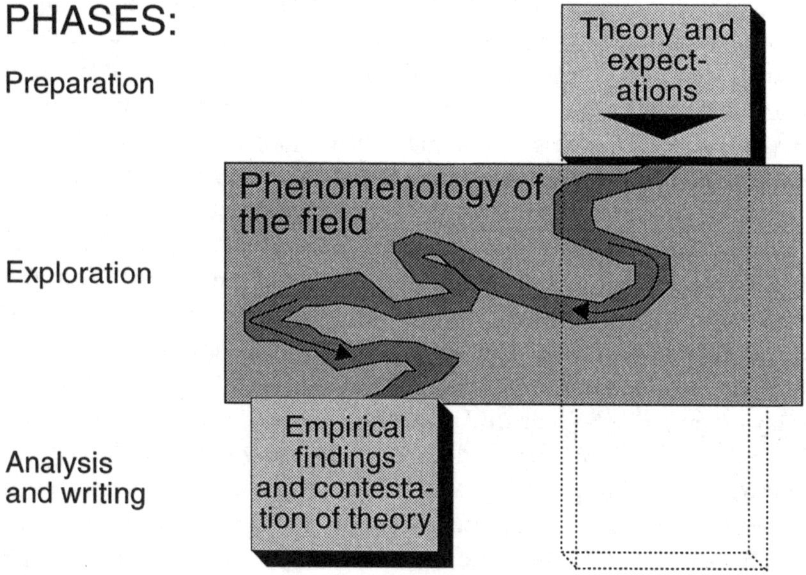

As *the production project* demonstrated, this intensive involvement in the field implied that the conception of the specific company's logic, the micro-theoretical rationalizations on the nature of companies, the habitus of production managers and the workers' skills needed to be modified. The assumptions about Denmark had to be modified. As a result of this discrepancy between expectations and findings, the researcher is still working on adjusting the meta-theoretical discussion about specialization and mass production – still striving to understand the nature of industrialization. In other words, using his sociological imagination in the project's first phase has stimulated a new, expanded sociological imagination. His project resulted in an excellent source of inspiration for writing.

9. The Researcher and the Field: In »*Das Ding an Sich*«

Is Reality Comprehensible?

Researchers embarking on the exploration of social fields are confronted with the most essential issue of all science: is reality in any way comprehensible? What does it imply to explore a social field scientifically?

In the Aristotelian tradition of knowledge, such issues were quite simple. According to this tradition, the gods had equipped humans with the ability to develop concepts that captured the essence of the matter: if only the researcher used these concepts to argue logically (this was the very essence of the art of science), they would reveal the »truth«.

Descartes and Bacon rebelled against the belief in the inherent truth of concepts. Such common-sense concepts were labelled *notiones vulgares, praenotiones,* or *idola* by Bacon. According to him, they occupy the position that justly should be occupied by the things themselves – *das Ding an sich* – or by empirical facts – data. These *idola* resemble

> »...a type of ghost-like creature, which distorts the true appearance of things, but which we nevertheless mistake for the things themselves. Since this imagined world offers no resistance, the mind, feeling completely unchecked, gives rein to limitless ambitions, believing it possible to construct – or rather reconstruct – the world through its own power and according to its own wishes.« (Durkheim 1982: 62).

How does one get to the bottom of the true aspect of things? Bacon's advice was to reject *notiones vulgares* and make direct observations, experiments, and measurements, that is, to manipulate *das Ding an sich* to reveal its secrets. This method later proved to be very successful – reaching its peak during the Newtonian revolution. Natural science revealed concealed forces that no one had been able to discover through *notiones vulgares*. Who would have imagined the presence of gravitation, electromagnetism, or natural selection before these concealed causes were revealed through the scientific search for truth?

Durkheim's Methodology

Thus, the father of sociology, Émile Durkheim, had very good reasons for stating in his book on methodology from 1895 that »The first and most basic rule is to consider *social facts as things*« (Durkheim 1982: 60). The purpose of his book on methodology was to apply Bacon's revolution to sociology. Therefore, Durkheim's first methodological corollary is: »One must systematically discard all preconceptions« (Durkheim 1982: 72).

Discarding preconceptions also implies that the researcher must avoid involving herself emotionally in the object of research. The problem of the sociologist is that

> »We become passionate in our political and religious beliefs and moral practices... Consequently this emotional quality is transmitted to the way in which we conceive and explain our beliefs.« (Durkheim 1982: 73)

Durkheim dissociates himself from this feeling of solidarity that emerges when using one's emotions to understand how other people feel, think, and act. We are to apply rationality rather than feelings. Who would prefer »the immediate and confused syntheses of sensation rather than the patient, clarifying analyses of reason« (Durkheim, 1982: 74)?

Humility and Empathy

To the question: »What distinguishes a poor field researcher from a good one?« *the authors of the four tales* answer unanimously: »Humility for and empathy with the human activities characterizing the field.« Humility and empathy have much to do with the syntheses of sensation and a feeling of solidarity. These are the very qualities needed in order to avoid the field study taking a course such as the one outlined in Figure 6.1 (see Chapter 6).

There are at least two reasons for developing this humility and empathy:

- the altered relationship between researcher and social field; and
- the principle of complementarity extended to comprise the social field.

The Altered Relationship Between Researcher and Social Field

Compared with Durkheim's epoch, the relationship between social science and social fields has been altered radically. Durkheim claimed that practical reflection and creation of concepts precede science, and that this practical reflection merely employs ideas and concepts whose »main purpose is to attune our actions to the surrounding world; they are formed by and for experience« (Durkheim 1982: 61). These common-sense concepts (*notiones vulgares*) are created and developed to perform a useful function in practical life, but from the perspective of scientific insight they may be erroneous or inadequate. Consequently, the researcher should not take a point of departure in these practical concepts but, quite the contrary, approach »things« directly.

Today, the objects of scientific reflection are in many cases scientific concepts that have been developed within the academic field and have been subject to much scrutiny in the academic discussion machine. Too often the academic field has tended to be self-sufficient. Currently, social science theories are often mistaken for »the thing itself«. And the social scientist is surprised by the false consciousness, incomplete information, ignorance, and irrationality she encounters in social fields. »False consciousness«, »irrationality«, and »incomplete information« are rather evidence of the researcher being locked in the cage of the theoretical apparatus of the world of science. Science has distanced itself from everyday life to the extent that the researcher has difficulty in re-establishing a relationship between scientific and common-sense concepts. Often there is only a weak relationship between »things« in the conceptual world of social fields and the academic field. This separation derives from the independence and institutionalization of social science. Therefore, the researcher who embarks on a social field study has to go though a training process in order to understand in any way the practical reality of the people populating the social field to be studied.

The Principle of Complementarity Extended to the Social Field

Durkheim was of the opinion that sociological theories must express the »exact nature of things« and not only the subject matters that are pragmatically advantageous or disadvantageous (which are usually the domain of common-sense perceptions). Contemporary researchers are of a different opinion. Kant has made it difficult to believe that the true nature of things is comprehensible. At best, theories will ascribe qualities to the things that emphasize certain aspects of them. Therefore, Niels Bohr argued in favour of researchers applying multiple complementary theories to reveal several aspects. The realm of atoms cannot be understood either in terms of particles or waves. Approaching the matter by employing both theories yields a much better understanding than merely applying one of them. The sociology of organization, too, now recommends applying complementary perspectives for retrieving complementary data on organizations (Scott 1992; Morgan 1986).

However, the art of reasoning on things and phenomena equally well through a range of scientific theories is difficult. Extending the principle of complementarity to encompass the social field itself adds to the difficulties. It entails that the researcher recognizes that the social field's creation of meaning and use of common-sense concepts represent a process by which the inhabitants develop theories, which make it possible for them to cope with their everyday life. The social field's theories represent practical aspects of things and phenomena. If we accept that scientific theories are merely capable of capturing limited aspects of the things themselves, the theories of the field must be granted a status at least similar to that of the academic field. The practical theories of the field studied contribute *de facto* to structuring the actions that affect the development of this part of society. They are part of the concealed forces determining the axioms of society. This view of the social field's development of theories constitutes, among other things, the basis of field researchers working within the tradition of grounded theory (Glaser & Strauss 1967; Barton 1988; Strauss & Corbin 1990).

The ability to think in terms of complementarity is thus one of the most important means for developing the humility and empathy necessary to create the »synthesis of sensation«. The researcher does not merely accuse the social field of »false consciousness« and »irrationality«; on the contrary he or she is interested in the workings of this consciousness and the reasons used to justify the appropriateness of observed behaviour. The researcher wants to understand how the field develops an understanding and perceives of itself and to listen to how people express their worries, among other things in order to understand on what dimensions they diverge from the theoretical themes of the research field.

The Methodology of Phenomenologists

We have now reached the dictum of phenomenologists: systematically, researchers must capture the concepts by which the social field itself understands its actions. Or in the words of Alfred Schutz:

> »The participant observer or field worker establishes contact with the group studied as a man among fellowmen; only his system of relevancies which serves as the scheme of his selection and interpretation is determined by the scientific attitude, temporarily dropped in order to be resumed again.
>
> Thus, adopting the scientific attitude, the social scientist observes human interaction patterns or their results insofar as they are accessible to his observation and open to his interpretation. These interaction patterns, however, have to be interpreted in terms of their subjective meaning structure, unless he is willing to abandon any hope of grasping 'social reality'.« (Schutz 1962: 40).

Schutz' phenomenological perspective settles with the school within case analysis which uses a case to illustrate a given theory (cf. Figure 6.1) and with the »open ethnographic project« (Figure 6.2). Schultz' field researcher operates with dialectics between his »system of relevances«, theories, or themes and the field's inherent »subjective structure of meaning« and problems.

This perspective has implications for:

- the relationships between theory and field
- the nature of the field.

Implications for the Relationship between Theory and Field

It is important that the researcher, when planning a field study, operate with a theoretical perspective that focuses on relevant historical or social scientific themes. This tool will enable the researcher to establish a set of expectations from people, things, and phenomena in the local environment. Using her sociological imaginative competence, the researcher constructs a system of hypotheses, a micro-theory, about how general historical and societal trends translate into a local environment. The purpose of this system of hypotheses is not necessarily to find evidence in support of the assumptions. Some of the hypotheses are likely to be proven false – others confirmed, resulting in the emergence of a new understanding. A new and more realistic micro-theory about the field as a social system starts to develop. The system of hypotheses of the preparatory phase is thus used to extract response from the field on as many dimensions as possible. These responses are employed to develop a new micro-theory, which makes it possible for the researcher to reason, in the same manner as the field, about the themes he or she has selected as relevant.

The ability to attempt to reject the original expectations (those constructed in the beginning by the researcher to the best of her abilities) demands fighting an inherent, human propensity. This propensity consists of reducing most of our experiences to normal, standard events and seeing our expectations confirmed. Normally, this is a useful quality that makes it possible to economize on one's concentration in everyday life. However, in order to counteract it, the social scientist must consciously attempt to develop techniques that limit or eliminate this propensity for confirmation. Karl Popper (1973) has argued in favour of hypotheses or systems of hypotheses being formulated so precisely that they can be disproved. There is every reason to bear Popper's advice in mind during the preparatory phase. During the explorative phase the researcher ought to demand of the study that not only the original micro-theory can be disproved but also that it is possible to construct a new theory rooted in the field's subjective structure of meaning.

Implications for the Field

This demand on the study stems from the nature of the social field. Compared with natural scientific phenomena, social fields are unique in that they are shaped by symbolic interaction and exercise symbolic interaction (Blumer 1969: 2-26). According to Blumer, field researchers are simply unable to study social objects and phenomena directly (the things themselves). What the researcher can do is to study social systems in which human beings engage in symbolic interaction. Society is constructed through this symbolic interaction by which things become things and social phenomena are realized and ascribed meaning (Berger & Luckmann 1971). In relation to the field study, »the thing itself« is a field of interaction between human beings who try to understand themselves and others (through, among other things, local theories: working hypotheses about how individual behaviour may affect others, etc.). Through this interactive understanding, the human beings of the field ascribe things and phenomena properties that make their routine or enquiring behaviour more or less meaningful. By interacting with themselves and others, humans create in a social field a set of individual and collective actions that together evoke the social field's method of functioning.

The Dynamics of the Field

The dynamics of the field is our label for this method of working, the sum of relationships, subjective and inter-subjective creation of meaning, and individual and collective types of behaviour. A social field is a complex and multifaceted interaction between multitudinous dynamics, which no one has been able to describe, understand, or analyse in full. Depending on which theoretical themes we are interested in understanding, specific aspects of the field dynamics are relevant to the individual study. In accordance with the dynamics of the field, these themes are likely to be attributed a meaning and character quite different from that embedded in the theoretical arguments from which they originally emerged. In short, the themes are judged by a logic quite different from that on which the original formulation rested. Their relevance is quite different and they are part of the social field's development in a way quite different from what we imagined. When we are able to argue within our theoretical themes through logical manipulations of the perceived field dynamics, the field is about to be satisfactorily explored in terms of our limited objective.

There are numerous ways of constructing the field dynamics. In *the wind turbine project* the technical nature of wind turbines creates the frame of reference for understanding the actions, the projects, the in-order-to motives, and the interaction of a whole industry. By putting himself in the field's shoes, the author creates a new point of reference for assessing industrial and technological policies. In relation to the dynamics of the wind turbine field, this point of reference comes to play a role quite different from that intended by the authors of the political instruments. In *the hospital project* the logic of the field is constructed through the individual staff groups' roles and role perceptions. The analyses of alienation and power are used to explain the individual role occupants' worries in regard to fulfilling their expectations of themselves and others in the hospital hierarchy. In *the drug addict project* the profound insight into the biography of drug addicts is used to construct some typical life paths of drug addicts, which are then used to develop an understanding of the dynamics characterizing the interplay between treatment centres and drug addicts. In *the production project* the interplay between individuals from different units and their interaction within the institutionalized frameworks of management, control, and wage systems creates the antagonistic dynamics that drive the organization to attempt to achieve both flexibility and large-scale operations.

In the Field

Getting Access to the Field

Getting access to the desired information from a field is often a very crucial and time-consuming activity. It is often difficult to get access to organizations – private as well as public – and there is not much literature on this subject. However, Buchanan, Boddy & McCalman (1989) treat the subject in terms of how to negotiate access, how to establish fruitful relationships to the field, how to conclude such relationships, and how to make sure than one can return to the organization for supplementary data.

Negotiating Access Has Become Increasingly Difficult

During the two to three decades we have been engaged in research and teaching, it has become increasingly difficult for students and professional researchers to get access to organizations and institutions. This development is due to several circumstances. First, both among students and researchers at institutions of higher education, it has become increasingly common to design and conduct studies based on the collection of empirical data from various organizations. Second, the number of individuals engaged in such activities has grown immensely during this period. Both of these factors have placed heavy strains on the organizations' resources. On top of this, students often choose to study the same organizations in certain periods, which has made the organizations adopt a more restrictive policy about to whom they are willing to grant access. Rejections are most often justified with reference to an on-going project – or that a project investigating similar themes has just been concluded. Buchanan, Boddy & McCalman (1989) had similar experiences in the United Kingdom.

The Behaviour of Researchers

Apart from the above, both the public and the private sector have been subject to increasingly tightened finances. There is a growing trend among managers to decide that their staff have no time to spend on unproductive academic research.

In some cases, the attitude of both researchers and students to collaboration or attempts to collaborate with organizations has caused problems. Researchers and/or students have displayed a poor sense of situational intuition – have shown no consideration of the evident rules and traditions – or have been outright hostile towards the organizations studied.

There have been cases of breaches of professional confidentiality, loyalty and anonymity. There are examples of individuals shouldering the blame – not necessarily intentionally but because the researcher or student was not sufficiently mindful of how easy it might be to identify individual statements. There have also been examples of direct breach of explicit or implicit agreements. There are examples of organizations being smeared by the media because of the researcher or student's sensational findings. Events like these – albeit they are few – have contributed to the door being slammed on researchers and students for several years. Unfortunately, it does not take much to slam the doors – and incredible efforts to reopen them.

The Language of Researchers

We have earlier mentioned that the researcher has to act on her personal customs (habitus) and her sense of human interaction; however, we wish to warn the researcher against transferring the habitus that is usually tied to the academic discussion machine, lectures, etc. At best the natives will perceive this attitude as a ludicrous attempt to establish a teacher-pupil relationship. Thus it is always better to rephrase one's question than to accuse the interviewee of having misinterpreted it.

The language researchers use to communicate with peers is not immediately comprehensible to the public in general. Many researchers are not aware of this. If you use professional terminology when you contact organizations, the staff will often perceive this negatively. There are usually three types of reactions to the incomprehensible language of researchers:

- the researcher is subject to ridicule, which is, in reality, the best situation viewed from the researcher's perspective;
- embarrassment; or
- annoyance.

The last two reactions are certainly not advantageous for promoting collaboration between the field and the researcher.

What Can the Researcher Offer the Field in Exchange for Data?

Another important issue is the terms of exchange – what will the parties gain from the collaboration. Preferably, the relationship should, over time, be one of reciprocity. This is often not the case, mainly due to the researcher's deficient or incomprehensible feedback to the field. And if a researcher submits a report on her study to the organization, it is, in most cases, much too long. As a result, no one reads it. Business is used to the expediency of the one-page memo.

It is important to agree on the rules of the game for collaboration right from the beginning. In some cases, such agreements are formulated in terms of a written contract, in other cases they are merely verbal agreements. What is important is that contracts of cooperation be negotiated in an early phase of the project.

According to Buchanan, Boddy & McCalman (1989), organizations usually ascribe significant importance to three issues: (1) the amount of time the staff is expected to spend on the activities related to the project, and hence (2) how long a period of time the organization will commit itself to participation, that is, the total time schedule of the project. The final issue (3) is confidentiality – how will the researcher handle confidential information? These issues should be discussed at an early stage of the project on the initiative of the party who wants access to the organization.

When the Project is Underway

After having negotiated the terms of collaboration, one of the subsequent issues is (Buchanan, Boddy & McCalman 1989) how to gain access to the participants.

One problem that often arises between the investigator and the investigated is that the latter feel poorly informed about what they will gain from the data collection. Usually, they are very curious about the study, especially as it is about themselves. For several reasons it is a good idea to make sure that the informants receive feedback. They are usually not interested in theories, explanations, and conclusions. They are primarily interested in descriptions of themselves (not as individuals but as a aggregate) and of their organization. It is a good idea to exploit this interest. Hand over your descriptions to the participants and ask them to comment on your interpretation of the information – both in terms of correctness and sensitivity of material. You will discover that such a process yields valuable information. Most of the comments are corrections of information that are important for writing a report that is as accurate and as »true« as possible.

In some cases it is beneficial to establish a permanent reference group of representatives from the organization and the project team as a forum for discussing on-going themes and processes (see Chapter 10).

Ending the Fieldwork

Buchanan, Boddy & McCalman (1989) mention three important issues:

- Acknowledge the organization's collaboration on the study – usually in terms of a written report presented at a meeting.
- Make certain that it will be possible to revisit the organization to follow-up on the themes of the study.
- Adhere to the agreed deadlines.

Concerning the report, ask the organization what type(s) of report(s) they want and what issues they are particularly interested in. Organizations have little or no desire to receive scientific reports filled with sophisticated concepts and references to theory, literature and other researchers. They are first and foremost interested in descriptions. Thus, our recommendation is to write a short description of the organization. If the organization wishes, the report may conclude with issues for consideration and a short description of how other organizations have tackled similar problems. But do not offer your advice unless you are asked to do so. It may produce a backlash. The report should be presented and discussed at a meeting in which the project team or representatives of the team participate. Preferably, the report should start out with an executive summary – no more than one page. This summary should contain all the important information in the report. Many people in an organization do not want to read a description of 10-20 pages, but they do not mind reading one page.

It may prove necessary to revisit the organization, either because you need supplementary data or because you want to extend the project. Revisiting the organization requires asking once again for access to the organization, unless this was part of the original agreement. If it is a project covering several years, the most appropriate approach will be to negotiate the collaborative conditions every year. This leaves the organization with a legitimate reason for withdrawing from the project, if it finds the project too arduous. Very few organizations are willing to participate in lengthy studies.

One precondition for sound collaboration between investigators and organizations is that the agreed deadlines be observed, which also makes it easier to prolong the agreement if necessary. Researchers are usually not subject to tight deadlines, which is why they tend not to take agreed deadlines seriously. It is imperative that researchers keep to the agreed deadlines – otherwise they will lose their reputation as experts capable of efficiently managing and implementing a field study project.

Fear and the First Encounter with the Field

Fear is probably unavoidable when taking those last steps before crossing the threshold into the field: »What will they think of me? Do I look stupid in this sweater? I should have worn a suit. I am too tired today and definitely not in the mood for this. What if the interviews dissolve halfway through? Have I remembered my interview guide; how much of it do I remember? How do I introduce myself? Are they at all willing to discuss the issues I want to discuss? Do they think academics are ludicrous? And isn't that exactly what I am: a ludicrous academic on my way to the `bush.' Actually, it is so nice to just have one of those days when I sit, frustrated, in front of my PC trying to write ... I would even prefer facing a hundred hostile students to this uncertainty!«

Worries are justified. It is the researcher's task, to the best of her imaginative abilities, to try to reduce the distance between herself and the natives of the field. The researcher is not the only individual in the field who is making observations. This stranger is a welcome object of stories among the natives. The researcher's appearance is subject to interpretation from the moment she arrives on the scene. It is not a good a idea to park your car at 9:30 in the morning next to the entrance reserved for management, if you are going to interview labourers who have to walk a mile from their parking lot when they start work at 7 in the morning. This behaviour clearly signifies managerial affiliations and creates a distance to labour. You can do a great deal to avoid forming too glaring a contrast to those people whom you are going to interview. In *the hospital project* the researcher puts on a white coat and integrates with the natives. In other cases this type of assimilation would have had the reverse effect. The machine workers in *the production project* would have found a researcher dressed in a boiler suit ridiculous. You have to adjust your personal appearance and behaviour to a level that makes it possible to move about in the entire field. Henslin (1990) offers some very illustrative considerations in connection with planning a study of the homeless, in which he was to move among prostitutes and interview institutional staff.

However, the moment you press the doorbell and the door to the field opens, these worries must stop. At this moment, the project's articulated curiosity is put to a test. You must change your frame of mind and let yourself be filled with the curiosity the project laboriously has accumulated, like capital in the bank. You must let yourself be totally seized by this curiosity, by your honest interest, and repress all other thoughts, in order to avoid projecting the impression of a sick old woman who thinks that she is wasting her life. Turn the switch to »On«. Now you are simply captured by the issues and there can be no room for worries, tactical tricks, or planning of strategies. Come what may: here I am and I am ready: a working self (Schutz 1962: 216).

Three Important Dimensions of Fieldwork

You must behave in the field as a complete subject, practising the customs and the feel of interpersonal communication that you, for better or for worse, have acquired in a lifetime of habits and routines. In short, an authentic person who does not enact a prefabricated script (interviewer-respondent, observer-observed, researcher-native), but who tries to empathize with the field. This identification may involve different levels of depth and duration and the application of a varied repertoire of methods for generating data. We use the term intensive field studies about projects characterized by the researcher combining these three dimensions in order to empathize with the field studied.

Adler & Adler (1987) have designed a progressive taxonomy for the depth of the researcher's involvement with the field (Figure 9.1).

In our four research projects, we not only observed but also interacted with members of the field and, to a certain extent, also participated in the field's activities. However, only in *the hospital project* did the researcher go so far as to assume the role of a peripheral member of the field. In *the drug addict, production and wind turbine projects*, the researchers remained observers and only acted in the field as interviewers and collectors of data.

Figure 9.1. The Continuum of Field Research Involvement (Adler & Adler 1987: 33).

```
Observe members
   Interact with members          }
   Participate with members       }   ......Chicago school
      Investigate participation        ......Existential Sociology
         Membership role
         peripheral member
         active member
         complete member
      Good faith membership       .....Ethnomethodology
```

This demonstrates an important limitation placed on the experiences we were able to accumulate during our field studies. Our depth of involvement in the field was thus not the deepest possible (Whyte 1991), probably because there is no tradition for doing so in our educational environment. It is our impression that this attitude is symptomatic of recent years' social science field studies in Denmark. The more extensive forms of involvement had a renaissance in the early 1970s in connection with the emergence of action research and in the wake of the student revolt. Since then, the researchers' involvement within the fields studied has typically been confined to the upper categories of Figure 9.1. – with perhaps certain exceptions in contemporary studies on (organizational) cultures.

Although our studies implied a limited degree of involvement, they were of a considerable duration – at least for as *the drug addict, the production, and the wind turbine projects*. Of the four authors, three of us are senior researchers, and we have worked within our respective fields for a considerably longer period of time than that necessary to complete a Ph.D. study.

It is possible that the current restrictions placed on Denmark's Ph.D.

programme (a specification of a 3-year education) have in effect reduced the candidates' degree of involvement with the field and perhaps compel a limited duration as well. However, the youngest of us is still involved with the wind turbine industry, which seems to demonstrate that it is possible for contemporary young researchers to develop field studies of a longer duration via a continued and dedicated involvement with a field without wasting time on the impossible: that is, trying to get a grant to conduct a 6-year study.

Like McCracken (1988), we emphasize the use of interviews – although we disagree with him on some points. We want to emphasize, however, that we utilized other methods of data generation in our projects, and our interviews should, therefore, be interpreted in relation to a broad spectrum of data:

- *The drug addict project.* Participant observation in treatment centres, conversations with informants, intensive interviews with the physicians, social workers, etc., and drug addicts, documentary material (such as case records) and literature studies.
- *The hospital project.* Participant observation in the hospital, conversations with informants, interviews with hospital staff, documentary material, literature studies, surveys, intervention, and a follow-up study.
- *The production project.* Pilot study, literature study, documentary material including trade specific statistics; pilot studies in various organizations, intensive field studies including sojourns and observations; and interviews.
- *The wind turbine project.* Literature studies, trade specific statistics, a survey, telephone interviews, interviews with key informants, visits to the field, and documentary material.

Thus, we have not merely used one technique – the interview – to gain insight into the field. But through the interview, the researcher compiles explanations and information that provide her with such profound insight into the field, that the other data seem secondary.

The Interview as a Dialogue

The interview is a fragile situation that may easily assume perverted, ritualistic forms such as examination or ritual politeness (Borum & Enderud 1981: 335). If the researcher has decided to conduct the interview in a specific room where the table is clad with pencils, pads, tape record-er, etc., it is difficult to create a situation of equals. If she furthermore starts out by lecturing the victim in alien terms on the purpose of the study and its methodology, and what she expects from it, she is bound to create an impossible situation (compare Colling, Harboe, Jacobsen, Larsen & Wegens 1992: 29). Only if the interviewee shows an interest in these issues are they legitimate topics. If not, you should rather ex-plain, in as few and simple words as possible, towards what your curios-ity is directed. The general rule is: the less you need to say, the better. The important thing is, as quickly as possible, to make the native relate to and reason on the themes you are interested in studying. In the same way that you are often nervous about whether you have anything to ask, the native is just as nervous about not having anything to say. It is im-portant that you be able to sense when the interviewee misunderstands what you are getting at, since misunderstandings can create a situation that enables you to take a new point of departure in order to evoke a di-alogue.

You risk ruining the possibility of evoking a dialogue if you, through behaviour, facial expressions or eye movements, reveal a tactical or stra-tegic frame of mind. If you think that information on sensitive issues can be obtained by using tricks (Colling, Harboe, Jacobsen, Larsen & We-gens 1992, Chapter 4: 26-39) your body language will reveal to the in-terviewee that certain issues are sensitive, and like a self-fulfilling proph-ecy the interviewee will adopt a strategic and tactical position on these issues.

Hunt's Methodology

This view is close to what Jennifer C. Hunt (1989) calls the existentialist approach. This approach allows the researcher to react emotionally dur-ing interviews and other types of interaction with the natives of the field. Apart from being almost inevitable, such affective involvement demon-strates to the native that the researcher is a fellow human being merely reacting spontaneously in a dialogue of equals.

Hunt's analysis of the psychoanalytical aspects of fieldwork is a mar-vellous account of the incredibly complex processes occurring in the researcher's subconscious while conducting field studies. It is a pro-found human process during which both hostilities and friendships emerge, and during which both the researcher and the natives are sub-ject to culture shocks. It is a process evoking anxiety and joy that touches on the deep layers of the researcher's subconscious. In her book, Hunt describes how the researcher's dreams during her sojourn in the field are evidence of a an intensive, psychological process of change and learning. This process not only involves the researcher's empathy with the field but is also a challenge to her world view and self-perception. Thus, the Chicago school within field studies has developed a set of techniques to prevent researchers from transferring their loyalty to the field and abandoning their research career (Adler & Adler 1987).

It is important to be aware of the psychological processes, but we find that Hunt's analysis confirms that the researcher must behave as authentically as possible. This method of approaching field studies will determine what you learn as a researcher. Also, it will determine the type of data generated, what is remembered and what is neglected. To evoke a dialogue with a native by being present in the situation and demonstrating sincere curiosity is not only a tool for registering as much data and as many impulses during the conversation as possible. It is, as indicated earlier, also a way of making the interviewee forget the script he or she has prepared for this performance. It is the researcher's task to make the native put aside this script and act on his or her own volition. The ambition of a good dialogue, which only in a formal, technical sense is an interview, is to become mutually involved in understanding one another's actions, projects, and ways of interacting with others in the field (Schutz 1962).

The Mutual Project of the Researcher and the Native

Such a dialogue develops from layers that are easily exposed to those that are less readily revealed. As the dialogue proceeds, it will gradually touch on the layers that the native had not imagined to be significant. The dialogue must gradually evolve into a mutual project in which the empathetic researcher helps the native understand him- or herself in order for the researcher to understand the life of the native. The researcher learns to think like the native, at the same time that the native discovers his or her own manner of thinking and acting. Between the two of them they share a series of »Aha!« experiences.

It is, in principle, impossible to satisfactorily conclude such a mutual project. Anyone who has endeavoured to understand all the facets of one's spouse has to admit that it takes more than one lifetime to explore fully the universe of just one person. Anyone who has tried to put herself in the place of another human being and imagine how this person thinks has realized that this is unfeasible, unless you share precisely the same living conditions.

But merely lifting a corner of the veil covering the universe of another human being, which is possible by transforming the interview into a dialogue, will reveal to the researcher the worries, the hopes, the projections, and the criteria for self-esteem (in-order-to motives) to which the interviewee resorts to explain himself. However, the researcher must fulfil other demands, apart from that of being present, to be able to transform the interview into a dialogue.

The Interview Guide

It is important that the researcher be fully aware of what she is looking for so that she does not have to remind herself continuously of interests, systems of relevances, theoretical intentions and hypotheses. If the dialogue is to evolve into a mutual project, she must gradually interpret her interests in view of the subjective creation of meaning that the interviewee participates in constructing during the dialogue. Consequently, questions raised by the research project have to be transformed gradually as an effect of the individual interview – they have to be changed from one interview to another. This principle touches on one of the most widely used techniques of field researchers, that is, preparing oneself for the encounter in terms of an interview guide.

The researcher often uses the interview guide as a practical means of preparing for the encounter with the field and of placing the field within the relevant theoretical framework of the project. For these purposes, it is a good exercise. If the project implies various researchers visiting various field sites in order to collect data, the advantage of the interview guide is that they return with commensurable data. To the individual researcher entering the field, knowing that her briefcase contains an interview guide may be far more reassuring than having ten unclear questions in mind, and it may constitute a serious means to combat the anxiety one is often subject to in this situation.

However, if the researcher starts by asking the first question and proceeds through the interview guide step by step in an attempt to get the interviewee to answer the questions in the given order, the interview is bound to be institutionalized as an interview. The dialogue, in the shape of a mutual explorative project, will never materialize. Both the researcher and the respondent will be caught in a trap of reasoning along the lines of the researcher's theoretical themes, never escaping from the a priori logic from which the theories emerged. The subjective universe of interpretation that the respondent – the potential dialogue partner – applies to understand these themes will forever be hidden from the researcher. The researcher continues reasoning along the project logic lines that she carries into the field and does not get one step closer to field dynamics.

The important thing is to get the native to talk about issues that fascinate him or her, whether they concern current problems with improving a *wind turbine,* the most recent insult by the superior member of *the hospital staff,* the price of drugs and how *drug addicts* get them, or the hopeless situation of *production firms* due to the fact that they simultaneously want to introduce flexible production and maintain individual piece rates. It is simply a question of revealing the focus of attention. What occupies the minds of the people with whom the researcher is going to spend a shorter or longer period of time? From this perspective, the researcher should always be prepared to travel in time – back into history and forward into the future. It is also within this context that the researcher will find even the tiniest clues for combining themes of the research project with current problems of the field. How do the natives explain the emergence of these troubles or problems? To what are they connected? Who are the responsible parties? Why aren't these problems merely resolved – what are the obstacles?

But why is the native engrossed with these problems right now? How do they affect his or her actions? Which other activities and projects is he or she involved in? With whom is s/he collaborating? Is he or she in conflict with others? How does his or her present situation affect his or her past and future life? How does the present situation fit into his or her current life? Why is s/he here and what is the purpose in acting as s/he does? These are perhaps the most important questions. Their answers will furnish the researcher with a life story that is the precondition for getting a clue about a life form or a personal career pattern. This is the very precondition for understanding how individuals perceive possibilities for affecting the construction of both the micro-field and macro-society. What does it mean to a native to realize dreams and what are these dreams?

This is the framework for understanding why certain things worry the native. At the same time, it is important that the researcher begins to understand the status of the current job, private situation, etc., in the life of this human being. This is one of the best means for combining the current situation with the issues and phenomena that the researcher is interested in studying.

The Importance of Life Stories

Life stories play yet another important role to the researcher's work. A mutual dialogue about life stories entails that the involved parties begin to understand and respect each other as human beings. We know of no other tricks that are more apt to provoke mutual trust and the desire to be frank. However, it takes a mastering of the subtle balance between acting as an intruder and getting so close that one starts to reason based on the logic that inevitably arises from the native's life form in terms of worries, projections, incidents, and patterns of interaction. This empathy means, to some extent, becoming fascinated by another human being's specific identity, skills, and biography.

The dialogue on life stories creates the trust that is a precondition for talking about the interaction in which the interviewee participates in the social field. However, the dialogue on life stories is also a condition for understanding this interaction. According to Schultz, natives of the field understand one another because they share or have overlapping biographies.

Researchers often tend either to become irritated over or simply accept the fact that natives explain conflicts and patterns of collaboration (interaction) by referring to individuals' biographical habitus. It is from this perspective that natives want to explain friendships and hostilities, with whom and about what they interact, and thus profile themselves in relation to the field's collectivity. On her entry into the field, the researcher's preconceived notions about the actors and their interaction patterns are bound to be conventional in terms of interest groups, formal divisional groups, etc. The art lies in getting the native to talk about the patterns of interaction, the underlying group structures – the outline of which the researcher knows nothing – and to crystallize the world view by which the native divides his or her social world into good and bad, heroes and villains, the serious and the frivolous.

Within this incredibly personified division of the world, the researcher may capture a few glimpses of the human beings populating the field as well as the way in which a native classifies them. Capturing this world and world view is almost impossible, and there is only one thing to do in the first interviews: use trial and error and acute concentration to aid in understanding how the individual's current world is defined by a certain set of elements and a system of various relationships. This is one of the situations in which the researcher can test whether or not her originally formulated hypotheses were sufficiently clear and concrete for use in directing the dialogue. Likewise, preconceptions can be tested to see whether they point in the right direction. The awareness by the researcher that the hypotheses are changing during the dialogue is the best proof that the researcher is at least trying to view things, phenomena, and problems through the eye of the native.

Individuals develop their own strategies in relation to their interactions. Individuals are always in interaction at a conscious level in at least some relationships. Therefore, they continuously contemplate how they should tackle the problems and phenomena that are important to them. What are their plans? Are they at least slightly related to the phenomena, problems, and issues in which the researcher is interested from a theoretical perspective (the researcher's themes)?

This series of questions is a standard for being able to identify with a certain individual's way of relating to other people in the social field and to the phenomena and problems that are the very basis for initiating the field study. This standard is an attempt to reconstruct a kind of dialogue behaviour. It is a kind of post-rationalization, but hopefully the reader has realized that this standard does not conform to most interview guides.

Revealing the Language Code

The first interview is incredibly important. For the first time, the researcher begins to grasp the language used by the native in relating problems. The researcher may adopt this language and use it in when needed in the field. It is a tool that makes it easier to evoke another dialogue with another native. By using the logic of this language code, to the best of her abilities, the researcher will be subject sequentially to corrections and hence come increasingly closer to the themes she has ascribed to the field. This gradually improved ability to evoke the dialogue also illustrates why a prepared interview guide is, at most, the scaffolding around the building (dialogue).

Field Studies Require Many Interviews

For that very reason, many interviews are better than few. However, a field study requires many interviews for other reasons. It is important to move around in the field to the various groups of natives who, through their interaction, produce the dynamics that define and determine how the researcher's issues and phenomena are part of the total field. By talking to as many natives as possible, interaction is described from many different perspectives. Only by understanding the system through these multiple perceptions can the researcher understand how elements of the system affect other parts, and how totality is shaped through this interacting whole. It is this myriad of interacting worlds that produces all actions in the system. Gradually, after having uncovered the first clues, the researcher will better understand this entirety and the resulting dynamics. Thus, the earlier mentioned process of defining and redefining hypotheses may occur before, during, and after every single interview.

Mapping Out Gravitational Fields for Social Interaction

During the series of interviews, the researcher begins to sense that there is something that unites and divides – that social interaction in the field is structured in terms of gravitational fields of intensive interaction. Interaction between these and other gravitational fields is less intense: the organization is composed of several organized aggregates, and the many individual forms of logic combine to create a group logic. This, in part, implies that others are rejected. Some natives do not fit into these aggregates nor are they members of any subgroups.

Only gradually does it become apparent where the individual is placed in this pattern of interaction between groups of interacting individuals. Hence, the pieces of single groups' definitions of issues and phenomena relevant to the project slowly fall into place in the social field.

During the interviews it is important to try to locate the interviewee on a map of the gravitational fields for social interaction. This will make it easier to interpret individual statements and get a picture of the texture of the social groups.

Nevertheless, this construction is no insurance against falling into a trap: one may end up only having studied a single group from whose perspective the remaining groups' pattern of interaction, way of thinking, and logic are described.

Watch Out for the Satellites!

The situation is even worse if, caught in this trap of misrepresentation, you become infatuated with the satellites in a system that float around without any close affiliation with any of the groups. Individuals whose position in the organization is uncertain have chosen to act against the aggregate, and hence want to complain about the present situation. Such individuals are often willing victims for the researcher. They are easy to interview because they are not pressed for time, they do not need to legitimize themselves in relation to a group, and they want to tell killer stories: »Switch off the tape recorder and I'll tell you a juicy one.« A few of these stories may be fine, but if they accumulate, the researcher may be turned into a priest or ombudsman for the complainers, the oppressed, the hungry, and the homeless.

On the other hand, other satellites may be extremely good informants. Apprentices in *production companies*, orderlies or domestic workers in *hospitals*, police officers, *drug-addicted* bank counsellors, etc. may prove to be very rewarding to talk to, as they, by means of their social roles, travel in and between many groups without belonging to any of them and without being rejected by any of the groups. These satellites are often good at drawing comparisons between the various groups, including their nature and ability to collaborate. They are often capable of keeping a distance by not taking the interaction aggregate too seriously, and they are still able to spot the idiosyncrasies that gradually have become the norm for those who are integrated into the single groups.

Everyone constructs an understanding of the social field of which they are a part. Everyone finds evidence that their understanding is true. We caution you not to embrace – uncritically and untested – their true understanding of the field.

Many field studies directly convey management's portrayal of the organization. We are not saying that this portrayal is altogether inaccurate. Maybe this is the portrayal by which management establishes its interaction with the remainder of the organization. Therefore, it is important in order to understand this group of natives' manoeuvres and reactions in relation to the organization. But it is only a single group of natives in a pattern of interaction in which other groups' definitions of the situation and manoeuvres toward management are not to be compared to a stimulus-response situation.

The Synthesis of Empathy

Every individual interview will reveal specific aspects and contribute to understanding an interaction aggregate and its components. The researcher will gradually pick up a veritable sensation that the clues are leading her to a conclusion. The outlines begin to emerge for a key to understanding the tale. The synthesis of empathy has, in spite of everything, been at work.

But it is not only that the researcher gradually feels that she has the key to understanding. The sense of being able to tell the story in a different language gradually grows. According to some ethnographers, the dynamics of a social field should ideally be described in terms of the field's own concepts. Only by describing a field in a way that represents the field's description of itself can the researcher claim to have completed the task of empathy – if not fully, then adequately.

To describe a social field in terms of the field's own concepts is important in order to capture how various sections of the social field understand themselves and the interactions that result in mutual actions. However, it is not enough to have captured the dynamics. The dynamics, the system, or the pattern require an overview at a higher hierarchical level. This usually implies an understanding beyond that of a single individual in the social field. Laziness or a deficient and inappropriate panorama often results in this phase being analysed in terms of theoretical frameworks. However, we assert that the ideal is to construct the dynamics in terms of the field's concepts, fully aware of the fact that none of our research tales lives up to this ideal. By representing the terms in which the field understands itself, the researcher defines her position for action in regard to historical challenges and problems. It is in this language that the field will be able to construct its own relationships of understanding field-experienced concerns and the themes that the researcher thus far has only been able to formulate from a theoretical perspective. Such understandings will make it possible to construct macro-developments out of micro-behaviour (cf. Knorr-Cetina's (1988) discussion of this complex theme).

10. The Researcher in Her Den

Change of Scene:
Returning from the Field to the Institute

One day the fieldwork is over. Either temporarily or permanently. Even though we argued against a sharp distinction between data generation, analysis, and writing, we must acknowledge that returning from the field to work at the desk – at the institute or at your home office – implies a profoundly different working situation.

Fieldwork demands a social behaviour that is acceptable to the field's actors. This may take a certain amount of chameleon-like adaptation, since you have to function in different social settings and with different groups. Most of the practical, craftsperson-like tasks have to do with bringing interesting and analysable data home. Discussions primarily involve members of the social system studied. The actors' common-sense interpretations are brought face to face with those of the researcher, and possible, practical implications will come to light.

Work at the institute also implies certain demands on the researcher's social behaviour, although such demands have more to do with commitment to professional environments or networks and balancing the priority of research with other activities. The situation is often characterized by conflicting pressures. On the one hand, the research project constitutes a core asset that the researcher wants to have taken seriously. On the other hand, she is expected to teach, administer, and be socially visible. It is just as important to acknowledge and act on these demands as to act on the field's demands for appropriate behaviour.

The craftsperson-like tasks change from data generation to data processing – analysis and reporting. Here the professional network, or the environment, operates within a set of conventions. They represent the environment's aggregate learning – accumulated knowledge – some of which may stem from earlier generations of researchers. There are two courses of action: either these norms for analysing data must be met, or, if you want to deviate from the prevailing norms and want to be taken seriously by colleagues, a solid argument is imperative.

Discussions with research colleagues differ in many ways from discussions with practitioners. First, they typically emphasize how conclusions are reached just as much as what the conclusions imply. Research is a knowledge-generating process that is much more formalized and governed by rules than everyday generation of knowledge – according to Weick (1989), it is »disciplined imagination«.

Figure 10.1. The Diamond of Research

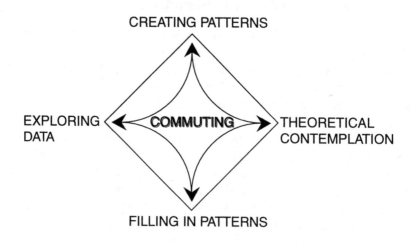

Second, discussions with colleagues take place in a universe of time and space. Discussions occur in the mind, or on paper, with other writers, contemporary, as well as deceased, who are important to your present analysis, from an empirical or a theoretical point of view. You discuss things with colleagues, friendly or hostile, near or distant from your own discipline or from other disciplines, all depending on the course of the research process and the occasions that present themselves.

Third, the researcher will continue mentally to go over the discussions that occurred during the fieldwork and will play off the discussions against the more theoretical analyses and conclusions. Some of them will be incorporated as elements of the final analysis after having been tested and refined.

The Secret of the Craft: To Create a Puzzle

Kuhn (1970) has characterized research as puzzle-solving. It is, however, a misleading metaphor in so far as it assumes that someone else has defined and solved the problem beforehand and that the puzzle has only one solution. In the case of intensive field studies, the puzzle not only has to be solved but must first be constructed.

Therefore, we prefer to talk about the researcher's analytical work as the creation of a puzzle, that is, creating and filling in patterns. Creating patterns is the same as creating a comprehensive narrative, and filling in the pattern means documenting this narrative. The two activities interact: ideas for the overall pattern may emerge from playing with a detail. An overall pattern is an aid for coping with and organizing complex data. Attempts to fill in the pattern may lead to insoluble dissonance and, thus, rejection or modification of the pattern. They may also lead to the creation of a consistent – or satisfactorily coherent – universe.

In principle, both activities involve alternating between exploration of data and theoretical contemplation.

Scrutinizing data is necessary, given the fact that the project is about exploring an empirical field that you have tried to encapsulate via data. Even if data are subject to interpretation while in the process of generation, such interpretations will be preliminary and, for the most part, constitute ideas and inspirations for the subsequent, main analysis. This analysis comprises both a search for additional inspiration and ideas, questions, themes, concepts, and explanatory patterns, and a strict analysis as a means to identify and prove or disprove coherence and variations.

Theoretical contemplation is what profoundly distinguishes research from common-sense analyses. Concepts, models, and theories that have emerged from previous research are a resource that may all constitute a source of inspiration, and thus enrich your own analysis, and save you the trouble of having to start from scratch. Existing theoretical literature is a treasure chest of knowledge. Using the results of other researchers' hard work and contemplations saves a lot of time. Literature provides access to more clarified schemes of interpretation. The idea may seem mundane, but our research projects, as well as the behaviour of others, reveals a tendency to draw insufficiently on the existing literature.

We are not refuting the fact that data (statements from the field) are rich in concepts and explanations, but they are often suggestive, ambiguous and less stringent.

The research process is thus characterized by alternating, or switching, between activities of creating patterns, filling in patterns, exploring data, and theoretical contemplation. Ideas and inspiration emerge from these interacting activities that focus on different aspects. An attempt to realize these ideas and inspirations is thereafter achieved by applying your resources of data and theories. As a result, ideas are rejected, modified, or realized. Together, the four major activities constitute the diamond of research (Figure 10.1).

Creating Patterns

The activity of determining the basic pattern, or overall theme of the analysis, is critical and difficult to define. Often the idea emerges from muddled and intangible processes characterized by uncertainty about goals as well as means.

According to Thompson & Tuden (1959) inspiration in this situation is the process leading to decision. Inspiration is characterized by the feeling of suddenly seeing the light- the »Aha!« experience. The feeling is not only intellectual but also emotional and leads to feeling high or stoned – the conviction that something unique is being experienced and that no one else has experienced it in quite the same way.

No of the authors has any doubt as to the nature of that experience, but it is difficult to determine exactly what it is that triggers this situation. The supposedly obvious idea may emerge from conscious attempts to find a overall theme. But it may also emerge from hard work with some mundane data, from reading or discussing literature at random, or from attempts to fill in a pattern that may result in the emergence of a more attractive pattern. Mills' (1959) point is that the sociological imagination can be stimulated by craftsperson-like working procedures. This idea is consistent with the classical description of problem-solving as a new way of combining known elements. Mills' recipe for »intellectual craftsmanship« (Mills 1959: 211-217) contains the following major ingredients:

- Keep a diary of personal experiences as well as of professional activities, current as well as planned studies. The diary reminds you of your intellectual activities and personal experiences. It is also a source of inspiration for finding new patterns and combinations of elements.
- Play with definitions, phrases and words to find the exact connotation that fits with your analysis.
- Try to develop types and typologies. Use cross-classification as a method.
- Think in extremes, ideal types, and oppositional categories.

- Try to break with your sense of proportion and see what difference it makes.
- Try to get a comparative grip on the data.
- Think in terms of issues and problems, and general themes. Formulate them as clearly as possible and clarify how they relate to one another.

But even if it is easy to recognize the feeling of »Aha!« when it is occurring, the inspirational idea for a pattern may prove inadequate during the subsequent process of filling in the pattern. It is just as important to be able to fall in love with your own ideas as it is to be able to reject or modify them as the analysis proceeds. The feeling of »Aha!« may contain an element of self-deception – you want to come up with a brilliant idea and to escape an unpleasant deadlock. And even though the feeling is genuine, many ideas prove inadequate when subjected to closer scrutiny. But treat the ideas seriously! Write them down in clear-cut formulations. Writing down your ideas is partly a manner of testing their substance and partly a necessary precondition for being able to use themes dynamically. It is necessary to see whether they crumble or need to be modified, and the best way of discovering that is to formulate them explicitly.

As our four research tales demonstrate, overall patterns and themes are dynamic entities that are modified and clarified or whose nature changes completely as the process unfolds.

In *the production tale*, the overall theme turned out to be international restructuring from mass production to flexible specialization, and Denmark was considered to be an ideal experimental laboratory for carrying out empirical studies. This macro theory was translated into micro theories, signifying expectations of the behaviour of medium-sized companies. The fieldwork fell short of these expectations, but this did not result in a rejection of the basic point of departure. Instead, attempts were undertaken to explain deviations as a consequence of the actors' specific, national characteristics.

In *the hospital tale*, the comprehensive theme turned out to be the internal structure's alienating effect on the employees. Alienation is hardly a concept that one immediately associates with working in a hospital. This type of work is often perceived of as humanitarian and in itself meaningful and rewarding – a calling. The very idea of applying the terminology of alienation to summarize how the employees perceived their situation had a certain element of novelty and provocation. But to make any sense at all, this systems analysis required that alienation as well as internal structure be translated into more concrete elements that made it possible to link the overall tale to the actors' statements.

But this comprehensive systems tale merely dealt with the first part of Berger & Kellner's (1981: 13-14) statement:

> »Not only is the world not what it appears to be, but it could be different from what it is.«

Therefore, in order to facilitate the shift from analysis to intervention, the theme had to be elaborated with a theory of change that was consistent with the new systems concept. Components of power and conflict theory proved useful as the basis for a theory of change, which could be defined as an alternative to the prevalent theory of the time of organizational development, which primarily was consensual. Finally, in collaboration with the staff of a hospital unit, it was possible to prove the practical relevance of a power-based strategy for change.

In *the wind turbine tale*, the original theme of the grand narrative was to uncover the need for new industrial policies and corresponding political and administrative instruments. This was translated into a study of product development among Denmark's wind turbine manufacturers. The theoretical concepts, the technological system, and learning by using proved suitable for uncovering central elements of the development activities of the wind turbine industry. At this point, the tale had changed radically and the grand narrative turned into something quite different: the story about the development and exchange of knowledge and immaterial resources within an industrial network. The final tale turned out to be a decomposition of the widespread linear model of scientific research preceding technological development.

The drug addict tale is another example of a radical change in theme that went from an evaluation of institutions' therapeutic programmes to an analysis and typification of drug addict careers. The first potential narrative stressed that the therapeutic measures offered by the institutions represented different belief systems in terms of assumptions about causal relationships. Each institution offered a standard package of therapy that was not tailored to the needs of the individual drug addict. Furthermore, this tale contained a critique of previous studies' methods for measuring the effects of therapy.

The final tale turned out to contest the stereotype perception of drug addicts as a group of individuals with identical characteristics. By mapping out the career of drug addicts, a typology for the careers of abusers was developed. Identifying the complex interaction of events related to turning points in life demonstrated that it was impossible to point to one factor that triggered off or was decisive for a drug addict career. By now there was only a weak link back to the first narrative, since the therapeutic institutions merely acted as intermediate stations in the drug addict's career.

The tale is thus exposed to constant changes, since it is only by realizing it that you can test its validity. The theme must be modified or possibly replaced as problems emerge, which makes it difficult to maintain a convincing translation between the theme and the concrete analyses based on empirical data. However, continual attempts of thematization prevent the analysis from deteriorating into many incoherent subanalyses.

Exploring Data

The purpose of empirical exploration is to answer the questions or issues you have formulated in relation to the empirical field, and through argumentation, produce a coherent interpretation of the social system explored.

Empathy with and loyalty to the empirical field require that the empirical data be taken seriously. The question: »What do data say?« serves as an important tool for the researcher executing her craft. It is like the professional carpenter who respects the material – she examines the wood, its pattern of colour, grains, knots and irregularities. She strokes the wood, bends down to it and tries to assess its limitations and possibilities.

Which informants and statements hold the key to the field? Which perspective should be imposed on the field? Which system boundaries should you choose? What is the body of analysis, and what can and should be excluded? Which ideal-type categories can be derived? Which theoretical concepts and models are adequate for this type of data, and how can they be matched?

Silverman (1985: 156-177) has outlined four positions for the interpretation of interview data: positivism, interactionism, ethnomethodology, and realism. We find these categories very useful for describing various potential interpretations of interview data and the relevant demands for validity. However, our position does not fall within one of these specific categories, since the interview, in our opinion, is a data resource that can be subjected to many different, purposeful analyses.

The hospital project did not begin with a theoretical framework, and in *the wind turbine project*, it was only embryonic. Thus, data became very important as a driving force in the search for the overall pattern. The interviewees' exciting or telling accounts and interpretations led to a search for more well-founded theoretical frameworks capable of capturing conflicts or patterns inherent in the data.

The theoretical point of departure of *the drug addict tale* was much more clear, but after the data were analysed, radical reformulation was necessary. In the case of the production tale, the theoretical basis proved to hold, albeit it had to be modified.

Through reading and by turning data over and over – with or without the help of theoretical concepts – you become familiar with them. Ideally, you have the ability to appreciate their nuances and potential for various interpretations. You produce sub-analyses that may not go very far but that later prove fruitful as components of a larger tale.

One example is *the hospital tale* in which role analysis as a guiding concept was abandoned. Nevertheless, several of its elements could be recycled as components of the pattern of alienation. Another example is *the drug addict tale*. The first account of treatment centres produced several elements that could be recycled within the framework of the final tale of drug addict biographies.

Whether or not you read data from the field with an open and focused mind, you have to select among the vast store of generated material. Even if you choose to work with the complete set of data, you will never be able to find an analytical framework capable of capturing the totality of data. The craftsperson-like judgement decides what to reject, and the resulting product is a dramatic test of the quality of this judgement.

While the researcher is working with data, it is important to pay attention to the difference between factual information and interpretation. Factual information may be more or less correct and must be checked. In *the wind turbine and the drug addict tales*, for example, much work was invested in reconstructing the history of the industry and the individuals, respectively. Historiography was in part a goal in itself and in part the basis for the subsequent interpretation.

In *the production and hospital tales*, the respondents' statements contained descriptions of the structure and the function of the social systems that to some extent were contradictory, uncertain, and incomplete.

Thus, modelling the two systems required considerable work in terms of data triangulation and incorporation of several sources.

The data in all four research projects contain multiple fragments of the actors' interpretations of:

- which factors were significant for the development of the *wind turbine industry*, and what effects came from subsidies;
- which incidents were important to *drug addicts' life paths*, and what role did treatment play;
- what characterized innovation processes in *production companies*, and which people played a key role in these processes; and
- what were the main problems at *the hospital*, and which external and internal actors and structures were the cause of these.

These interpretations are an important resource for the researcher, providing inspiration or components for a more formalized explanatory pattern. However, the actors' interpretations are extremely varied with regard to elements of knowledge, emotion, and speculation. Furthermore, such interpretations are bound to be coloured by the actors' background and position in the field – including the implied interests, resources, information, influence, and room for action. Thus, the researcher ought to adopt an open, but always critical, attitude to explanations from the field. If you adopt the informant's interpretation, it must be done consciously and be justifiable.

However, it is also important to be aware that the issue of the study may displace the boundary between the two categories of data: factual information and interpretations. For example, some actors' interpretations (experiences) in *the hospital tale* were categorized as hard, factual data as a result of the applied theories of alienation and roles. It is easiest to support an individual's feeling of being alienated if it is possible to point to fragments of the interview that demonstrate this feeling. If variation in the statements furthermore can be traced to differences in role position within the field, the interpretation gains credibility. On the other hand, the respondents' interpretations of the causes of the present situation – and the possibilities for changing it – were viewed as explanations from the field closely tied to the actors' backgrounds and interests.

The key point is to keep the analysis of data at a typified level. The goal of interpretation of the social field is not to explain the unique acts of unique individuals (Schutz 1962: 36). On the contrary, data are interpreted based on a formalized, typified model of the field. Such a model will, in principle, make it possible to deduce a subset from the data's complexity and subjectivity, which can be interpreted as an expression of one type of actor's creation of meaning, the interplay between types of actors, patterns in types of interaction, etc. This is possible; we do not claim that the process is easy or problem-free.

In *the hospital tale*, the actors' accounts were interpreted as an expression of views related to role types: physicians, nurses, nurse's aides, and orderlies, and of role positions: manager, middle manager, superior, subordinate, and student. Also, the interplay between the types of actors was formalized into interaction between physicians and nursing staff, superior and subordinate, the nursing groups internally, etc. Interaction was typified to comprise interaction important to the actors: rounds, case records, conferences, ward unit meetings, coffee breaks, etc., and the abstract categories: processes of communication, management, and decision-making.

Correspondingly, *the other three projects* established typologies for patterns of interaction and actors. Note that, even in *the drug addict project*, which focused on drug addicts' life paths, both the concrete biographies and drug addicts were typified.

Thus, the data are interpreted in terms of a scientific model of the world, the creation and function of which Schutz describes as:

> »[The researcher] begins to construct typical course-of-action patterns which correspond to the observed events. Thereafter he co-ordinates to these typical course-of-action patterns a personal type, a model of an actor whom he imagines as being gifted with consciousness. Yet it is a consciousness restricted to containing nothing but the elements relevant to the performance of the course-of-action patterns under observation and relevant, therefore, to the problem under scrutiny by the scientist (Schutz 1962: 40).
>
> Yet these models of actors are not human beings living within their biographical situation in the social world of everyday life. Strictly speaking, they do not have any biography or any history, and the situation into which they are placed is not a situation defined by them but defined by their creator, the social scientist. He has created these marionettes or homunculi to manipulate them for this purpose. A merely plausible consciousness is conferred to

them by the scientist, which is constructed in such a way that its presupposed stock of knowledge at hand (including the ascribed set of invariant motives) would make actions originating from it subjectively understandable, provided that these actions were performed by real actors within the social world. But the marionette and his artificial consciousness are not subjected to the ontological conditions of human beings.« (Schutz 1962: 41)

Even though Schutz' formulations are jarring to the contemporary ear, we agree with the content. If you do not develop a simplified model prior to – or during the act of – exploring data, you will be unable to discriminate between data and unable to produce an interpretation of the field independent of the field's own explanations.

Theoretical Contemplation

In *the production and drug addict projects*, existing theories played an important role early in the research process for generating the overall tale.

Opposition to existing input-output models was an important driving force in *the drug addict project*. This may often be a fruitful way of producing an overall pattern: create a theoretical scarecrow (bogeyman, if you please) in the shape of an author, or a school of authors, that can be used as a sparring partner.

On the other hand, existing theory provided a constructive approach in *the production tale*. Even though the subsequent in-depth analysis of data led the author to contest the theory, he did not abandon it. Instead, the analysis was reformulated in an attempt to dissolve the apparent paradox between theoretical expectations and factual observations. Thus, in this project, the theory of flexible specialization played an on-going heuristic role.

These two projects demonstrate how theories and assumptions about cause-effect relationships and more coherent, paradigmatic perspectives on empirical phenomena can play significantly guiding roles.

In *the hospital and the wind turbine tales*, theory played an important role too, but not until later in the process, and then as a supplier of concepts and models that could capture and facilitate a sharper interpretation of significant empirical observations. Here, theoretical concepts functioned as words that facilitated and led to a dawning understanding.

In *the hospital project*, this was the case in the concept of alienation, which captured significant aspects of the hospital staff's dissatisfaction and pointed towards its structural causes. Similarly, the normative part of the project was released through the term power, which served as a means to create a critical distance from existing literature on change and facilitated the formulation of elements for an alternative change strategy.

In *the wind turbine project* the technological system and learning by using turned out to be the keys to a better understanding of some empirical, experience-based learning processes, as well as elements for confronting the research and development perspective on industrial innovation processes. Furthermore, top-down versus bottom-up technology development provided a dimension that could be used for a comparative classification of national technology policies.

These latter two tales illustrate how theory plays an important role as a supplier of concepts (Thomlinson 1981) that can function as »sensitizing devices« (Giddens 1976). Blumer (1969: 163) has assigned three central functions to scientific concepts and conception in the researcher's perception of the studied field:

- it introduces a new orientation or point of view;
- it serves as a tool, or a means of transacting business with your environment; and
- it makes possible deductive reasoning and so the anticipation of new experience.

In relation to the first two functions, concepts are of decisive importance to the generation of knowledge. This is supported by our experiences from the four projects. In Blumer's words:

> »Throughout the scientific inquiry concepts play a central role. They are significant elements in the prior scheme that the scholar has of the empirical world; they are likely to be the terms in which his problems are cast; they are usually the categories for which data are sought and in which the data are grouped; they usually become the chief means for establishing relations between data; and they are usually the anchor points in interpretation of the findings. Because of such a decisive role in scientific inquiry, concepts need especially to be subject to methodological scrutiny.« (Blumer 1969: 26)

Blumer furthermore emphasizes that a significant characteristic of scientific concepts is their dynamic nature:

> Scientific concepts have a career; changing their meaning
> from time to time, in accordance with the introduction of
> new experiences and replacing one content with another
> (Blumer 1969: 161-162).
>
>   In the first stage, the concept represents merely a primitive conception applied to some situations requiring solution or adjustment. It is in the nature of a hypothesis; its value is suggested but unknown. It promises some comprehension and control, and it is used on the basis of this promise. ...
>
>   In being refined, the concept functions none the less to aid activity, but its function changes character somewhat. Its field of operation becomes more definitely understood, its possibilities better gauged, and the consequences of its use more secure... one significant value of the concept lies in its possibility of deductive consequences. ...by reasoning from the concept one may gain a new perspective and visualize problems and procedures which transcend the immediate problems which have given rise to the concept and in response to which it functions as a tool. (Blumer 1969: 166-167)

All of our research tales contain examples of this of which two will be mentioned.

In *the drug addict project*, the introduction of biographies was a conceptual leap that resulted in a shift of focus from the institution to the individual. At first, the concept made it possible to systematize various events that may have affected the drug addict's life. Consequently, the focus shifted to turning points in life and the combination of incidents that these may have triggered. The resulting typology included two dimensions: personality and subculture affiliation. The conceptual development facilitated a discussion on the prevailing myths about drug addicts and of the treatment offered at that time.

In *the hospital project*, the concept of alienation was narrowed by choosing Blauner's (1964) conception of alienation, but omitting the dimension of self-alienation, which data were unable to support, and operationalizing other dimensions adequatery in relation to the data. As to the concept of power, the principal decision was to choose the theory of power bases. However, since this rests on individual psychology, it had to be expanded to comprise a collective dimension. Furthermore, focusing on change required a dynamic reformulation of the concept of power bases. Finally, the conceptual development was a precondition for gaining the ability to argue in favour of the relevance of the field analysis to the hospital system in general.

Filling in the Pattern

Some say that creative work consists of 80% perspiration and 20% inspiration. You have constructed a pattern that must be tested. The time has come to fill in the pattern – like a jigsaw puzzle. But unlike the pieces of a jigsaw puzzle, your puzzle's pieces are not preshaped. They must be generated from data on the field and borrowed from other empirical studies and theoretical works.

At one point in *the drug addict tale*, the team worked with an idea for a pattern – careers – and a series of interviews containing information about the life on drugs and the background of these drug addicts. Filling in the life pattern of each drug addict required patiently coding each interview and deducing the main categories of events. However, this was merely one of several steps taken towards developing a more general typology.

In *the hospital tale*, the confused researcher found consolation in the concept of alienation based on a more intuitive interpretation of data. What remained was merely to listen to the tapes, to read the transcripts, to develop a stringent notation system for interview quotations, to translate multifaceted interview statements into one-dimensional statements about alienation, and finally to evaluate the appropriateness of the chosen conceptual apparatus.

The process requires trust in analytical skills and the ability to make appropriate judgements, much hope for success, and much love for the overall pattern chosen to govern the process.

The are many potential traps – and much doubt: how far can you reasonably go in pursuit of a theme or a pattern? How much dissonance reduction is justifiable? When should you give up on the puzzle and attempt to create a new pattern? This is not a process for delicate souls. It requires persistence and stubbornness and the ability to endure a long, lonely struggle.

This process can be particularly difficult, especially for the junior scholar. When it comes down to it, faith in what you are doing is decisive for the process.

What can be done to avoid going wrong in the process of filling in the pattern – either in terms of a good pattern being abandoned or wasting too much time pursuing a poor pattern?

First, you must be explicit and you must externalize! Only by making clear (that is, in writing that is comprehensible to others) what is implied by filling in the pattern is it possible to retain your overview and thereby avoid logic displacements, intellectual jumps, inconsistent data processing, and treating aspects that do not seem to fit in too leniently.

Second, it requires craftsperson-like integrity – not only to make the analysis, but also to persuade the scientific community to accept the intensive field study. In most cases the study depends on the scholar conducting it, and others have to assume that she has not cheated or cut corners. They must be able to assume, for example, that conflicting or ambiguous data have been subject to meticulous treatment. And this must be clarified! In principle, there is nothing wrong with filling in gaps in data with background data (such as own observations) and with data and lines of reasoning originating from similar studies. But only if this is stated explicitly and if the reader can test whether this invisible mending is justifiable.

When filling in the pattern, you must be open to the possibility that the puzzle may disintegrate. The outlined, overall pattern is based on a preliminary concept, the design and validity of which are tested through the trial-and-error process of filling in the pattern. Even though you may have to give up filling in the pattern, the work is rarely wasted. You have gained a deeper insight into the empirical field and a section of the possible theoretical universe. In addition, the process has yielded some sub-analyses that may be used as components of other patterns. Don't get caught up in a panic situation because you have to give up filling in a pattern! The next attempt will probably prove to be easier because learning has resulted from the previous process.

In most cases it is easy to discover whether you have compromised your craftsperson-like integrity: a feeling of shame arises. The rule is easy: do not use methods and techniques that you will not accept others to use.

Aside from all these scruples, it is also – or in any case can be – fun to fill in a pattern. You become captured by the process. You live through and triumph over frustrations. It is satisfying to see a pattern emerge. In the end, it may prove less amusing: you know the final solution and what remains is merely the tedious work of completing the picture. Nevertheless, most of the process contains amusing moments. If the field analysis offers no amusing elements and occasional moments of play, it is very likely that you are pursuing the wrong clue. Such a clue should be abandoned – no matter how long it has been pursued, and no matter how close the approaching deadlines.

However, there is another inherent and important problem of filling in the pattern: retaining an overview of a large number of components – concepts as well as data. A pattern consisting of, for example, just five components may result in numerous pages of text in relation to 20 interviews of each 15-20 pages with different types of respondents. The simple solution to this problem is to try to reduce the complexity by applying techniques such as:

- modelling, such as breaking down the pattern into levels
- drawing and visualizing the pattern
- formulating the pattern in terms of a typology.

After all, humans are only capable of comprehending a limited number of elements at one time. Perception theory operates with an upper level of seven (plus or minus two) elements. This also applies to researchers.

On Writing

Sooner or later, the results of the efforts have to materialize. It is not enough to think, analyse, make jigsaw puzzles, find patterns, etc. The dissertation must be written.

The initial manoeuvres

After many enriching experiences in the field and discussions with colleagues, it is time to close the door to the workshop. Finally alone! Not that the fieldwork and the discussions are over and done with: as the four research tales illustrate abundantly, fieldwork alternates with institute work and other activities. Furthermore, fieldwork has a tendency to flow outside of its planned boundaries.

However, finally you succeed in squeezing in some time between all the other required activities. It is now time to focus on the essential: get down on paper all that dawning recognition from the field and develop a coherent explanatory pattern. Finally, you have time to do what you have been longing for!

> The pens are all arranged neatly. Paper on the desk. Books from the library are organized according to subject. The disk is formatted and has a brand new label with the title of the project – in capital letters. I made it on this fantastic, new, PC which I have borrowed temporarily. OK, this all took me two and a half hours but it looks smashing. New files are lined up filled with various papers, notes, bibliographies, etc. The coffee cup and pot are ready to brighten a busy new day in which I have decided to take the initial steps to write my dissertation. Oh. That's right. I ran out of lead for my pencil. What type is it? 0.5 millimetre? Yes, I think so. I'd better go get some immediately. Then I can also mail the envelope with all my bills to be paid via the giro account – it's almost too late. Where did I put the giro forms? That's odd, they're not where they normally are – what's this – an old reminder from the library! Something is wrong. I returned those books 3 weeks ago – didn't I? Perhaps I didn't – I'd better check this out...

Everyone who has been engaged in creative writing of one sort or the other is familiar with this or similar situations: the difficulty of getting started. Preparations are used as an excuse for avoiding the unavoidable: to write. »I have not tidied up and cleaned the house for a long time. I can't work in this mess!« The excuses are infinite.

In other words: you stop before you get started. The divine inspiration fails to materialize and you become restless and start to feel inept (Rienecker 1991: 45-49).

The four of us have all shared this experience – not only in connection with the four research projects described but also later in our careers. We have identified four mechanisms that trigger this writer's block:

- problems of readjusting from one work situation to another
- exaggerated expectations of the result
- not recognizing that the process of writing is a process of learning
- no obligations to meet deadlines.

But we have also learned ways to unblock.

It is only a passage

Few of us go from one life situation to another without spending some time and energy on adjusting to the new situation. We switch regularly between working 5 days a week and having the weekend off – and in most cases we spend the time with different people, which is why it's fairly easy to adjust. Nevertheless, most of us have established certain routines and rituals connected with Friday and Sunday evening.

It is our shared experience, agreed on by our colleagues, that it usually takes approximately half a day to get started on the job of analysing and writing. This is hardly surprising: mentally you have to adjust from other types of activities that are predominately social – whether it is fieldwork, teaching, administrative tasks – to an antisocial task requiring contemplation and concentration. You have to shut yourself off from other disturbances: keep the door to the office closed – or ideally – stay away from the institute and work at home. (Provided that the family leaves you alone.) However, apart from this physical shift, there is also a mental shift.

Rites of passage may help you shift from one work situation and its symbolic domain to another (Schultz 1991). Without revealing which of us does which, these are some of the elements of our rites of passage: a leisurely breakfast, casual attire, pleasant music on the stereo, a properly brewed cup of coffee or tea instead of »industrial instant« and a stroll in the neighbourhood. The next thing to do is to wipe the slate clean, which typically means doing all the practical things you have postponed. Checking up on your private finances, calling the plumber, writing down what to do tomorrow, rearranging your files, etc. Finally, unplug the phone. So far so good: comfortable surroundings and you feel the day has started well, even though 3 hours have disappeared in doing other things than what you were supposed to do.

Becker (1986: 2-5) confirms this observation. When he discussed this subject with his Ph.D. candidates, it turned out that each of them had developed their own rituals for the process of writing. In his interpretation, they are what anthropologists call magical rituals. They are performed in an attempt to effect processes over which one has no rational control. This sounds very sensible in relation to the process of writing. Any attempt to control this process rationally is superficial, whereas the very essence – writing and creation of meaning – remains obscure.

Rituals – those of passage as well as magical ones – take time. Thus, rather than becoming depressed about not getting started on the actual research immediately, you should try to observe and understand the process you are going through: how long does it take, what does it consist of, how does it effect one psychologically? Is it possible to make the ritual more amusing, shorter, or more efficient?

Sit down at the desk – organize your paraphernalia. Start by reading something – theory, data or notes. Time passes. Now and then write down some ideas. Suddenly it is lunch time. Panic: half a day has passed with no visible results!

It is our experience that this unpleasant feeling is unavoidable but surmountable. You have to live through the unpleasantness. Escaping it merely implies that you have to start all over the next day by adapting yourself to the process of writing and going through the rites of passage once more. But how do you get through the process?

You start to write! It is almost unimportant what it is, just as long as it is related to the research project. They may be wild ideas or beautifully composed, grandiloquent sentences that proclaim you to be the master of the empirical field and the social sciences, or they may be an unpretentious description of the problems of getting started and your doubts about your capabilities.

Write a letter to someone on the subject. This is what the American journalist Tom Wolfe did. For some time he had been doing research on the »Pralford« cars, automobiles pieced together at home by many Americans. The subject was good, but he was unable to come to grips with his article. He then wrote a long letter to his editor explaining everything. The editor deleted »Dear X« and printed it. This was the beginning of the so-called »New Journalism«. Try Tom Wolfe's experience. Write to someone you trust and let go of your ideas. The point is not that Wolfe's letter was printed. The point is that by putting down his ideas in a letter, it became easier for him to express himself (Kock 1988: 27).

In the beginning it may be necessary to force yourself to get going. You decide not to get up from the chair until x number of pages have been produced. And you sit there until the boredom of remaining inactive exceeds the reluctance of starting to write. Don't be critical about what you are writing. You don't have to show it to anybody. It is primarily a matter of getting into the habit of writing, of removing things that obstruct the writing process. Motivation often increases as you become absorbed in the writing process. You can literally write yourself into a sweat.

Write – and throw away. But write. It is not the final product. Later in the process there will be time for correction. The important thing is to get started.

The Taming of Expectations

It is important to put yourself into the right frame of mind for the task. Our experience shows that it's useless to tell yourself that »now I have to be creative«. On the contrary, this attitude obstructs the writing process since too much self-criticism occurs.

Creativity is intangible and complex and is burdened with expectations of writing something exciting, transcendent, ground-breaking, mind-expanding or whatever terms you can come up with that have a positive connotation. Without being aware of it, you may create personal expectations that are far too great compared with your realistic level of performance.

How many of the above-mentioned positive terms spring to mind in relation to our four research tales? Right. Also, bear in mind that the environment rarely perceives of a scholar's work as particularly creative or exciting. Outsiders focus instead on the process and the appearance of the product (book or dissertation). Only a limited number of peers and students read it, as it is often incomprehensible to non-specialists. The outsider can observe that the scholar is working on something that is common within that field – and that it later materializes in the shape of a written product. Thus, somehow the scholar masters a production process during which various materials and tools are combined, resulting in articles, books, reports, etc. The connection between the point of departure, process, and outcome is not obvious to the outsider. The scholar has capabilities that have slowly been developed through her education and research practice.

Aside from defining the task as a craft to yourself, your expectations probably become more realistic and focus on relevant dimensions, such as professional expertise, which you either possess or want to establish.

However, in the beginning you have to be prepared for a slow process. It takes time to get into the subject. It may feel like a waste of time, but this period is best viewed in terms of start-up costs. However, it is often easier to get started if you begin to write about the aspects you immediately feel most competent at approaching. This is not necessarily the introduction. In other words: start with subjects you feel like writing about.

Many people find it much easier to express themselves verbally than in writing. Another way of getting started is therefore to record your thoughts and ideas and later transcribe them. Instead of a tape recorder:

> »you can use a reasonably intelligent and interested person in your immediate surroundings as a sparring partner or secretary: you »draw a portrait and explain« while the sparring partner writes down in terms of key words the essence of what you are saying and then reproduces it. This way it becomes possible for you to elaborate and clarify what you have already said which the sparring partner also writes down. Returning home, you sit down and write a draft based on the sparring partner's notes.« (Enderud 1990: 171)

Only by experimenting can you discover which works best. As soon as the writing process has started it becomes self-propelling and results in a greater motivation to write.

> »The detailed outline is often suitable for gradually approaching the actual writing process. By continuously supplementing and working on the key words in the outline, the writer often realizes that suddenly he is no longer working on the key words but also writing a coherent account. The writing process has acquired its own dynamics. It is like decorating a Christmas tree: one starts with a fairly naked stem and wispy branches but gradually the tree begins to look »lush«.
>
> In the same way that the tree can be redecorated – if time allows for it – so can the manuscript be redone before the deadline. Until then the writer is not responsible to anybody – not even himself. Thus, there is nothing to be afraid of.« (Enderud 1990: 172).

The Writing Process as a Learning Process with Its Own Dynamics

Postponing the writing process until after the data collection (see *the hospital tale*) is a sure way to create writer's block. Such blockages can be counteracted by starting to write early in the process – while collecting data – or prior to collecting data (cf. *the production tale*). Many suffer from the delusion that everything must be settled mentally – problem formulation, choice of theory, data collection, and methods of analysis – before putting pen to paper. This perception is both erroneous and unrealistic. The writing process is exactly a learning process and an important part of developing the substance of the dissertation. By starting the writing process earlier, the search for information becomes more focused. Much of what you read does not really seem important, and reading becomes a passive rather than an active process of gaining knowledge. There is, thus, a correlation between defining the problem, reading, analysing, and writing. Therefore, these phases should be run parallel with other project activities.

The moral is: start to write before you have determined your final objective. The writing process itself reveals how much you know and do not yet know. You can actually start to write your dissertation or research report when the first idea for a problem formulation emerges. The subsequent writing phases are merely a matter of continuing to write, adding to what has been written, reformulating, and throwing away. Working your way through the theoretical material and analysing existing empirical data, you realize that additional information is required. This is collected and the results are incorporated into the existing text. The problem formulation is sharpened, and the limits of the subject are made more explicit.

The writing process sharpens the process of knowledge production. Having to formulate your thoughts in writing often makes you realize that the argumentation lacks logical consistency as well as documentation of formulated assumptions, and this is not always obvious when things are formulated verbally. Therefore, the writing process should be an integral part of the total research process.

During this integrated writing process, you realize the shortcomings of the initial points of departure. Consequently, the research process becomes an iterative process during which you are forced to return to earlier phases of the work process or to work with several phases simultaneously. In other words, the process is one of searching, of going forward and backward rather than taking a direct route.

Recognition or, if you prefer, knowledge generation emerges from the interplay between the following four fundamental elements (Figure 10.1):

- problem formulation and questions
- theory

- empirical data
- conclusions and answers.

These four elements constitute a spiral of recognition. We ask questions (formulate problems), search for information (theory/empirical data) and attempt to come up with answers (conclusions). Through this process we move into a new level of recognition asking ourselves supplementary or imaginative questions, search for additional information, etc. (Andersen & Enderud 1990: 23-25). In principle, this process is infinite.

The continuous writing process reflects this process of recognition (Figure 10.2).

Figure 10.2. The Main Elements and Work Process of Knowledge Production

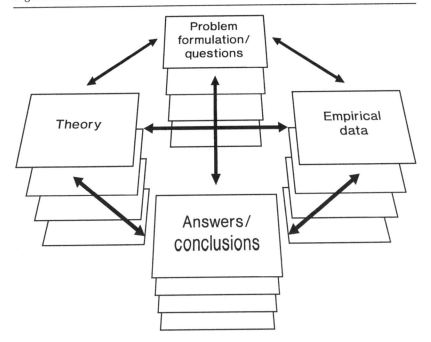

During the early phases, you come up with a number of ideas – most of which probably should be forgotten and a few remembered. The latter is usually only the case if they are written down. Mills (1959) emphasizes the importance of taking ongoing notes when reading and collecting or analysing data. Furthermore he emphasizes (Mills 1959: 197 ff.) that it is wise to establish and repeatedly update a master agenda that sum-

marizes the comprehensive issues and plans to which your research activities can be subordinated. When you are forced to take a break from
writing, a few tricks may make it easier to resume the process the following day or after a longer break:

- stop writing when you feel you still have a great deal to say; and
- list, in terms of key words or short sentences, what is on your mind
  and use these notes when resuming the writing after a break.

This makes it easier to maintain involvement in the continuous writing
process. It is like a serial – it always stops at the most thrilling moment
(Rienecker 1991: 49).

Write continually, every day, and write as much as possible: facts, fiction, speculations, about the process and about the content. This confused writing process implies comprehensive editorial work, which is
fairly uncomplicated technically in the age of word processing. Find out
which periods during the day you are most creative and pick these periods for the most difficult writing tasks. Tasks such as reading and editing
can be accomplished at other hours of the day.

Any written product needs to mature. Put it aside for at least a day –
preferably several days – and forget all about it. Then read it again from
beginning to end and make the editorial changes.

Simultaneously with going over the manuscript for the last time, trim
your language; delete empty words and phrases. Try to persuade someone to edit the language, as the writer is often blind to her own problematic phrases.

> »Close to deadline!
>
> The last dash of the (writing) project starts when the
> deadline threatens on the horizon. The deadline is often
> decided externally – as in the case of, for example, award-
> ed papers, dissertations, or project reports. Sometimes you
> simply feel that the project has been running long enough
> and set a deadline in order to conclude it.
>
> No matter who has been responsible for setting the
> deadline, the last dash always creates the need for getting
> a quick survey of the situation: What do I still need to do,
> how should I spend my remaining resources given that I
> only have a given number of work days left? Now it really
> becomes crucial to close down various activities, i.e. to

structure the remaining work process rigorously. No more brilliant ideas, reading, data, etc.

Now you use what you have and work towards the end. Any attempts at perfectionism must be brutally smothered. The best is the enemy of the good! The positive aspect of a deadline is that you can see the end of the marathon which in itself is a motivation for calling up your last resources. Most people are surprised by how much they can get done in the last dash.« (Enderud 1990: 1985).

On Planning Your Activities

Deadlines Are Necessary

Deadlines are not at all bad. In principle, each of us could easily have spent his whole life on the four projects. It is difficult to justify the conclusion of a project by solely referring to the knowledge acquired. In principle, research projects can continue indefinitely as indicated by the spiral of cognition (Figure 10.2).

Fortunately, as scholars, we are working in an environment that sets concrete (and sometimes unreasonable) deadlines for our activities. A Ph.D. dissertation has to be concluded within 3 years in Denmark if one wants to get a job. The deadline may be set by the research council or the foundation that has granted money for the project. You may be committed to other activities or under obligation to the people who have let you into their world and made themselves available as informants, interviewees, or collaborators. Your family may expect you to spend vacations and holidays with them or is anxiously looking forward to the day you start acting normal again.

If deadlines are not dictated by the environment, they must be invented: promises to present preliminary results at conferences, workshops, (Ph.D.) seminars or informal meetings are good ways of establishing mild external pressure. These types of occasions played an important role – perhaps too important – in the drive of *the wind turbine project*. Deadlines should also be tight in order to create an appropriate level of stress, but not to the degree that you block. It is important to ensure some leeway to avoid the project breaking down if some deadlines are exceeded – which is surely going to happen! It is, however, important psychologically to play such tricks with yourself. Even though you know that some of the deadlines are not really serious, you should take them seriously, or they are not going to fulfil their most important mission: to channel additional energy and attention to the project.

It is important to make deals with others – family, friends, colleagues, supervisors, and others. First, agreements with others are more obligating than those you make with yourself. Second, it is easier to resist pressure from colleagues when you can refer to existing commitments with others. Agreements should also be made with individuals within the social system studied: in part to show that you appreciate that they opened the doors to their world and in part because the field's reactions to the researcher's interpretations contribute strongly to the generation of knowledge.

We all have similar experiences from working in an environment characterized by competing activities (such as teaching, development tasks and administration) that constantly exceed the environment's capacity. Being subject to these circumstances, you are forced to set your own deadlines – otherwise well-intentioned colleagues will book up your dairy.

Planning your time combined with practical arrangements to reduce interruptions are thus important measures. In order to ensure that you get on with the analysis and writing process, you have to be able to cut off yourself from other activities for days or weeks. Apart from protecting yourself from other activities, it is also a matter of getting into the habit of working regularly with these tasks – and mentally to let yourself become absorbed in an inner world – go into a trance in which you are so absorbed that the ink flows (Enderud 1990: 172-173).

We have emphasized that by organizing your time in a way that leaves you with coherent working periods, less time and energy are wasted on readjustment activities. Another aspect is that physically and mentally you live with the project for continuous periods. Problems are turned over and over; information is processed; ideas emerge while working with other, secondary things. It is incredibly productive to work with the project in an uninterrupted state.

However, it is just as important to establish a project plan that is reconsidered at least each month. In projects such as *the drug addict project*, planning functions as a means of coordinating the team's work tasks. Furthermore, a project plan is often necessary if there is to be any hope of obtaining external funding.

The research process should be designed in such a way that deadlines or milestones focus attention on results and make it possible to evaluate whether the project is progressing satisfactorily.

The drug addict and hospital tales are examples of projects that stretched over an inappropriate period of time. One important explanation was that the projects were periodically superseded by other, more urgent, routine activities, such as teaching and administration. Inadequate recognition of the necessity of project management in projects that include several individuals contributed to prolonging *the drug addict project*. In addition, the complex conditions related to data collection and the shift of focus made it difficult to predict the duration of the project.

Even experienced researchers often grossly underestimate how demanding it is to implement a larger research project in terms of time, energy, and attention. Designing plans that are not merely pipedreams requires that you try to estimate the duration of the various activities. Activities such as fieldwork, data collection, and preliminary analysis are often underestimated because you do not bother to sit down and calculate activities that are not particularly complicated (Borum & Enderud 1981: Chapter IX). As a result, you can count on having to face long nights of work and delays – that has been our experience.

The project management literature offers various techniques for planning and implementing research projects that can be used as an inspiration. We stress inspiration, as most project management literature is based on a very rational approach.

Even though research projects cannot be reduced to approximated rational processes, our advice is to plan and manage the project as if this were the case. It helps you to think in terms of the future and to contemplate alternative and potential consequences of current actions. Such future-oriented exercises are imperative if there is to be progress in a project.

Project Management

According to Mikkelsen & Riis (1985), a project process requires three important managerial tasks:

- goal attainment
- communication with interested parties
- management of resources.

These are illustrated in Figure 10.3.

Figure 10.3. Important Project Management Tasks

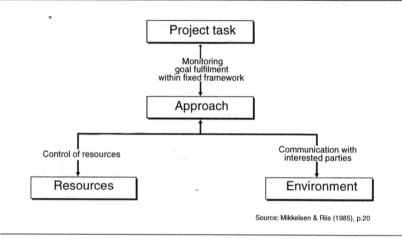

Source: Mikkelsen & Riis (1985), p.20

Managing Goal Attainment

Goal attainment is primarily a matter of determining and defining the project's goals and formulating the issues to be addressed.

Communication with Interested Parties

Research projects have traditionally been perceived as a cognitive project for the individual researcher and not as a project with several interested parties.

The fact is, however, that intensive field studies often mobilize several interested parties during the process. Access to the field mobilizes some interested parties and the research field and financing of the project mobilizes others (Scott 1965: 265).

These interested parties often have different and sometimes conflicting demands for and expectations of the project. Handling these situations requires analysis of the interests of the parties involved. Also, it may be necessary to establish one or several communication forums in order to ensure the communication and to balance the demands of the various interested parties against each other. But doesn't that interfere with the freedom of research? Well, in a way, but our four research tales have also demonstrated that the field researcher in most cases is subject to pressure – both from the occupational field and the research field. Such working conditions may prove more or less favourable.

The production project illustrates that being aware of the potential problems of getting access to the field compels the researcher to develop a contact and communication strategy that prevents the problems from arising. The means are not a formal project structure but open and informal interaction with the interested parties of the field.

For *the hospital project*, on the other hand, this turned out to be a problem, as it was part of a larger project governed by a formal structure. This strongly reduced the possibilities for acting in relation to the specific hospital and almost forced premature termination of the project.

The drug addict project was populated by several potentially interested parties: institutions, drug addicts, treatment staff, and politicians. However, the tale only seems to indicate one problem: access to registers of psychological case records and the possibility of combining information from registers containing information about the drug addicts. Otherwise the project seems to have taken place within an empirical field that was characterized by openness and the absence of blocking, organized interested parties.

The wind turbine project, however, does not seem to have had any problems in relation to the empirical field. On the other hand, this tale illustrates the amount of time and energy spent on interpreting and handling demands from the research system during a Ph.D. project – and especially from the supervisor(s).

All four projects must be viewed as falling within the category of projects over which the researcher has a high degree of discretion *vis-à-vis* the interested parties: probably considerably more than in most Ph.D. projects.

Management of Resources

Resource management is first of all a question of managing time, finances, equipment, and staff. Which resources should be allocated to the various project phases in order to reach the desired goals? A research project usually depends on external grants. Writing applications to potential research councils and foundations for financial support forces you to calculate the project beforehand – and it needs to be done properly, as it is usually very difficult to obtain anything other than modest additional grants.

Planning the Process of the Project

The general approach is:

- Consider the whole project from beginning to end. Define the various phases or activities of the project.
- Divide the project into appropriate main activities or phases.
- Define the time limits (start and end) of the individual main activities or phases.
- Define when essential decisions have to be made within the project team and outside the project team.
- Define who is responsible for the various main activities or phases.

On the Importance of Discussing with Others

The four research tales show that minor crises or breakdowns are inevitable during a project. Sometimes the crises are so serious that you cannot resolve them alone. You are stuck – paralysed – and your mind starts to go around in circles.

One way of preventing such situations is to make sure that the project is embedded in a supportive social environment. It is important that the process does not become a long, lonely inquiry into a social system. You need others with whom you can discuss your ideas: individuals apart from your supervisor or the other members of the project team with whom you can conduct a domination-free dialogue. It is important to make sure that there are others to consult: colleagues, older or younger, practitioners within the system subject to analysis, friends, family – or others in whom you have confidence.

Individuals who are not directly involved in the study are often able to spot clues that you cannot see and indicate whether your own clues are dead ends. You may become hypnotized by data and develop distorted and outright erroneous interpretations. A social test can prove most effective, and sometimes it is the only way of escaping the vicious circle.

Notice, however, that the three types of sparring partners mentioned possess quite different capabilities. The colleague may take a critical position on the chosen theoretical perspective, your operationalization of it and way of combining theory and data. The practitioner may take a critical position on the presentation and analysis of the empirical field, including whether the analysis is too offensive, too »twisted«, etc. Furthermore, the practitioner is particularly interested in normative conclusions. The category of confidant usually comprises the individuals with whom you dare to confide your inner thoughts: your doubts and anxieties. They may prevent you from falling into the black hole.

If this happens – you fall into the black hole – social activities are the very means to escape it. Talk to others, exploit your personal network and the resources available in the professional milieu. Spend time with other people. Reach out for the non-committing and non-threatening, but fruitful, discussions – for example, over lunch. And if you are really down, it is highly recommendable to avoid potentially threatening, formalized discussions.

Talk to your supervisor. Talk to others. Talk to somebody who is not connected to the project at all and thus not tangled up in your line of thought. Seek reassurance that neither the world nor you will fall apart because the project is facing problems. Plunge into activities that have nothing to do with the world of research – get some fresh air. Get drunk, go to the theatre, read a good book, get some physical exercise. Nourish yourself and your family.

The Result

Suddenly it is over and done with: the dissertation, the report, or the book is finished.

Did it turn out well? That is for others to decide: colleagues, reviewing committees, practitioners and students. Most often the reaction is delayed, ambiguous, and unsatisfying compared with what has been invested in the project mentally and physically. One way of evaluating your own outcome of the project is to develop an explicit set of achievement norms, regardless of the fact that it is difficult to distinguish process from result and to dissociate yourself from your work.

If you are unable to dissociate yourself from your work, it is hardly a good idea to set yourself up for a career in the world of research. The final product can always be subject to criticism – and usually is. This reflects the very nature of scientific activity: you try to meet the unattainable ideals of knowledge production. The insight and understanding you gain are always temporary and risk being refuted later.

Thus criticism, even if it hurts, should not be taken personally. You have lived through a process and produced visible results or knowledge that can be subject to scrutiny – and from which you probably have learned something that can be used in future projects. Compared with others, who merely have the end-product to relate to, the generator of the knowledge can learn much from the comments and criticism of others.

What then characterizes a good research product? It has an impact in and of itself, even if the author is not present to interpret the text!

The good scientific text is a tale that captures the reader. Second, through a series of arguments or interpretations, the critical reader finds it intriguing to pursue its line of thought. This aspect is supported by Latour & Bastide's (1986) and Law's (1986) analyses of scientific products, which have revealed that the composition of scientific reports and books that attract attention and interest is very similar to that of fiction.

In other words, a good research product is a story that captures the reader and makes him or her curious. There are several ways of making the reader interested. Davis (1971: 310) mentions:

- findings that prove or disprove hypotheses;
- clues that indicate how to resolve the problems;
- aesthetic descriptions that provide us with a more varied perception of phenomena;
- analogies that make it possible to distinguish the known from the unknown; and
- models that facilitate the analysis of complex relationships.

To Davis, an interesting social theory makes the reader question his or her perception of everyday phenomena and their interrelations. Only by challenging this perception and the daily practice supporting it is it possible to strengthen the reader's awareness and attention (Davis 1971: 311, 313-326).

However, even though this may seem to be a somewhat unscientific, journalistic way of writing, it is important to the very generation of knowledge. First, fostering a story is a way of making yourself interested and of turning your research into a novel task. Second, placing the story in the context of existing theories or empirical analyses makes you more attentive of elements of these that may or may not be applicable. Third, a research system depends to a certain degree on market mechanisms: only by selling your product on the market is it possible to influence the formation of knowledge. A precondition for being able to market the product is that it has a certain novelty value.

The story must comprise a theme capable of capturing the reader (theorist or practitioner). The reader must decide whether we have succeeded in accomplishing this task in our four tales. Even in this post-modern epoch we are convinced of the potential of the intensive field study for creating a grand, coherent narrative that breaks the case story's limitations of time and space.

Another important condition – that the product can convince the sceptical reader – is only fulfilled if the basic norms for knowledge generation are observed. Explicitness, consistency, and progression are universal norms to be observed.

Explicitness means that premises, arguments, and conclusions must be explicit and not merely hinted at or implicit. The reader should not be required to decode or interpret the text. Likewise, gaps in the data or weak aspects of the argumentation should be made explicit. There is a world of difference between the way in which researchers and salespeople handle the advantages and disadvantages of a product.

Consistency is partly a question of general analytical rigor: the line of reasoning must be coherent and not characterized by gaps or jumps in level of abstraction. Inferences and derivations must follow logically from the premises (empirical as well as theoretical) and argumentation. It is necessary to distinguish between value premises and analytical premises, and the former must be handled with great care. In general, the intensive field study is characterized by great degrees of freedom to choose which issues to treat. In this context, values are quite legitimate and important.

Phrases such as »I think«, »I believe« or »I'm convinced« often indicate that the lines of reasoning unconsciously have been affected by value premises – typically in order to reinforce weak links of argumentation.

Progression has to do with the composition of the story. A story has a neatly worked-out plot, and the reader must be able to detect the progression. If the final chapter might as well have been the first, then the text is circular and the reader will protest. This is not an uncommon problem with scientific texts and has to do with the nature of the process of generating knowledge. A scientific text is the result of a process, but in most cases it does not reflect the process itself. The final text must be consistent, and the problem formulation must be revised during the process as the author grows wiser. This is not being dishonest – it is simply a basic characteristic of the research process. However, the ultimate consequence of this continuous adaptation of problem formulation and conclusion is that the final item to be written is the final problem formulation. The risk of these perpetual adaptations may be that the author becomes incapable of distinguishing head from tail.

Part 4:
Conclusion

11. An Ideal Type of Field Research

In the introduction to this book, we indicated two weaknesses in the current methodological literature: the objectification of the researcher and the perception of the research process as an approximated rational process.

The objectification of the researcher is inherent in the attempts of classical methodological literature to develop universal objective methods for research in the social sciences. The approximated rational process is the result of attempts to manage the research process by design. Thus, these two weaknesses are closely coupled to the general, overall goal of traditional methodological literature: to confine research to a process manageable by calculations and a limited amount of judgement. This brings us back to the typology of Thompson & Tuden (Scott 1992: 296) as cited in the introduction's Figure 1.1.

But perhaps it is a bit unreasonable to characterize these as two weaknesses of traditional methodological literature. Wouldn't it be more accurate to regard them as fundamental features and strengths? Is not methodology, after all, an attempt to develop methods that rise above characteristics of the individual research project and the idiosyncrasies of the individual researcher?

Our answer to these two questions is a qualified confirmation!

The strength of traditional methodological literature is also its weakness: it attempts to eliminate distortions that the researcher may bring into the project by making a distinction to methods that depend on the individual. Thus, Yin (1984: 21-22) clearly distinguishes between case studies and ethnography. But this also implies that the methodological literature refrains from treating the problems that are tied to an intensive field study in which the researcher is forced to deal with issues of ethnography.

Attempts, via design, to reduce the research process to variations of an approximated rational process also represent a more mechanistic research tradition. The more open and susceptible nature of field studies creates problems and considerations that go beyond the traditional methodological literature.

Using our four research tales, we have stressed the gap between the practice of field studies and traditional methodological literature. It should hardly be surprising that a gap exists between theory and practice. When practising a profession, you can rarely live up to the ideals with which you were indoctrinated during your studies. Nevertheless, ideals still guide and affect actions.

With this book, we have created an empirical basis for arguing that the deviations are not the usual ones found in the dichotomy of ideal versus practice. Rather it is a question of categorical differences. The intensive field study cannot be reduced to an approximated rational process independent of the individual researcher. Our four research tales demonstrate that a methodology needs to be developed based on an understanding of the research process that is basically different from the traditional one.

In the previous chapter we developed some elements of a methodology of intensive field studies. This concluding chapter spells out our basic understanding of field research and deduces some implications for the training of researchers.

Field Research Depends on the Individual

The intensive field study's demand for empathy with the empirical field makes the individual researcher a key factor in the successful outcome of the project. In Chapter 9, we reflected on how this empathy could be included in the execution of the interview – the very situation of generating data, which has been of decisive importance for our understanding of the field. Our prime message was that the interview should develop as a dialogue between the researcher and the native. This involves demands that some researchers (and researchers to-be) are not able to meet – and that we were only able to meet roughly.

Application of more intensive ethnographic methods – participant observation and long stays in the field – places additional demands on the researcher as an individual. But since we applied very few ethnographic methods in our projects, we cannot discuss this issue in detail.

Our research tales show that the four authors are temperamentally very different. The reader can safely conclude that we behave very differently in the field. Working with this book has made us aware of the importance of our different temperaments and educational backgrounds. The different paths taken by our projects and our accounts of them reflect individual applications of the outlined methodology to our specific empirical projects.

The working conditions of the field researcher acting in the tensional sphere of project, research field, and empirical field make additional demands on the researcher. You must be capable of handling conflicting pressures and changing expectations by directing your focus and becoming absorbed – not by escaping or distancing yourself. It is a very special work situation, and you do not know whether you can handle it until you have tried it. We will leave it to the reader to decide whether our performance in the four different projects were acceptable variations. On this issue, too, we were struck by the impact of our different temperaments and educational backgrounds: none of us would have been able to act like the others!

Data analysis and the process of writing the report are other features that show that field research depends on the individual. Each of us recognizes that rational, analytical working methods are necessary tools when the puzzle must be made to form a convincing pattern. But our ways of carrying out the analysis and writing up the results vary greatly. By no means do we argue in favour of standardizing these dimensions, but it is important to be aware of their impact and to accept your own idiosyncrasies.

Field Research is a Continuous Learning Process

The projects were conducted during different stages of our professional development. *The hospital project and the wind turbine project* were conducted as Ph.D. projects and were thus educational projects to a greater extent than the other two projects. Only the wind turbine project, however, included formalized research education in terms of courses and supervision. We are not in a position to infer any conclusion about the impact of educational courses for researchers. The working conditions of Danish Ph.D. students have been and still are subject to radical changes.

Nevertheless, our experience indicates that any research project contains an educational dimension – even when it is conducted by a senior researcher. For the two researchers in *the drug addict project and the production project*, the processes implied significant elements of learning. This has also been the case in our subsequent field studies.

An additional argument in favour of this viewpoint is the fact that most researchers only find time to conduct a very limited number of intensive field studies during their professional career. Combined with the strongly varying contexts and working conditions of field studies, the result is that no field study can ever rely on applying the previously acquired routines of a certain paradigm.

Compared with Argyris' (1970) classification, intensive field studies are doomed to belong to organic and not mechanistic research.

We therefore conclude that the metaphor of the learning process captures some fundamental aspects of the research process that are beyond the reach of the traditional rational process metaphor.

The difference between the two conceptions of research are summarized in Figure 11.1.

This basic conception of research as a learning process emerged from our discussions in the joint process of writing this book. According to Flyvbjerg's (1991, vol. 1: 24-39) interpretation of Dreyfus' model, our projects set us on an expedition rediscovering at least the first four of the five stages of human learning (Fig. 11.2) (Flyvbjerg 1991: 35):

To us, the crucial point of this model is the qualitative leap that occurs

Figure 11.1. Two Ideal Type Conceptions of the Research Process

	(Approximated) rational process	**Learning process**
Objectives	clearly defined beforehand	tentatively formulated beforehand
Function of objectives	define limits, exclude noise, can be marginally adjusted	heuristic means, initiates discovery, exchangeable
Theory, models and concepts	determined beforehand and operationalized	adaptive, pliable
Process dominated by	calculation and judgement	inspiration and judgement
Function of process	a means to answer questions formulated beforehand	a means to produce knowledge about the field and develop research competencies
Researcher's learning process	perfection within the paradigm	development of individual methods for generation of knowledge between two cultures, learning related to paradigm boundaries
Researcher's self-perception	distant observer, expert	existentialist, craftsperson

between level three and four. The difference between a competent and a skilled researcher is the significance of intuition and context.

With this book, we have attempted to penetrate the domains of intuitive and holistic thinking. It was our unshakeable feeling that there were shared elements behind our different ways of conducting and conceiving field studies. But they were tacit and therefore inaccessible. Through the process of writing this book, we laboriously worked at making the intuitive accessible to analysis.

Not that we think that it will ever be possible to capture fully what is intuitive by means of an analytical approach. But we hope that, by identifying and discussing the intuitive, we have not reduced it to mere approximated rational contemplation.

Figure 11.2. The Five Stages of the Human Learning Process Source: Flyvbjerg (1991)

Stage	Characteristics
1. Beginner	General elements and rules as basis for behaviour
2. Advanced beginner	Experience-based, contextually dependent elements supplement general elements independent of context
3. Competent performer	Objectives and plan are consciously selected with the aim of reducing complexity. Selection is non-objective and imperative. Performer invests himself in the results.
4. Skilled performer	Intuitive problem identification and intuitive selection of objectives and plans from an experience-based perspective. Intuitive selections are evaluated analytically.
5. Expert	Intuitive, holistic, and synchronous identification of problem, objectives, plan, decision, and action. Fluid, easy performance, uninterrupted by analytical considerations.

References

Adler, P.A. & P. Adler (1987): *Membership Roles in Field Research*. Newbury Park, CA: Sage (Qualitative Research Methods Series, Volume 6).

Allison, G.T. (1971): *Essence of Decision. Explaining the Cuban Missile Crisis*. Boston: Little, Brown & Co.

Andersen, E.S., B. Lundwall & B. Johnson (1978): *Industriel udvikling og industrikrise*. Aalborg: Aalborg Universitetsforlag.

Andersen, I. & H. Enderud (1990): Vidensproduktionens arbejdsgang i hovedtræk. In I. Andersen (ed.) *Valg af organisations-sociologiske metoder – et kombinationsperspektiv*. Copenhagen: Samfundslitteratur, pp. 23-35.

Andersen, I. & P.W. Hansen (1984): *Narkomaners livsløb*. Copenhagen: Gyldendal.

Andersen, I., P. Bauter, E. Gregersen, E. Hultzrantz & J. Kirstein (1972): *Materiale til en vurdering af dansk stofforskning*. Copenhagen: New Social Science Monographs.

Argyris, C. (1970): *Intervention theory and method. A behavioral science view*. Reading, MA: Addison-Wesley.

Argyris, C. & D.A. Schoen (1978): *Organizational Learning: A Theory of Action Perspective*. Reading, MA: Addison-Wesley.

Barton, L. (1988): *Basics of Qualitative Research: Grounded Theory Procedures and Techniques*. Newbury Park, CA: Sage.

Becker, H.S. (1986): *Writing for Social Scientists*. Chicago: University of Chicago Press.

Berger, P.L. & M. Kellner (1981): *Sociology Reinterpreted. An Essay on Method and Vocation*. New York: Anchor Press/Doubleday.

Berger, P. & T. Luckmann (1971): *The Social Construction of Reality*. Middlesex: Penguin Books.

Blauner, R. (1964): *Alienation and Freedom*. Chicago: University of Chicago Press.

Blumer, H. (1969): *Symbolic Interactionism. Perspective and Method*. Berkeley: University of California Press.

Borum, F. (1976): *Organisation, magt og forandring*. Copenhagen: Handelshøjskolens Forlag.

Borum, F. (1979): Interviewanalyse i praksis. In T. Broch, K. Krarup, P.K. Larsen & O. Rieper (eds.) *Kvalitative metoder i dansk samfundsforskning.* Copenhagen: New Social Science Monographs, pp. 297-337.

Borum, F. (1990): Om valg af organisationssociologisk metode. In I. Andersen (ed.) *Valg af organisations-sociologiske metoder – et kombinationsperspektiv.* Copenhagen: Samfundslitteratur, pp. 39-62.

Borum, F. (1995): *Organization, Power, and Change.* Copenhagen: Handelshøjskolens Forlag.

Borum, F. & H. Enderud (1981): *Konflikter i organisationer.* Copenhagen: Handelshøjskolens Forlag.

Borum, F. & P.H. Kristensen (eds.) (1990): *Technological Innovation and Organizational Change – Danish Patterns of Knowledge, Networks and Culture.* Copenhagen: New Social Science Monographs.

Bourdieu, P. (1987): *Outline of a Theory of Practice.* Cambridge: Cambridge University Press.

Bourdieu, P. (1990): *In Other Words. Essays towards a Reflexive Sociology.* Cambridge: Polity Press.

Broch, T., K. Krarup, P.K. Larsen & O. Rieper (eds.) (1979): *Kvalitative metoder i dansk samfundsforskning.* Copenhagen: New Social Science Monographs,

Bryman, A. (ed.) (1989): *Doing Research in Organizations.* New York: Routledge.

Buchanan, D., D. Boddy & J. McCalman (1989): Getting in, Getting on, Getting out, and Getting back. In A. Bryman (ed.) *Doing Research in Organizations.* New York: Routledge.

Burgess, R.G. (ed.) (1990): *Studies in qualitative methodology. Reflections on field experience.* Vol. 2. London: JAI Press Inc.

Carroll, J.S. & E.J. Johnson (1990): *Decision Research. A Field Guide.* Newbury Park, CA: Sage Publications.

Christensen, P.M. (1988): *Teknologi mellem stat og marked.* Århus: Politica.

Cohen, A. (1966): *Deviance and Control.* Englewood Cliffs, NJ: Prentice-Hall.

Colling, H., S. Harboe, P. Jacobsen, H.H. Larsen & J. Wegens (1992): *Følsomme Emner – belyst gennem det kvalitative forskningsinterview.* Copenhagen: New Social Science Monographs.

Conant, J.B. (1947): *On Understanding Science.* New Haven, CT: Yale University Press.

Dahrendorf, R. (1959): *Class and Class Conflict in Industrial Society.* Stanford: Stanford University Press.

Davis, M.S. (1971): That's interesting! *Philosophy of Social Sciences 1*: 309-344.

Dosi, G. (1982): Technological Paradigms and Technological Trajectories. *Research Policy 11*(3):147-62.

Durkheim, E. (1982): *The Rules of Sociological Method.* New York: Free Press.

Eco, U. (1984): *The Name of the Rose.* London: Pan Books.

Enderud, H. (ed.) (1984, 1986): *Hvad er organisations-sociologisk metode?* Vol. 1 and 2. Copenhagen: Samfundslitteratur

Enderud, H. (1990): Skriveproces – arbejdsproces, skrivning er en integreret del af arbejdsforløbet. In I. Andersen (ed.) *Valg af organisationssociologiske metoder.* Copenhagen: Samfundslitteratur, pp. 165-186.

Flyvbjerg, B. (1991): *Magt og rationalitet.* Vol. I. Copenhagen: Akademisk Forlag.

Fielding, N.G. (ed.) (1988): *Actions and Structure. Research Methods and Social Theory.* London: Sage.

Freeman, C. (1982): *Economics of Industrial Innovation.* 2nd edn. Cambridge, MA: MIT Press.

Frøslev Christensen J. (1992): *Produktinnovation – proces og strategi.* Copenhagen: Handelshøjskolens Forlag.

Frøslev Christensen, J. & F. Valentin (1986): *Dynamisk specialisering og erhverssystemets udviklingskompetencer.* Copenhagen: Institute for Industrial Research and Social Development, Copenhagen Business School.

Garrad, A. (1988): The Future Needs – Close copperation between Mathematicians and Manufacturers. *Windpower Monthly.* April: p. 22-55.

Giddens, A. (1976): *New rules of sociological method.* London: Hutchinson.

Glaser, B & A. Strauss (1967): *The Discovery of Grounded Theory.* Chicago: Aldine.

Groth, A. (1984): [Book review.] *Ugeskrift for Læger 23* (June 4): 1754-1755.

Hammond, P.E. (1967): *Sociologists at Work.* New York: Anchor Books, Doubleday & Company.

Hegland, T.J. (1971): Buråkratiet – egenskaper, problemer og alternativer. In T.J. Hegland (ed.) *Strejftog i organisationsforskningen.* Copenhagen: New Social Science Monographs, pp. 21-45.

Henslin, J.H. (1990): It's not a lovely place to visit, and I wouldn't want to live there. In R.G. Burgess (ed.) *Studies in Qualitative Methodology. Reflections on Field Experience.* Vol. 2. London: JAI Press.

Hunt, J.C. (1989): *Psychoanalytic Aspects of Fieldwork.* Newbury Park, CA: Sage.

Karnøe, P. (1986): *Opbygning af populationen.* Copenhagen: Institute for Industrial Research and Social Development, Copenhagen Business School (Working Paper No. 2, Project Dynamic Specialization).

Karnøe, P. (1989): Mitsubishi kvæler dansk vindmølleindustri. Børsen 31 May: 29.

Karnøe, P. (1991): *Dansk vindmølleindustri – en overraskende international succes.* Copenhagen: Samfundslitteratur.

Kline, J. & Rosenberg, N. (1986): An Overview of Innovation. In R. Landau & N. Rosenberg (eds.) *The Positive Sum Strategy.* Washington, DC: National Academy Press.

Knorr-Cetina, K. (1988): The micro-social order. Towards a reconception. In Fielding, N.G. (ed.) *Actions and Structure. Research Methods and Social Theory.* Newbury Park, CA: Sage.

Kock, K. (1988): *Mål og mæle.* Copenhagen: Modermål-Selskabet.

Kristensen, P.H. (1986): *Teknologiske projekter og organisatoriske processer. Strategier og strukturer under forandring i danske virksomheders drift mod fleksibel specialisering.* Roskilde: Forlaget for Samfundsøkonomi og Planlægning.

Kristensen, S.B. (1987): *Dansk industripolitik – med særlig henblik på danske erfaringer.* Copenhagen: Samfundslitteratur.

Kuhn, T. (1970): *The Structure of Scientific Revolutions. 2nd edn.* Chicago: University of Chicago Press.

Kvale, S. (1992): *What is Anthropological Research? An Interview with Jean Lave.* Aarhus: Centre for the Development of Qualitative Method, Aarhus University (Nyhedsbrev no. 10, June).

Lassen, M.J. (1983): *At vikle sig ud af stofmisbrug – En kvalitativ-, eksplorativ undersøgelse.* Copenhagen: University of Copenhagen.

Latour, B. & F. Bastide (1986): *Writing Science – Fact and Fiction.* In M. Callon, J. Law & A. Rip (eds.) *Mapping the Dynamics of Science and Technology.* Basingstoke: Macmillan, pp. 51-66.

Laudan, R. (ed.) (1984): *The Nature of Technological Knowledge.* D. Reidel Publishing Company.

Law, J. (1986): The heterogeneity of texts. In M. Callon, J. Law & A. Rip (eds.) *Mapping the Dynamics of Science and Technology.* Basingstoke: Macmillan.

Layton, E. (1978): Millwrights and Engineers, Science, Social Roles, and the Evolution of the Turbine in America. In Krohn, W., E. Layton & P. Weingart (eds.) *The Dynamics of Science and Technology: Social Values, Technical Norms and Scientific Criteria in the Development of Knowledge*. Dordrecht: D. Reidel Publishing Company.

Lundvall, B.-Å., N.M. Olsen & I Aaen (1984): *Det landbrugsindustrielle kompleks*. Aalborg: Aalborg University Centre (SIU no. 28).

March, J.G. & J.P. Olsen (1989): *Rediscovering Institutions*. New York: Free Press.

McCracken, G. (1988): *The Long Interview*. Newbury Park, CA: Sage.

Merton, R.K. (1962): Foreword. In B. Barber (ed.) *Science and the Social Order*. New York: Collier Books.

Mikkelsen, H. & J.O. Riis (1985): *Grundbog i projektledelse*. Copenhagen: Promet.

Mills, C.W. (1959): *The Sociological Imagination*. New York: Grove Press.

Morgan, G. (1986): *Images of Organization*. Newbury Park, CA: Sage.

Morgan, G. & L. Smircich (1980): The Case for Qualitative Research. *Academy of Management Review 5*(4): 491-500.

Nelson, R. & Winter, S. (1982): *An Evolutionary Theory of Economic Change*. Cambridge, MA: Harvard University Press.

Organisationsudvalget (1974): *Organisationsudvikling på et hospital*. Copenhagen: City of Copenhagen Hospital Service.

Pavitt, K. (1984): Patterns of Technical Change: Towards a Taxonomy and a Theory. *Research Policy 13*(6): 343-373.

Pedersen, J.D. (1980): *Historisk analyse af det danske narkobehandlingssystem*. Copenhagen: University of Copenhagen, Institute og Sociology.

Phillips, E.M. & D.S. Pugh (1987): *How to Get a Ph.D.* Buckingham: Open University Press.

Piore, M.J. & C.F. Sabel (1984): *The Second Industrial Divide. Possibilities for Prosperity*. New York: Basic Books.

Polanyi, M. (1969): *Knowing and Being*. Chicago: University of Chicago Press.

Popper, K.R. (1973): *Kritisk rationalisme. Udvalgte essays om videnskab og samfund*. Copenhagen: Nyt Nordisk Forlag.

Rienecker, L. (1991): *Tekster til tiden*. Copenhagen: Dansk psykologisk Forlag.

Rosenberg, N. (1976): *Perspectives on Technology*. Cambridge: Cambridge University Press.

Rosenberg, N. (1982a): *Inside the Black Box: Technology and Economics.* Cambridge: Cambridge University Press.

Rosenberg, N. (1982b): Technological Interdependence in the American Economy. In Rosenberg, N. *Inside the Black Box: Technology and Economics.* Cambridge: Cambridge University Press, pp. 55-80

Rosenberg, N. (1982c): Learning by using. In Rosenberg, N. *Inside the Black Box: Technology and Economics.* Cambridge: Cambridge University Press, pp. 120-140.

Rosenberg, N. (1982d): How exogenous is science. In Rosenberg, N. *Inside the Black Box: Technology and Economics.* Cambridge: Cambridge University Press, pp. 141-159.

Rothwell R. & W. Zegveld (1985): *Reindustrialization and Technology.* London: France Pinter.

Sabel, C.F. (1982): *Work and Politics. The Division of labor in Industry.* Cambridge: Cambridge University Press.

Sahal, D. (1985): Technology Guideposts and Innovation Avenues. *Research Policy 14*(2): pp. 61-82.

Schein, E.H. (1987): *The Clinical Perspective in Fieldwork.* Newbury Park, CA: Sage.

Schultz, M. (1991): Transitions between Symbolic Domains in Organizations. *Organization Studies 12*(4): 489-506.

Schutz, A. (1962): *Collected Papers.* Vol. I: The Problem of Social Reality. The Hague: Martinus Nijhoff.

Scott, R.W. (1965): Field methods in the study of organizations. In J.G. March (ed.) *Handbook of Organizations.* New York: Rand McNally, pp. 261-304.

Scott, R.W. (1992): *Organizations. Rational, Natural and Open Systems.* Englewood Cliffs, NJ: Prentice-Hall.

Silverman, D. (1985): *Qualitative Methodology and Sociology.* Aldershot, UK: Gower.

Stoddard, F.S. (1986): The California Experience. Presented at Danwea 1986, Proceedings available from the Danish Wind Turbine Manufacturers' Association, Copenhagen.

Strauss, A. & J. Corbin (1990): *Basics of Qualitative Research: Grounded Theory Procedures and Techniques.* Newbury Park, CA: Sage.

Thomlinson, R. (1981): *Sociological Concepts and Research.* New York: Random House.

Thompson, J.D. & A. Tuden (1959): Strategies, Structures, and Processes of Organizational Decision. In J.D. Thompson et al. (ed.) *Comparative Studies in Administration.* Pittsburgh: University of Pittsburgh

Press, pp. 195-216.

Tyler, S.A. (1986): Post-Modern Ethnography: From Document of the Occult to Occult Document. In J. Clifford & G.E. Marcus (eds.) *Writing Culture*. Berkeley: University of California Press.

Valentin, F. (1990): *Når virksomheder lærer. Innovationer og videnudvikling i mellemstore virksomheder*. Copenhagen: Institute for Industrial Research and Social Development, Copenhagen Business School (Report II, Project Dynamic Specialization).

Van Maanen, J. (1988): *Tales of the Field. On Writing Ethnography*. Chicago: University of Chicago Press.

Vincenti, W. (1984): Technological Knowledge without Science: the Innovation of Flush Riveting in American Airplanes 1930-1950.. *Technology and Culture 25*(July): 540-576.

Weick, K.E. 1989: Theory Construction as Disciplined Imagination. *Academy of Management Review 14*(4): 516-534.

Whyte, W.F. (ed.) (1991): *Participatory Action Research*. Newbury Park, CA: Sage.

Winks, R.W. (ed.) (1968): *The Historian as Detective. Essays on Evidence*. New York: Harper & Row.

Yin, R.K. (1984): *Case Study Research. Design and Methods*. Newbury Park, CA: Sage.

Index

1
2
3
4
5
6
7
8
9
10
11
12
13
14
15
16
17
18
19
20
21
22
23
24
25
26
27
28
29
30
31
32
33
34
35
36
37
38
39
40